A LONGING
IN THE LAND

A LONGING IN THE LAND

Memoir of a Quest

ARTHUR GREGOR

Schocken Books · New York

First published by Schocken Books 1983
10 9 8 7 6 5 4 3 2 1   83 84 85 86
Copyright © 1983 by Schocken Books
All rights reserved.

Library of Congress Cataloging in Publication Data
Gregor, Arthur
  A longing in the land.
  1. Gregor, Arthur—Biography—Youth. 2. Authors,
American—20th century—Biography. I. Title.
PS3557.R434Z473 1983   811'.54   82–17043

Designed by Nancy Dale Muldoon
Manufactured in the United States of America
ISBN 0–8052–3834–4

Lines from "Voyages" from *The Complete Poems and Selected Letters and Prose of Hart Crane,* edited by Brom Weber, are copyright 1933, © 1958 1966 by Liveright Publishing Corporation and are used by permission of Liveright Publishing Corporation, New York, and Granada Publishing Ltd., London.

Lines from "The Paper Nautilus" from *The Complete Poems of Marianne Moore* are copyright 1941, and renewed 1969, by Marianne Moore and are used by permission of Macmillan Publishing Co., Inc., New York, and Faber and Faber Ltd., London.

Lines from "For Bill and Eleanor Monahan" from *Pictures from Brueghel and Other Poems* by William Carlos Williams are copyright © 1955 by William Carlos Williams and are used by permission of New Directions Publishing Corporation.

To Sri Atmananda, Presence that abides
To Susheela Dayal
And in memory of
Benjamin and Regine Goldenberg, my parents

The land was ours before we were the land's.
. . . .
Something we were withholding made us weak.

—Robert Frost in *The Gift Outright*

The image must be of the nature of its creator.

—Wallace Stevens in *A Mythology*
Reflects Its Region

Contents

Illustrations

I

ARRIVAL

► 1

The experience of uprootedness, of cultural loss, loss of the familiar—how many innumerable times had occurred to others what was occurring to me then, in New York harbor, on that grey day in September 1939, two weeks after war had broken out in Europe?

. . . Europe! How I began to feel, to live the sound of that word as though saying it for the first time, how different its meaning for me when weeks later I trudged through fallen leaves down streets totally unlike any I had ever known, and the word of the continent lost to me rose from within like the name of someone taken for granted, an essential closeness, part of oneself, unobserved until separated, removed and disappearing like a seafront's lights receding in a fog. Europe . . . Eu . . ropp! . . . Eu . . ropp . . p! How I had mouthed these syllables, these sounds, lingering over them at once lovingly and mockingly like utterances of betrayal, indignation, loss . . .

I suspect that this too was a repetition of what others had done, if unconsciously, somewhere behind their thoughts, almost routinely. How could it have been otherwise, how could they not have uttered dismay in some sounds, some gestures? For, to lose one's soil is grievous however urgent, imperative, even lifesaving, the removal. But the soul has its own temper; it does not necessarily concur with actions events force on us. I am reminded of Anna, my mother's jovial, distant cousin. I can still hear her laughter, as full as she was plump. I can still see her seated on top of a wooden chest where large pots were kept, in the kitchen of our apartment, laughing with other women who loved to gather there. Anna Lust, a woman of sturdy humor who refused to leave Vienna, let her husband go illegally to Yugoslavia, but would not go herself. "Even if I am killed"— and she was—"I will not leave these streets." And she stayed on, of all her sisters and brothers, alone with her old mother.

Arriving in America was the most dramatic in a sequence of events that had begun a month earlier at the Westbahnhof in Vienna where my father and Julie, our wonderful, our loyal *Mädchen*—maid, housekeeper—had seen me off on the night-express to Zurich where Fritzi, my three-years-older brother, had been living for over a year. He had been badly beaten by a gang of young Nazi hoodlums in the summer of 1938 when he was seventeen, and my parents soon after sent him off with a family who had been our neighbors and who were risking an illegal entry into Switzerland by taking a plane to Zurich. My mother had not seen me off. It was understood that the separation would be brief—my parents were to follow in about a week—and she had preferred to stay behind in our apartment rather than risk an emotional parting at the station. We were fortunate to have kept on living in our apartment until my parents left. It was large and expensive and had not been confiscated by some Nazi official who might have coveted it; many Jews had in this way been forced from their apartments into furnished rooms or flats shared with relatives or friends.

When we arrived in New York on September 14, we were four days late. A strike by the crew had delayed the ship's departure—it was the SS *Statendam*—from Rotterdam by a day; the first night out we had stood still in the Channel, funnels and decks ablaze in floodlights to identify the ship's neutral status (it belonged to the Holland-America Line) to German submarines; once out in the Atlantic the ship had detoured twice to pick up survivors from merchant vessels that had been torpedoed by Germans. The ship was, in fact, the first to reach the United States after war had been declared in Europe. But, as we stood still once again, this time at the Line's pier in Hoboken, it was not the enormity of recent events that possessed me, it was something else of gravity, an experience I could then not all take in, an end and a beginning, a decisive moment lived by countless others before me.

As we waited in line in the First Class Main Lounge where the U.S. immigration officials had set up their tables, as the man who examined and stamped my passport looked at me in astonishment (the way, a few months earlier, the consul at the U.S. embassy in Vienna had done, when I spoke to him in fluent and correct English); as holding my little dog, Fifi, a toy Doberman pinscher, and leaning against the railing on deck I shouted down to our relatives who had come to meet the boat, that this, namely Fifi, was our entire possession from our former life, everything else having been left behind; as we walked down the gangplank and without giving it any thought I set foot on the new world, our home-to-be: I did not then realize that I was re-enacting an event so momentous, so far-reaching in its significance, so beyond one's comprehension that it seems to occur almost outside one, like clouds passing, like standing by in a stupor of helplessness, as years later I have stood more than once, when a casket is lowered on heavy ropes into the ground. I did not and could not have realized then that a severe transition was taking place, that what had been absolutely natural and familiar in my fifteen-year-old life was over, was over with an irreversible finality. Could not have realized that everything I had taken for granted in my young life—where we had lived, how we had lived, how I had felt about living, the streets, the trees, the yards, the rooms, the faces, the feelings these had bred in me, and with which I had met new impressions of places, of people, intimations of first and powerful experiences—that all of this was over, over as though a laborer, his work done, rubbed his hands to show that he was finished, a bit of dust drifting toward the ground. I could then not have realized how severe was what was happening, a finishing off, a beheading of the past, for with us the severance was enforced; and I could realize even less that this was a kind of rite undergone by millions before me, a rite at the altar of the new, a trauma of displacement, of alienation at the root of this New World—none of this was, of course, then in my thoughts and could not have been. But that such was the nature of the experience, and that what became my personal dilemma was in fact also a collective one, has only gradually, over these forty years since that day in September 1939, become clear to me.

► 2

New, everything was new to me, new and different. Zurich and Paris had been new to me but the tree-lined streets, the houses—although in Paris higher than the four- to five-story buildings I had been accustomed to in Vienna—the parks, even the lakefront in Zurich were new only in the sense that I had not seen them before. They did not appear strange, I was familiar with their look; the cities seemed to me to be variations of what I already knew. The differences were all part of a familiar pattern. Even the sea which I saw for the first time at Boulogne-sur-Mer—we were to have embarked there but didn't because war broke out and we hurried by taxi to Rotterdam—even the sea which I had feared seemed familiar as though a secret suddenly revealed, a long lost, forgotten terrain that now lay spread before me like an immense silver lake joined on the horizon to the sky. These and other impressions had been new but they were like something anticipated, further extensions of a knowledge already absorbed.

Not my first sights of America, however. The Manhattan skyline seemed familiar enough—I had seen it often on postcards, in newspapers and newsreels—though less impressive than I had imagined. From the highest deck of a large ocean liner, the sky-scrapers were not quite as tall, as august, as uncommon as I had somehow envisioned them. Still, in my anticipation of things, they were distinctly American, were, in fact, the European's image of America. But nothing else that confronted me that first day was; I had not been prepared for my first sights of vast industrialization, of a world whose physical aspects do not reflect a past but the modern, industrialized present. The harbor was teeming with craft of all sizes, smoke billowing from small and huge funnels; sirens, bells, shrill whistles filled the air. As my father's cousin Serge drove us across industrial New Jersey to my great-uncle's house in Newark, the streets once we left Hoboken and its shabby, low wooden buildings—I had never seen such before—were undulating ribbons of concrete which all around us crisscrossed the land high above ground. There were stretches of waste below, vast, dirty puddles, mountains of loose earth ground into grains, flames like slender tall torches atop refineries, piles of crushed metal, wrecks of cars, barges black as the coal they carried down narrow dirty waters, the outline of Newark's skyline in the distance, planes above us, descending or taking off, a high tower with red lights blinking, a train moving like a snake slithering, cars alongside us, streams of oncoming ones in the ribbon next to ours, and, as the day was quite warm and the windows slightly open, the foul odor of sulphur or some other rank chemical.

"Where are the streets, the *real* streets, the *real* buildings?" I asked my uncle Martin who had preceded us here by a year and who took me for a walk in the neighborhood, Newark's then-affluent Weequahic section, where my father's uncle lived. For we were not walking on what I had understood streets to be: habitations dense with a feeling of life being lived, a connected-ness, an intimacy observed and replenished, shouts from win-dows, the sounds of trams clanking, streets filled with people walking, women out shopping, schoolboys being rowdy, a shopkeeper in long apron sweeping the sidewalk, dogs sniffing around trees, streets that were rarely long and never straight, usually connecting with other streets, often merging into a square where traffic moved in a circle around a small park with a statue in its center, or a group of statues in a fountain usually not open, water trickling from one spout, just enough for children to drink. Nothing, nothing like this confronted me on my first walk through an American suburban neighborhood. The streets, such as they were, were straight, lined with trees and lawns; we were the only people walking, occasionally a child pedaled around a driveway on a tricycle, or an older boy or a girl shot out from between the houses on a bicycle. There were cars parked in some of the driveways or in front of the houses; here and there was a woman getting out of a car loaded with bags or packages; there were sprinklers rotating on some of the lawns: no denseness of life lived but an emptiness, a melancholy feeling as I looked up and down the streets and was sharply aware of the clear shadows cast by the thick trees across the wet lawns.

"Don't people live here in regular houses?" All I had seen so far were what my uncle called one-family homes, usually of white stucco with slanting roofs, or what he explained were two-family homes, many of which were made of wood with enclosed porches, constructions such as I had never seen before.

"And where are the stores? Aren't there any stores?"

"They are in what is called downtown; you'll see. It's all different here. Where people live they don't shop, and where they shop they don't live. There are some commercial streets even in residential neighborhoods like this. But you won't find any houses here like in Vienna or anywhere in Europe, not even in New York, you'll see!"

This was all strange to me. But it was not the newness, not the difference in the appearance of things, in the physical environment as it began to unfold before me that was disturbing and unsettling, it was something unfamiliar in the total atmosphere, something alien, and that—that quality of something alien—that condition I had never felt before.

Later that day, sitting at the window of one of the rooms my Aunt Greta, Martin's wife, had rented for us, on commercial Lyons Avenue in a flat above a candy store, looking out on a street so long I could not see its beginning or its end, watching the steady stream of cars, across from me the row of low buildings, stucco or wood with shops, signs, and displays also new to me, a bank on one corner, a bar on the other, a cleaner, a bakery, a liquor store, a greengrocer, a gas station, I felt an increased onslaught of this unfamiliar sensation. Other than when crossing the ocean, I had never seen the sky so vast, the clouds so low; probably because of the lowness of the buildings the sky seemed more vast, more exposed and, somehow, lonely; and for the first time in my life I sensed a feeling of loss and dejection, an acute loneliness as though in a dream I had awakened in an uninhabited darkness, no family, no human life, only a wasteland of stones and prickly shrubs. I felt lost, cut off. But why? And from what? What was it that gave me that sense of grim departure? After all, I was not alone, I was with my parents, brother, aunts, uncles, cousins; moreover, we had escaped the Nazis and the war, we were free . . . why then this dreadful dejection? I felt almost physically ill; I wanted to bring it all up, be rid of it, throw it up, if I could! Why? What had I experienced? What was it that was missing here and had caused this inner shudder?

▶3

Was it disappointment, finding the opposite of what I had anticipated, that gave me this most disturbing sensation? It could not have been that, for America had been a reality to me in only vague terms. Other than the Manhattan skyline and the contrast of how the rich and the poor live as I had seen in the film *Dead End Kids,* I had had no notion at all of visual America. Now that I look back on it and have thought about it for so long, how dread and despair had gripped me early that evening as I had looked out upon what I later discovered to be a characteristic scene of urban America, I feel that I experienced the reality of absence, and I am not referring to the physical absence of the continent I had then just left. I am referring to something that that continent contained and this one did not. I sensed, on that first day, an important characteristic of this, to me, new land. The eye had met newness, differences in the appearance of things. But that part of the inner being—the soul, if you like— that had always felt itself connected to what surrounded it as though the environment containing it were a reflection of itself, that part in me had not sensed itself reflected here, had not met itself here; it had met absence. How could I have known then that an inner communication was in fact occurring by the very lack of response; that I was experiencing America at its very core. What had been a fullness, a richness of soul in the very objects, the very atmosphere around me, was an emptiness here, an absence. At any rate, the other side of fullness, the other side of accumulations for centuries by means of human extensions, to the soil, the heavens, to each other.

II

VIENNA

► 1

Before arriving here America had meant a number of things to me, though each in a vague, abstract way. America was free, America was Roosevelt, America was jazz, was modern, was a place—as I had heard said in our house—one didn't live in unless one had to. Of these, its freedom and modernness engaged me the most. I had adored the world of my childhood—the baroque and nineteenth-century houses, the quays curving along the Danube Canal, the ornate monuments at the beginnings and ends of the many bridges, the splendid views of the surrounding hills from the parks and many other open spaces, the floral patterns in the formal lawns, the statues of emperors, war heroes, the great thinkers and artists, Goethe, Schiller, Beethoven, Schubert, Mozart, each in addition to its physical aspect of harmony conveying a contained mysteriousness—but despite these and so many other sights that had engaged my imagination and given me joy, I yearned for something else. My world had been heavy with the past, saturated, the present was little else than the evidence of the past, and I yearned for the new. I ran, whenever school, tutors, or violin lesson permitted it, to the Herrengasse in the *Innere Stadt,* Vienna's venerable first district, the inner city, its narrow streets crowded with the ornate palaces of the nobility, its few open spaces part of the former royal residences, to watch the construction of Vienna's first Hochhaus which, when completed, was by American standards a miniature skyscraper, for it consisted of no more than fourteen stories, I believe. But for me, it was spectacular; it was new and it was modern. This was not another replica of the old style I had seen all my life—as far as I was concerned even the revolutionary art nouveau buildings of Adolf Loos close by were of the old style—this was modern, straight-up, with terraces and recessed upper floors. This was our first skyscraper, our Manhattan, and to my mind the modern was entirely associated with the English language and America. I had studied English at home with a tutor and at school, but before I began to learn it I used to imitate it. It held an extraordinary fascination for me: I loved its sounds and associations, which for me meant the contemporary world. And the contemporary world was the English-speaking world, and the modern world, America.

I had gone to a very strict Gymnasium, the Chajesrealgymnasium. Gymnasiums, training students in the humanities and in preparation for the university, were all strict; there were, in Vienna, the far less difficult regular high schools for students who did not intend to pursue any of the professions or who were not bright enough and lacked the required stamina; but the school I attended was a Jewish Gymnasium. It was a private school supported in part by the Vienna Jewish *Kultusgemeinde* (Jewish community council) and was named after one of Vienna's outstanding rabbis. While it was by no means a religious school it also gave one, in addition to the standard curriculum, studies in Jewish history, and Hebrew was an added, obligatory language. By the time I was eleven I was studying Latin, Hebrew, and English and—had Hitler not intervened when I was in my fifth year and had I concluded with *Matura,* the diploma following the eight-year studi s—I would also have had Greek and French. But, as the school was a Jewish private school which had nonetheless to meet all the academic requirements of the state-supported schools, and was evaluated by the state periodically, the training and demands on the students were particularly rigorous and strict. In those days it was a six-day week in school and we did not have classes on Saturday but, for half the day, on Sunday.

Vienna had an excellent radio station. The programs were generally "cultured": frequent broadcasts from Vienna's "temple," the *Staatsoper,* and from the various music festivals, of live concerts and solo recitals; there were also frequent productions of radio plays which, on the whole, were riveting and were done extremely well by some of Vienna's best known stage actors—Vienna did have a great tradition of acting and had a number of outstanding repertory theatres. And of course there were also the operettas—Lehar, Kalman, Bernatsky, Stolz, and others—and other forms of light entertainment. But what had been of greatest interest to me, and what I had looked upon with the severity of a religious observance, was the weekly hour of jazz, American jazz, which had been relegated to the far from "prime-time" hour of eight to nine on Saturday mornings. So I was up early on Saturdays, my only morning for sleeping late; nothing could keep me from listening to the weekly hour of jazz. It was an important part of my adolescent—really early-adolescent—yearning; part of my worship of the new. And, in a way, I associated America with that weekly worship.

▶2

I did not go to school after June 1938. Our plans three months after the *Anschluss* were entirely unclear. My father held on to the notion that if this sudden and, to us, unwelcome intrusion by the Germans would not be over soon, *somehow* corrected—"They won't permit it," he would say, meaning the civilized defenders, the French and the English, "this is the center, the heart of Europe"—life under this new, imposed order would at least become tolerable once things had settled down; which was his way of refusing to accept the horrendous prospect of having to change his life, of having to give up a way of life he had loved.

So it was not because we were about to leave Vienna that I had not gone back to school but because the Nazi authorities had closed it. From June 1938 on there was no school for Jewish students. Soon after the Anschluss hundreds expelled from their Gymnasiums came to mine; the classrooms were bulging for the next three months. But after that the doors of education were shut—as were businesses, theatres, hotels, even the parks, where *Juden Verboten* was painted on the benches, or elsewhere hung as printed signs on gates, doors, windows. Also, by the time schools had opened in the fall for non-Jewish youngsters, thousands upon thousands of Jewish boys and girls had left, had had their dreadful departures at railway stations where groups of hundreds left at a time for asylum granted by England, Belgium, Holland; some, the fortunate ones, going as part of the Youth Alleya to Palestine. I saw two such departures, one of Trudie, the six-year-old daughter of one of my mother's cousins; the other of Eugen, my closest friend at the time.

Trudie was part of a group going to England. In those early days of the Anschluss, the English authorities permitted children to enter England provided they had relatives or family friends prepared to take them in. Trudie's mother had cousins in London and Trudie was leaving to go to live with them. Each of the hundreds of children on that train carried identification and travel permits in a packet hung around the neck, each clung to a parent, both parents, to aunts, uncles, weeping, never before having been separated for this long a period, experiencing the worst trauma of their early years. Assurances from parents, forced smiles, last-minute gifts to assuage sorrow, the reality of a nightmare, and then the children waving, crowded around the windows, the train slowly pulling out, the parents breaking down once the children were out of sight. For many, this proved to be the last time that they saw their children, and many feared it. Trudie's parents never saw her again. Both perished in a concentration camp. Eugen's departure was less tragic. He was fifteen and he was leaving to join his parents in Belgium; a year or so later, I saw him again, this time in Brooklyn. But even his departure had for me that curious aspect of unreality—or is it reality?—we experience when confronted by something beyond our control, something that runs entirely counter not only to our wishes but to what we are able to comprehend, and we stand by, utterly helpless, letting what is happening happen as though will had been wiped away, choice an illusion, and something we sense dimly as destiny has taken over, and what must be, is, and we can do nothing about it.

The last two weeks before he left, Eugen had stayed with us. His father had been arrested, as many Jews were, soon after the Anschluss, but fortunately released because an exit permit and entry visa to Belgium had been secured for him. However, he had to leave at once and he and Eugen's mother left Vienna a day or two after his release. Eugen's many aunts and uncles had also departed by that time, so he lived with us until he could join his youth group to Belgium.

I was very fond of him. We had between us—or, at least I toward him, for I could not be certain of the depth of his feelings—that strong bond of adolescent friendship and love that is perhaps never again matched in its naturalness, innocence, intense anticipation and enthusiasm for the mystery, the reality of the other individual. And the two weeks he stayed with us were uninterrupted, happy ones for me. However darkening, threatening, and incomprehensible the events encroaching upon us were, the quality of intimacy, of the heart being utterly at home and joyous in a combined state of contentment and anticipation, was unimpaired. Favorable outer conditions do not necessarily feed and enhance our inner being, and that the reverse is also true, that unfavorable outer conditions do not necessarily attack or alter our inner state of being: I was beginning to have my first intimations of such contradictory aspects.

I would stand by a window and look out upon streets where I had felt deeply at home. Almost unconsciously I would muse upon the wonder, the ever-unfolding, ever-increasing mysteriousness of life which continued, bringing every day new, first experiences of suggestions among shadows, of piercing looks in faces, of sexual stirrings. And though the doorbell was answered with great caution, if at all, for too many Jews had been arrested, too many apartments ransacked—I would see my Uncle Martin shaking with fear running from the toilet unzipped, his fly flopping about, because the bell had rung unexpectedly; it turned out to be a cousin come to visit and everyone roared with laughter at the sight of my disordered, fear-ridden uncle—though life was anything but normal and uncertainty hung over us like an ever-present mighty sword: I continued to feel at home, even oddly secure in my adolescent world, in which my dreams reached into reality and my life-to-be into my dreams. For the rupture had not yet occurred. I was still moving in familiar rooms, among familiar corners and darknesses; I was still looking out upon chestnut trees in the yard, as I had done for years on wakening, for there was a tree directly outside the window of my room. I was still rooted. My inner being was still connected to its source, a stem to its roots in the soil.

► 3

Soon after school was over, that summer of 1938, I had formed the habit of taking long walks along the same route. We had lived at Heinestrasse 31, corner Fugbachgasse, in the second district, called Leopoldstadt. Vienna has twenty-one districts, each retaining the name it was known by earlier as a suburb clustered around the inner city before becoming incorporated into Vienna in the last century. Leopoldstadt is a district separated from the center by the Danube Canal. In my time it contained one of the oldest Jewish quarters, dark, narrow streets with tall buildings. But that was only a small section in the district; in other parts there were wide avenues, open markets, three large temples, many smaller synagogues and of course many more churches and chapels, two railway stations, hotels, a circus, the renowned Dianabad (a year-round health institution), some good cafés—my parents' wedding reception was held in one, the Café Fetzer, in 1919; the district also contained a theatre and the famous Prater, the amusement park at the edge of an enormous *bois,* the Hauptallee, a wide avenue lined with dense trees and cafés with large terrace-gardens, and surrounded by meadows, thick bushes, ponds; it led to Vienna's racetrack and in the days of the empire was the favorite promenade of the aristocracy on foot, followed by their carriages, or driving in their open equipages. Hence, there were scattered around the district townhouses of the lower nobility and a good many stables. Our street was one of the district's wide avenues. In addition to the sidewalks there was on each side a path for bicyclists or, formerly, for horses as they pulled carriages into and out of the buildings; following this path was on each side a mall where rose giant, dense chestnut trees, shading the benches between them; next came the cobblestoned, main part of the avenue where the always slight traffic flowed and the tramway—which the Viennese pronounced *tromveh*—ran. There were few shops along the street, some corner cafés; the buildings were comfortable late eighteenth- and nineteenth-century apartment houses, though there were a few former palaces, in my time shut and inhabited only by caretakers on the ground floor inside the yard. Opposite our building were former royal stables, then empty, where horses were changed for the long rides through the Prater woods. The avenue ran from Taborstrasse, a long winding street, to the Praterstern, a circle where a number of wide avenues converged and in whose center stood a high, needle-like, lighted monument to Tegetthoff, an admiral honored for the defeat of the Danish and Italian fleets during the long reign of the Emperor Franz Joseph. In spring and summer the monument stood as a symbol of shining importance to pedestrians and cars approaching on the converging avenues; for during the warm seasons the Viennese and the tourists came in great numbers and the bright

Praterstern beckoned as the gateway to the Prater, popular for its amusement park, outdoor cafés, for strolling down the Hauptallee, and for clandestine purposes.

At the Praterstern was a building of enormous attraction to me, the Tegetthoff Kino. I went there many a Sunday afternoon, whenever a film was being shown to which I could be admitted. Film ratings were strictly observed and until I was fourteen I could never see a film *verboten* for anyone under sixteen. But by fourteen I was tall enough and with the aid of black crayon applied above my upper lip to fake the beginnings of adolescent fuzz, I often managed to be admitted to films deemed proper only for adults. In the days before Jews were barred from cinemas, there was always a two-part Sunday afternoon ritual to my film-going adventure. The first was mildly humiliating, the second pleasurable and often enriching. My brother and I were by no means spoilt. Not by our parents, certainly. Aunts and uncles were less strict, and the most permissive of all was Julie, who at twenty-five had strong sympathy with our adolescent interests—which she fired to no little degree and often indulged us in mischievously. But, unlike the situation common in American homes, we were not the center, our needs and interests did not dominate the house. We were given what bourgeois children were generally provided with— good schooling, tutors if needed, music lessons, adequate and appropriate clothing (always tailor-made), summers in the country—but what was not deemed essential by our parents we had to struggle for. Seeing American films—and American ones were at the top of my list—was not thought essential, nor were any kind except for harmless sentimental or educational ones. And so, the struggle began on Sunday afternoon whenever I needed to obtain the shilling for admittance to the Tegetthoff Kino. A shilling—or *schilling* in the German spelling—was not an insignificant sum in 1937 and early 1938. For a schilling and a half one could get quite a decent meal in any number of *Wirtshäuser*—a sort of local pub where food was served.

I usually went to my mother first. "May I have a schilling?" No reply. I repeat. "May I have a schilling?" After a long while, "What for?" "The movies." No reply. She would go on reading or knitting or daydreaming; she used to love to stand leaning against the floor-to-ceiling tile stove in the small dayroom next to the kitchen, her eyes closed, enjoying some form of revery. Often, when I was with a tutor in the next room, she would stand in that position in her favorite spot, half listening to the lesson, mostly absorbed in whatever she was thinking—but nothing escaped her, she was always aware of what was happening in the next room, in the kitchen, in the large rooms in the front of the apartment, hearing Julie answering the doorbell, the telephone, giving orders from her state of revery without moving. "Tell him I am not in," "I'll ring back," "Give him ten groschen," "We don't want his soap but give him a coin," "Tell him to wax the floor next week," "Auf Wiedersehen, Frau Aberbarch. Is he improving? I know, he'd rather be at the Tegetthoff Kino. He'll never speak Hebrew like his father."

"Mama, I need a schilling for the movies. Please, Willie is going, please." "Finished with your homework?" "Yes." "Why do you have to go to the movies so often? Why don't you read your Tolstoy?" As a Bar-mitzvah present the previous December, I had been given the complete works of Tolstoy, in which my mother was reading, or re-reading, and I read in intermittently. "Not now. I want to go to see the new film with Willie." "You and your Willie, you and your god, always doing what he does." All this said with her eyes closed and standing against the stove. "All the other boys at school go to the movies on Sunday, please!" Silence. Silence. Then, without opening her eyes, like the oracle speaking, in low, slow tones, as usual: "Go ask your father." The routine had started. I was being shuttled back and forth. My mother sending me to my father; my father, at first imperturbable in *his* Sunday afternoon—after dinner—revery, at last answering me and telling me to go and see my mother. In the end, I always got the schilling, telephoned Willie, and embarked upon the second, the pleasant phase of the movie-going ritual. We were off to the Tegetthoff Kino where, like so many of my generation, I received my education in things and ways American.

School taught us next to nothing about the New World. The history curriculum touched only briefly on the American Revolution. In language, we were taught English in the British manner; we were not encouraged to read American authors and those we did we read on our own. My mother had been reading the books of Shalom Asch and she had passed them on to me. It was from him that I learned something, for the first time, of the American immigrant experience.

And we, my mother and I, also read Dreiser's *Sister Carrie,* and others. But as far as the regular school program was concerned, modern America did not yet exist, didn't belong in our studies. Still, my class sat in rapt attention in the term's first history lesson in the fall of 1937, when Professor Roser told us, informally, of her American visit. She had gone there during the summer on her wedding trip. What seemed the most outlandish to me, in her descriptions of New York, was her account of Times Square, a landmark I knew well from the movies and newsreels. New York's entertainment center was so crowded, she related, the sidewalks so jammed that the only way one could move ahead was to clear a path for oneself with one's elbows by pushing people aside. I thought this extremely odd and funny. Accustomed to a leisurely pace, a politeness to strangers, to streets rarely crowded, I couldn't imagine this; not the dense masses and, mostly, not this manner of people pushing each other in order to walk. I was also impressed, favorably this time, with her account of an opposite attitude, the patience of the public when waiting in line, whether for a bus, in a bank, or in a store. I was neither accustomed to the inconsiderateness of the pushers nor to the considerateness of people forming a line. This contradiction amused and startled me, and from all of what Professor Roser told us of her exotic story, it stood out above all. (A year or so later, she made the journey again, this time not as a honeymooner but an immigrant.)

But despite such first-hand accounts, and there were others from friends and relatives who had visited America, nothing was as immediate and instructive as the American films, though most of those I saw were either historical adventure films like *Anthony Adverse,* sentimental musicals like *Maytime,* or the modern, glamorous dance films with Fred Astaire and Ginger Rogers. And, of course, there was Shirley Temple, for whose films I did not have to apply crayons to my upper lip in order to be admitted. And *The Dead End Kids* with Sylvia Sidney, the most telling film yet of life in modern New York, which had made a lasting impression on me. But regardless of subject and period, they were glamorous all, and the stars memorable: Frederic March in the adventure film; Tyrone Power, his perfect handsomeness, his elegant manner; Astaire and Rogers, their swift, dashing, stylish modernity; Sylvia Sidney, sorrowful, tormented, and brave; Jeanette MacDonald and Nelson Eddy, romantic, picture-book perfect. We talked of them between classes, on our walks home from school, whistled their songs, imitated their accents. For the movies, along with visits to the Opera and the Burgtheater (Vienna's famed classical theatre), the latter two sponsored by parents and approved by teachers, were our extracurricular education, our direct confrontation with life's hopes and dilemmas expressed in an art form.

Whether we realized it or not, and we could hardly have done so then, our imagination was engaged fully and richly from early on. The physical reality of the city itself fed the imagination. The city's outstanding aspects had been conceived of in artistic terms. There was even something artlike about its situation between gentle hills, sloping vineyards, a fertile plain stretching from a broad, romantic river; and life lived in a city thus surrounded, the style aspired to, had about it the manner of art. At its best, this atmosphere was conducive to artistic genius, and there is more than enough evidence that it did flourish there for over a hundred years. At its worst, it produced an excess of artificiality, in manners, in customs which finally degenerated into superficial slightness and the deceptive charm, horror really, of *Gemütlichkeit*. But for a child born and raised there, for a child as open to impressions as I was, it was a rich terrain for the imagination. Things were not as they seemed. There was mystery about the order of classical lawns, clipped hedges, cone-shaped bushes, about the opulent decorativeness of baroque facades, the silence of an *allée* of statuary, especially of fountains with nothing but the leaves from trees in their dry basins. Things were not as they seemed; I sensed this early on from the physical qualities of the world, of both the natural and man-made world around me. What were they, if they were not what they seemed? What was it that inhabited them that gave them the aura of mystery that so fired and soothed the imagination? Of course, I did not ask such questions then. But this was the nature of the atmosphere I imbibed, and because it suggested questions and with them a yearning for something answered, and because I sensed somehow that what was real, or had been real in the things around me, was out of reach, that the core of the glimmer still apparent was in the distant, distant past: I yearned for what was apprehendable, for things not as they seemed but as they were and, somehow, this is what American films gave me. The sense of *now*—although some took place in bygone periods—American films meant *now,* and America was *now.* I felt that with certainty. And when I sat with Willie, who was my best friend then and with whom I shared the intimate closeness later transferred to handsome Eugen ("An Adonis," my Aunt Grete had gasped when she first saw him in the entrance hall of our apartment), when on Sunday afternoons we sat in the comfort of the darkness in the Tegetthoff Kino, close to each other, and were totally absorbed by the film, as though our physical beings had been transmuted by some magic and had merged with the wide screen where the marvel of another life, a truer life as I thought then, the world of my life-to-be was the only reality—I felt that my anticipation had been somewhat assuaged, my imagination enriched in a new way. And felt, on leaving the cinema, that another world—other than that made up of strict, sour-faced teachers and long, silent museum rooms—awaited, lay ahead. Whether that was simply the world a young adolescent sees as the grown-up world, or in fact a changed world, other than the one in which I then lived, I could not tell. Just what it was was vague, but that something else existed, and that that something awaited me I felt strengthened in feeling, as I arrived back home. forced to think again of next day's classes. Alas, these movie-going adventures also ended by the time school in Vienna ended for me in June 1938 and I took to taking long walks, my only outlet then to allow the imagination to roam.

► 4

Before giving my route and telling of an "American experience" I had on one of those walks, I should describe in greater detail the location of our building. Its situation was in itself an expression of a coziness one finds only in the layout and character of certain European cities, a coziness compounded also of city sounds, the light bells from the corner chapel, the occasional clanging of the tramway, hoofs on cobblestones—horse-drawn delivery wagons were still in use—a car-horn, of voices of people strolling past the open windows, of boys playing soccer or girls throwing diabolo in the side streets. These were expressions of a daily, of an established pattern, of a continued connectedness. There was no sense of urgency or hurry about any of this. On the contrary it had a somnambulant quality about it, of repetitiveness, an unbroken routine that brought with it also more than a tinge of hopelessness, fatigue, colorless drabness—staleness as well as coziness. And the corner location of our apartment contributed to this nostalgic landscape. Directly opposite our building, two streets merged with Heinestrasse—Grosse

Stadtgutgasse and Zirkusgasse—providing an enlarged openness so that one had from our windows and especially the attic windows (a portion of the attic belonged to each of the apartments for storage, maid's rooms, or whatever purposes the occupants wished to use the space for), a view at once intimate and expansive: of habitations always in human proportions, of the historic monument at the end of the broad avenue, of patches of green and the top part of the *Riesenrad* (giant Ferris wheel) of the Prater beyond.

These many years, living principally in New York, I have had a series of recurrent dreams. Some are of people who have died, not only those who figured significantly in my life, like my parents or my great friend Jean Garrigue, but others peripheral to it. For example, for years I dreamed about two people who did not belong prominently in my childhood and whom I last saw in 1938, the sister and brother-in-law of an aunt of mine. Their sons survived, but they perished in a concentration camp. For a period of about ten years, they reappeared in the same dream, always sorrowful, always together, always alive, figures existing haze-like in a haze. My mother's brother, sister-in-law, two sisters and their husbands, and most of their children were annihilated, yet I never once dreamed of them—my blood relatives. But that couple, distantly connected to us, came to me again and again like a reminiscence of loss, a monument of nothingness that came, nonetheless, to convey its vanished though persisting reality.

Sorrow, loss, memory; of people, of place, of connectedness. Of something that has disappeared in its physical form but whose essence continues, breaking forth into sometimes magnificent symbols, illuminated moments in dreams. In this manner, the building we had lived in has repeatedly been the locale of my dreams. Approaching it from the spacious avenue, having come from the harmonious fields, the trees in white bloom, having walked toward it up the broad street of deep familiarity where there is no one but myself, the full length of the street entirely empty except for me; the sky, the street, the building as I near it covered in the colors of early sunset, and then, reaching our windows, lifting myself up to them, looking inside, remaining outside but looking in a window on the corner and seeing from there a row of rooms furnished and arranged in perfection and, once at least, on a bed, two shapes in intimate closeness. Or, in another recurring incident: It is after the war, my parents are back in our apartment, I wander again through the beloved rooms; my parents have never given it up, this place of my young adolescence, it has been ours now for forty, fifty years; and the rooms are arranged for receptions, windows and balconies filled with shady plants for there is always sunshine; and it is our home, has always been ours; it cannot be abolished—home, belonging, centered where you are meant to be.

No doubt, dreams these, promoted by exile. For the depth in us strives only toward the natural condition however strongly opposed by unnatural accretions. Building means home, and home means place and place means a drenched blessedness, the soil absorbed into a shining invisibleness that we speak of as the feeling of "feeling at home." Memory, harmony at the core. It is, therefore, not a place I once lived in that I dream of, but the place that has once existed and beckons still: the nostalgia for that which is. Which cannot be destroyed and is not lost, though we may suffer separation.

When I arrived in America, a little more than a year after I had started on my regular walks into the Innere Stadt, or simply, *die Stadt,* as the Viennese call it, what did I in fact know of the culture that had bred me? At fourteen I might have had intellectual potential but I had little information. I was not a good student, though I worked hard; I was, however, a much better dreamer, absorber of impressions than a learner of facts. My best subject in school, my only *sehr gut* was, as though by presentiment, English. But I did poorly in everything else despite the assistance of tutors. History meant dates and little more, all subjects were a process of drilling information, facts, and figures into my head until exams were over and I promptly disposed of them. Even literature was dreary for it meant learning Schiller by heart, reading Ceasar's *Gallic Wars* in Latin, and memorizing the opening chapters of Ovid's *Metamorphoses,* "Aurea prima sata est eitas quae vindice nullo. . . ." But it seems to me that I did absorb if not the facts the aura in which they existed, if not the stated information the unstated atmosphere surrounding them. If I was learning my culture poorly, I was absorbing it richly. And some of that process of absorption occurred along the route I took so often after June 1938 and until I left Vienna in August 1939.

▶ 5

Starting from our house, the route took me down Heinestrasse (after the Anschluss called Schönererstrasse in honor of Georg von Schönerer, one of Hitler's predecessors in virulent anti-Semitism) to the Praterstern, then along Praterstrasse, another wide avenue of shops and bourgeois flats with first-floor (second-story here) high ceilings and chandeliers visible from the street, past a statue of Nestroi, the nineteenth-century Austrian playwright, to the Danube Canal and a choice of bridges. Usually I took the Uraniabrücke which brought me to the Urania (Vienna's planetarium) at the beginning of the Ringstrasse, or the *Ring* as that famous, wide, tree-lined boulevard circling die Stadt is referred to locally; on either side of the Danube were the quays, also tree-lined, with narrow parks and solid, mostly nineteenth-century apartment houses, though many on the Leopoldstadt side were earlier. Or I could have taken the Schwedenbrücke which I would have reached passing my father's *Stammcafé,* the Café Fetzer—which he frequented regularly—and beyond it, directly below the bridge, the swimming pool in the Canal where Vienna's young bourgeoisie swam and sunned itself and where I was not permitted to enter as I was not wearing a swastika in my lapel, the signal instituted immediately after the Anschluss to announce one's Aryan blood to the world around one. This route would have brought me to the Schwedenplatz, a large square whose inside, gravelled space, separated from street and sidewalks, was taken up by a large, outdoor café where in the spring and summer colored umbrellas shielded the patrons from the sun. Next, turning right on Kohl-messergasse, where one of our relatives, a family with close ties of friendship to mine, had had a textile shop (but no longer, it was confiscated, as most prestigious Jewish-owned establish-ments were soon after the advent of Hitler), I would reach the Rotenturmstrasse, and the Hotel Excelsior at its corner, where, one sunny day, my "American experience" occurred. But of that, later.

That corner could also have been reached via another bridge that crossed the Danube Canal at the Dianabad, a large, imposing building complex that was a year-round institution for health. It would take a Fellini to convey its quality; his depiction of the spa in *8½* reminded me of it, as it did of another health resort—a true spa not just a building—where I used to accompany my mother when she took the cure there; but more of that also later. The Dianabad was a sort of health-palace, every kind of physical health therapy was possible there. It had numerous steam baths, gymnasiums, elegant shops and cafés in its arcades, escalators, saunas, and an enormous swimming pool in a hall the height of the entire building; this was surrounded by floor after floor of galleries from where one reached the lockers or private rooms and from where one could observe the people racing or just swimming in the pool, which had a well-known attraction: high, artificial waves, for fifteen minutes every hour. It was another kind of "temple" in Vienna—the Opera, or *Oper,* as it was called, being at the top of that hierarchy—and it was very popu-lar with the smart-set, both Austrian and international. The Prince of Wales used to visit there each time he was in Vienna, or so it was rumored. It was certainly, on my few visits there, full of foreigners, and had about it for me at the age of thirteen, when I first went there with my class from school, a novel mysteriousness, an awakening of erotic realities, of body-consciousness, and an excitement in the imagination that attended it. But on my walks in lieu of school I could not have entered there; like almost everything my young mind and body were ready for, it was off limits to me.

The point to which my tour invariably led, regardless of the bridge taken, was the Opera, that large, imposing building, or rather building complex on the Ring that had for so long been the focal point of Viennese attention. It was said that the collapse of the World Bank would make secondary headlines if Jeritza or another adored diva had hit a spectacular note in *Tosca* or another of the beloved "Viennese" operas the night before. The fact that Puccini was Italian mattered little to the Viennese, he was theirs, he understood their heart, and they loved him for it. This was not just *Schwärmerei;* the Viennese understood emotions—they were less good in their respect for feelings—and they did not hold them back. They saw life as a sad affair; time as the great devastator, love as betrayal, loss as a necessary, inescapable condition, and they loved to weep their eyes out over these inevitable human realities. Never mind that they had little use for genius. They loved art more than artists, though they did tolerate, even adore some in the performing arts. But genius was too unsettling, the *vie bohème* not popular, there was no place for it in their bureaucratic concepts. They did not like art as a vehicle of criticism but loved it as a spectacle.

They preferred those operas and plays that confirmed them in their suspicion that life cheats, cheats one of happiness, and they loved to have their hearts melted in these confirmations. They accepted human love as tragedy or sentimental triumph but had little taste for it as transcendence, or for its apocalyptic magnitude as in *Tristan*. They were mad about *Turandot* and on one occasion carried Jan Kiepura, then their favorite tenor in that opera (he possessed the required melting power), on their shoulders, paraded him up and down the Opernring, placed him on top of a taxi, and waved him away. My acquaintance with opera had started early: *Madama Butterfly* (another of the adored Viennese favorites), *The Bartered Bride, Lohengrin,* a memorable *Don Giovanni* with the famous Louise Helletsgruber as Donna Anna which I attended one Saturday afternoon in 1937 with Willie and his sister and younger brother. But, of course, now I could only stand outside the building and absorb its stateliness, the life around it, the sense of importance it gave off.

As I said, I could get to this point by various routes—up the Ringstrasse from the Urania, or up the Rotenturmstrasse past the Stephansplatz where stood St. Stephen's, Vienna's central cathedral, from there up the Kärntnerstrasse, then a fashionable street on the order of Fifth Avenue at its height, or of the Faubourg St. Honoré in Paris. (When I was in Vienna last, in 1974, this street had become a pedestrian mall, the once elegant shops replaced by bargain stores.) In 1938, regardless of the route I chose, each time I took this walk I was adding to my reservoir of impressions whereby I imbibed by a sort of cultural osmosis the character, the inner nature, much of the psyche of the world that bred me. If school could no longer cram dates and phrases into my head that were to add up to my *humanistische Erziehung* (humanistic upbringing), the churches, buildings, squares I crossed and passed on these walks, the faces I encountered on the streets or in the parks—Volksgarten, Burggarten where I strolled on occasion—transmitted to me impressions of cultural character and enlivened my imagination. This was education by suggestive transferrence—the education each person receives in the formative years no matter where born and brought up, no matter what the surroundings. But the suggestions of historic purposes and meanings, of human desires and frailties, which I received, were dense with human attributes and accomplishments. Above all they implanted in me the feeling that man was capable of his challenge: to do great things by virtue of patient though spirited cultivation of his best faculties. That life was foremost a human affair—this was the implication—mysterious and worthy of desire. That sadness is rooted in time but that the larger designs—expressed through heroic deeds and by genius through art, through floral patterns, marble, oil on canvas, sun in windows—are not so restricted; and that the interplay, the force of one against the other, time against timelessness, lives in the darkness of eyes, in gentle faces, movements of hands. The faculty whereby we receive these contrasts, the imagination that enables us to discern the changeless, invisible reality in the transitory visible world, was very much alive for me, vibrated richly in those days of my walks through beleaguered Vienna. For the dark destiny was also in the air, the black boots of the SS troops resounding on Vienna's pavements with ever-greater frequency. Still, the magic of the imagination won out over the dread world-realities and for a few months at least—until the infamous Kristallnacht of November 10, 1938, when more than Vienna's synagogues lay in ruins, all hopes for continued life there shattered like the glass littering the streets—I was able still to give myself over to the musings of a fourteen-year-old boy embarked upon the great reaches of the imagination and becoming dimly aware of the power and reality of the human spirit.

▶6

I was accompanied on these expeditions by my dog, Fifi, a two-year-old, pure-bred, female *Rehrattler* (toy Doberman pinscher), then a popular breed in Vienna. Fifi was black, had a brown-spotted head, fierce eyes, long, thin, slightly shaking legs, was nervous, high-strung, and intelligent. In German, the name Fifi did not have the silly, froufrou quality it has in English. It was a proper name for this type of dog, not small enough to be a lapdog, not large enough to scare toddlers in the park. Actually when my father had brought the dog home about a year earlier—her former owners, Russians, were leaving Vienna and could not take the dog along—her name had been Grete. But I had an aunt by that name.

I think every boy in Vienna must have had at least one Tante Grete; not only a parent's sister was called *tante* but cousins and close family friends as well. We had a mental picture of my somewhat snobbish aunt snapping at us upon hearing our new dog called by her name; so the dog was baptized Fifi. Of course, I adored her, we all did; she even came to America with us as I have already mentioned. I took her, in addition to my excursions, on her regular morning and evening walks; she slept with me, curled up in the crook of my legs bent, dutifully, to accommodate her, and she was in the habit, so my mother and Julie told me, of jumping frantically up and down below the window if she sensed that I was approaching or heard me whistling a few blocks away. At first my father had addressed her in Russian to ease the pain of transition for her; I did not know her former owners but she could not have been inordinately attached to them, for she became thus attached to us very quickly. She would whine and carry on when left alone with only Julie, whom for some reason she considered— as we certainly did not—an inferior member of the household, or had to be content to spend some hours in the afternoon with a visiting uncle or cousin. As she lay shivering in the depth of her sorrow on a divan in the sitting room, nothing could make her stop her whimpering sounds unless she could tell that one of us was coming home and was only a few blocks away. Then she would stand waiting at the heavy entrance door until the bell rang and Julie opened it, or we let ourselves in, and she would practically lift herself up into our arms.

When, some months later, my aunt Grete—who with her husband, my Uncle Martin, had emigrated to America in November 1938—wrote that we should under no circumstances go to the great expense of ordering what was called a "lift" to ship our furniture to America, a situation arose which put Fifi in a frenzy of confusion. Rooms over there, aunt Grete wrote, were not large enough to hold our large chests, beds, tables, sideboards, etc.; at least not the rooms we were likely to be able to afford. Consequently, once it had in fact been decided that we would go to America, my parents sold the furniture. Frantic, Fifi rushed back and forth and finally placed herself at the open entrance-door from where she could not be persuaded to move but stood there as though rooted to the floor, clutching in her mouth her favorite ball, fiercely holding on to it as the movers carried out piece after piece of our modern, only recently acquired, Swedish furniture my mother had watched over so carefully—my brother and I had never been permitted to sit on our new dining room chairs in our shiny lederhosen.

The fact that my parents had contemplated ordering a crate the size of a railroad car in which our heavy belongings were to be transported, as certain Jewish families had done, indicates a bourgeois characteristic that was part of the texture of life that had prevailed for so long a time. One cherished possessions. One lived with the things one owned and resisted changing them or disposing of them. To step into the salon of the neighbors whose family had owned our building since its construction in the early nineteenth century was to enter a Biedermeier world with, here and there, evidence of a more recent style; fringed lamps, Chinese vases, faded silks and carpets. It was perfectly in order to add things, but not to get rid of them. Things, objects, became part of one's physical self. One would no more throw out a sofa or a writing desk than cut off a limb, unless cracks, rot, or gangrene demanded it. I am reminded of Mme. Ranevsky in Chekhov's *The Cherry Orchard* whose first outburst of joy, having come home after years abroad, is to her nursery, her address to her beloved chest of drawers, a lingering part of her childhood. Likewise in my childhood world to dispose of an object that had surrounded a parent or a grandparent for years was to cause a tear in a fabric of secure familiarity. Moreover, this was a perfectly sincere emotion. For one had in fact lived with one's things as though woods and plasters and fabrics, even one's clothing, were animate, breathing realities. The materials had become extensions of, had been transformed into one's self. This feeling was genuine; it came from, and spoke in turn to, the heart. But it also created a resistance often at odds with necessity and always so with the reality of time and change. It made for a spiritless sameness and became a stubborn, unrealistic clinging on. When, only a few years before the advent of the Nazis, my mother had entirely redecorated our apartment, she could not endure giving up most of her old furniture and it stood crammed into two rooms until—when Fifi watched by the door and the new Swedish furniture was carried out like corpses—the old things were revived and we lived in them again until we left.

And so, Fifi accompanied me on those spring and summer afternoons of 1938. It was the first summer I had ever spent in Vienna; previous ones had always been in the country, either at a spa in Czechoslovakia or one near Vienna. Between the wars the city had been a popular attraction for tourists; this was especially so in the warmer months. I had formed the habit of playing a game guessing the nationalities of foreigners walking ahead of me. They were always well dressed; in those days only the wealthy Europeans traveled and I had developed a knack for distinguishing the English from the French, the French from the Italians, the Italians from the Roumanians, and so on. The easiest to spot were the Americans—from their casualness, their distinct manner of walking and talking—but I had discovered equally distinctive traits in others; for example, women with a tint of blue or pink in their greyish hair invariably turned out to be Italian or Roumanian. Once I had decided on their origin, I sped up my walk, caught up with them, slowed down as I passed them, heard them talk and knew then whether I had won or not. To let it be known to the international set in the fashionable streets of Vienna that I too was of their kind, was not limited to my native tongue but was as cosmopolitan as they were, and hence belonged to their enviable order, I would address Fifi either in the few Russian words I had learned when my father first brought Fifi to us, or in English, which I spoke quite fluently by then. To me what was foreign was glamorous. It meant travel, luxury trains and hotels, it meant wealth and privilege and at fourteen I was no rebel. Rather, I was myself addicted to the bourgeois addiction to aristocratic manners, the noble aura. I thought it natural for some people to exude and enjoy privilege and its air impressed me. Unlike my brother, who had for years rebelled against what he called "all this rot," I was all for the high-toned way of life. If not of my imagination—which even by then was far more serious—this was part of my adolescent fantasy: to be a *von,* to speak only English, to be modern, to drive up in front of elegant hotels. In this mood, I came one day upon a group of foreigners—I knew at once they were Americans—standing in front of a long, black car at the Hotel Excelsior. Porters were loading the car with elegant leather luggage. In the group, a family, I supposed, I spotted a boy my own age.

My first thought was, how *légère!* (The language of the Viennese with high-tone pretensions was peppered with foreign words, mostly French but also some English. *Légère,* in French *light* as in lightweight, was used to suggest casual, leisurely but elegant.) To be légère meant to be stylish in the *right* way—which, in turn, meant not vulgar—and to be thus in manner or dress was highly approved of by the Viennese eager to be part of the haut monde. The entire group was dressed in that way, but that agreeable quality soon dissolved into the overall appealing nature of their manner, the air of modernity and freedom that they gave off. At first I was curious, then startled, captivated, then enthralled.

I was, quite naturally, well dressed. One didn't venture out on a stroll through the Innere Stadt, the bastion of aristocratic tradition and dignity, unless one were. I wore a dark blue suit with short pants, appropriate for a boy my age, a tie, long socks, black, légère shoes. I had Fifi in my arms, she had to be carried from time to time, the walk was too long and tiring for her, her red leash wrapped around my hand. My hair was long, as was the style for boys, the right side falling down my forehead. I was the perfect specimen of a boy of Viennese bourgeois background, as though sculpted to order. I was, in fact, in the process of being finished into a statue, had perhaps already been shaped into one: a statue of middle-European attitudes, past and present, as I began to discover not long thereafter in my Newark transplantation. But I sensed this then and looking at the boy—his carefree hair, his open shirt, his casual, light trousers, his sandals, his unstockinged feet—I caught, in a split second, the image of what is possible in life: a free spirit.

It was as though the visage before me had caused me to dive deep within myself, behind the marble or iron cast, below the cultural accumulations, to find there its replica within me: I, transformed into a free being; I, emerged as what I also am, a free spirit, my hair messed up by wind and light, my shirt open, my feet bare. I was not standing; suddenly I was thrust upward and forward. I was leaving the heaviness behind me. I was off the ground.

I clutched Fifi as though to endure and prolong this headiness. She responded by licking my face, and this brought me back. Then I heard the group I had been watching, the boy's image that had mesmerized me, talking. He was helping the porters with the luggage. They were American, as I had suspected. I was right again, this time. I won the game. I could tell even without having heard them, from their manner. It was the manner entirely appropriate to the vision of freedom I had just experienced. Their movements were melodious, as were their words when I heard them; they were more than elegant: they behaved in a way I had so far not observed, or at least never as keenly before; they behaved like people who cared about other things than conventional formality and propriety. What they did care about seemed to me to be rooted in something else, something I vaguely perceived as being free, being themselves. But what was not in the least vague to me was that they were American. And from that day onward the curiosity I had always had about the new continent was intensified. From then on my desire to know it, to go there, was confirmed. America became part of my overall, vague, yet by then intensely felt, yearning.

I had had a previous encounter with someone who stood out from the rest and who had suggested a cultural character totally different from the one that had been projected around me. The person was a young American woman and the place where the encounter occurred was the Czech resort Lazne Luhačovice, in July of 1937.

Karlsbad, Marienbad, Baden-Baden, the best-known watering places in middle Europe, were by no means the only ones that drew people from all over the world to their curative springs. Luhačovice, of more recent vintage than those mentioned here, was a popular spa during the thirties, frequented largely by people from neighboring countries as well as Czechoslovakia; it had a large sanatorium for Czech labor unions which were then a strong force in that progressive country. Czechoslovakia, between the wars, became one of the most liberal of European republics. Tomas Masaryk, its founder and first president, had close ties with the United States; his wife, Charlotte Garrigue, was in fact a native American. The resort, modern, attractively situated in the foothills of the Tatra mountains, surrounded by pine forests and old villages, rich in springs that would soothe a variety of minor diseases and for a while cure a larger variety of imaginary ones, was filled to capacity in the summer months. It swarmed with women of all ages, obedient husbands, and children and teenagers like myself who, despite proper upbringing, were rowdy and noisy (for they were on vacation), and during the morning hours when their mothers lay packed in mud or were drilled in exercises, were mostly left to their own devices. My mother suffered from a minor bronchial condition which flared up usually when during the damp and cold late winter months the vision of a spa in the bright colors of summer was a welcome apparition. Her mild attacks—she did have some serious ones when we arrived destitute in Newark—made it difficult for her to breathe, and she would always have to sit up in bed and inhale medicinal vapors. Luhačovice was one of several spas that alleviated that condition, and starting in 1927, when I was three, we went there from time to time.

I remember little, almost nothing, in a distinctive sense, of my very early years. More than jumping up and down while holding on to the net around my *Kinderbett* (the children's bed that follows the crib) at the sight of my father returned from one of his frequent journeys; or sitting atop his shoulder holding on to his head while we played *Stockerl* (diminutive for walking-cane), another kind of jumping game; or, while on this unearthly height, I would point to the light overhead and would say with an immense grin of discovery and delight, "*Lichtie, Lichtie*" (baby-talk for "light, light")—more than that does not emerge from my overall impression of vagueness during these first years. But that overall impression is vivid still—as though life, as it began to take form for me, to break into myriad shapes, grew out of a flow, a stream wherein distinctions were only gradually occurring. So that the sameness, the living oneness behind things, the reality of *that* became my first and distinct experience and, hence, memory. And, as though I could almost see the shape of things grow from that stream, I delighted in this primordial play. First, there was nothing; then, there was something, and the something I watched take shape was always different. Eventually, to each was attached a name. And I was happy. I remember being happy. The occurrences of things coming to consciousness made me happy. And the grown-ups around me delighted in my—and their relived—elemental joy. And that condition of my early life I remember even now.

An incident occurred in Luhačovice in the summer of either 1927 or 1928 when that experience of that first, fundamental state came to a peak it had not reached before. (I must assume it hadn't, or I would have remembered it.)

Only the abstract, formless aspect of that experience lingers on, the details are again vague. For, as though that stream had been contained in a chasm like the sea rushing up, I felt its intense rush through me, erupting in me, taking me into a condition way beyond my years, beyond adulthood, beyond the measure of years. Some supreme expression of certainty, it was. I have since seen it conveyed as a stance in Indian classical dance when one of the divinities—Krishna or Vishnu or Rama—is victorious, has defeated a usurper, a pretender, and dances to give expression to this supreme, fundamental glory. In physical detail I recall only that it occurred in late afternoon or early evening outdoors near the house where my mother had taken rooms; I believe my brother was with me; I recall also a rush of water (there was a rivulet in the old part of the resort where we lived that summer) and that grown-ups came running to me (I must have done something in response, must have behaved in some odd way). But I do remember the opening up, the excitement in the body as though the body itself were the flow. No doubt, there must have been even then an erotic component to these rumblings, to this ecstatic vision and experience.

► 8

We did not go to Luhačovice in the ensuing years. The Depression in America had hit my father's business badly—his was a wholesale business of raw skins and furs—and summers were spent in moderate cottages in the *Burgenland (land of castles,* one of Austria's eight provinces) about two hours south of Vienna. But by 1935 things were improving and by 1937 we were again able to spend the summer in agreeable Luhačovice. This time we went only for the month of July, for I had to prepare for an exam in Latin at the end of August. I would fail the subject and, in that event, the entire year, my fourth, at the Gymnasium, unless I passed this extended oral and written exam. That was the strictness of the school system: one subject failed and the entire school year had to be repeated. So I had to be back in Vienna for a stiff training with my tutor during August. (I did pass the exam and went on to my fifth year—and last, as it turned out—in September.)

In the beginning of July, my mother and I took the train at the *Nordbahnhof,* the railway station near where we lived, for Luhačovice. We were traveling with close friends of our family, a mother and daughter. The Kemplers were former neighbors of ours and Frau Kempler and my mother had known one another for a good many years. Their one child, a daughter, Gertie, was a thoroughly spoilt, not especially pretty, fifteen-year-old *Backfisch*—which literally means baking fish, and is a term applied to well-brought-up, teenage young ladies. Gertie, who had a crush on my handsome, girl-crazy brother, was a giggly, chattering girl who loved to talk about her Josephine Baker records and to whisper stories with scandalous suggestions. While our mothers wept over the recent death of my mother's cousin—the one who had owned the shop on Kohlmessergasse I mentioned earlier, and who had left a young widow and two teenage boys, now orphans—Gertie and I stood by the window of the compartment watching the fields and villages fly by and shared stories appropriate for the condition in life we had in common, namely of puberty, on my side, starting (I was thirteen), on hers, settled, hence unsettling.

Our confidences were innocent enough. While, once established in the villas where each had taken rooms, our mothers were busy with their treatments from morning until noon, Gertie and I would roam the parks and forests for interesting strangers we were too shy to approach, or watched them with fascination in the pool. Gertie would flirt with the men—though they never knew it—and I would make up stories about their lives. We would confide our thoughts and adolescent experiences in sex, limited though they were then. But what interested us and absorbed us above all was the modern and glamorous atmosphere in the resort and the activities of the vacationers.

Until noon the resort was quiet except for the children and

young people who took walks, swam, or played tennis. Next followed the large, main meal of the day, accompanied by waltzes, gypsy tunes, and other light music played in the restaurant by a few strings and a pianist; those "flamboyant Hungarians," as the correct, haughty women around my mother referred to them, nothing could hold them back from jumping atop the tables where they had just dined and doing a czardas to the cheers of the orchestra and the embarrassed looks of most of the diners in the large, crowded restaurant we frequented daily. But it was later in the day, after the exhausted grown-ups had had their rest while Gertie and I scouted the windows of photography shops for snapshots taken of us the day before, that the resort came to life full-force. Late afternoon coffee and pastries in one of the many *Konditorei,* a concert in the *Kurgarten*—usually Wagner overtures, a Dvořák symphony, a Schubert work, or some such popular classical music—and in the evenings, many of the residents in evening clothes on their way to one of the nightclubs for dancing and American jazz. For me, a dizzying atmosphere of attractive grown-up activity!

But it was also 1937 and the headlines and newscasts were full of disquieting reports of threatened aggression, of appeasement, and while standing around the springs that spouted from the marble-covered ground under rotunda-like enclosures, and holding in their glasses health-restoring waters, the discoursing crowd of acquaintances and friends created a murmur of uncertainty and fear. One woman was telling my mother incredible tales—incredible to us then, believable and mild only two or three years later—of confiscations and restrictions imposed upon the Jews in Danzig, her home, to which she would be returning soon. There were rumors of men arrested, of concentration camps, of ash-containing urns received by families. It seemed distant to me, beyond comprehension. Yet the reports persisted. I had heard them even a year earlier, in the summer of 1936, in Bad Sauerbrunn in the Burgenland where we had vacationed then, from German Jews in Austria on a holiday. But these reports did not yet intrude themselves upon me, I accepted them like a horror-story or a bad dream. I was immune to them due to my curiosity and eagerness for the coming of the rich, full life that I felt certain lay ahead of me. And everything about that summer month in Luhačovice had the right look for that. The life that I viewed before me and upon which I would one day be entering was attractive, full of mysterious possibilities very much worth desiring.

In that mood I sat one day in the late afternoon on a folding chair in the Kurgarten where the *Kurorchester*—one of the leading orchestras in middle Europe—played one of its important concerts, broadcast around the Continent. Ahead of me and somewhat to my right—so that I could observe her in profile—sat a woman, probably in her thirties, whom I had noticed before and who I knew to be an American. She wore a small American flag like a pin on her left chest, and I knew that she belonged to the American delegation of the International Congress for Women meeting that year in Luhačovice. The participants had been very much in evidence for days, their meetings announced and their main events open to the public. I went to none—neither did my mother nor Frau Kempler—but I was intrigued by the foreignness of the ladies, especially of those in Indian, Chinese, or Japanese dress. The American lady had stood out among them, despite their more exotic costumes, when I saw them one afternoon walking through the English garden. She was tall, thin, much more slender than most women were those days in middle Europe, and there was something about her that I found entirely captivating. When, some years later, I read Thomas Mann's *Magic Mountain* and came to the part where Hans Castorp first observes Mme. Chauchat through the glass door in the dining-room, I was reminded of my first glimpses of the American woman in the summer of 1937.

During the concert I was able to watch her more closely. Her dark blond hair did not have the *Dauerwellen* (permanent waves) customary then but was straight, long, and fell to her shoulders in a natural, graceful manner like an evening cloak falling to the heels of ladies stepping from the broad staircase onto the marble floor of the Staatsoper's vast foyer, or like the tail-feathers of a relaxed peacock I had that day watched in the park; there was something innocent, untouched about this naturalness that appealed to me greatly. Her features were also long and fine, her face untampered with—no make-up as far as I could tell, perhaps just some lipstick. Her dark, light dress fell as well without any fuss in the natural way of its material, the only decoration a bright belt and a string of corals around her neck. Her legs were long and slender, her feet a bit large, and she wore flat-heeled, légère shoes. She gave off the same kind of casual elegance that I so admired, a year later, in front of the Hotel Excelsior. But she had another quality that captivated me: She sat in the most natural manner, her arms folded in her lap across her crossed legs and she listened—she *really* listened! There was no pretense about that, no air of being there because being there and being seen there was important, more so than the concert or even the performers whom, presumably, one had come to hear—an attitude I was more familiar with. For the concert-going Viennese the occasion was often more important than the content of the concert or the competence of the performers. The occasion was part of the decoration, the civilized way of living, but it didn't make listening obligatory. Furthermore, they considered listening intently, eyes and ear fixed on the speaker or performer, not part of the "good" style, which was to be relaxed if not downright blasé. They knew quality, or the lack of it, at once, didn't have to listen carefully; they were too expert in matters of culture for that.

But this woman listened! And the intensity of her absorption was apparent from the indrawn, almost cast-like quality of her face. I found everything about her graceful; another kind, a new kind of elegance: that of controlled naturalness. If her manner reflected conventions of the world she was from, then her world was clearly a different one from the one I had known until then. A reserve and an integrity that I sensed and came to know and appreciate in later years. It wasn't all that much later, in fact, that I observed these suggested qualities again: in the group outside the hotel in Vienna and, about a year after that, in September 1939, on the deck of the *Statendam* when my father introduced me to two Americans he had befriended—two "Yankee types," the father, around fifty, the son, in his mid-twenties, polite, formal, yet easy, not strict, approachable, and friendly though not a bit voluble, in no way excessive.

►9

And so my impressions of America, from sources other than films, were beginning to be formed. They were, however, not always as flattering, as stimulating as the ones I have recounted thus far. An expedition taken during that summer of 1937 with my mother, Frau Kempler, and Gertie contributed to the less favorable aspects.

Zlin, the home of Batia Shoes, a company town styled after such in America—Hershey, Pennsylvania, was mentioned in comparison—was an hour's drive from Luhačovice. The town was considered an experiment, the first such on the Continent, whereby the workers were in some, to me, vague way, co-owners with the company of everything in it. It was a model community, the way of the future, or so the posters, reports, and leaflets said; businessmen and tourists were invited, and they came in cars and busloads from all over Europe to see for themselves. One day, when our mothers needed a rest from their thermal baths and inhalation tubes, we rented a car—it turned out to be the same model open Fiat my father had at that time—and were driven there. (Of course, our mothers did not drive; even my father didn't but engaged a chauffeur whenever he needed one.) From the minute I saw the town—the buildings not spread out but huddled together like sheep in the valley—I was overcome by an acute sense of discomfort, some vague sense of dislocation. Portentous? It was only two years later that Cousin Serge drove us above the industrial flat-lands of New Jersey—and when we left after a few hours, I was appalled.

I had, just a few weeks before, seen the film, *Of Things To Come,* based on H. G. Wells' novel, and the model town through which a tour guide took us reminded me of its futuristic world. Everywhere the key word was *efficiency,* a productive utilization of time. Waste was sinful, productivity rewarded. I had the sense of an unjust imposition, a manipulation not in the interest of the individual in the community but of the company, and though I had never been exposed to anything like it, and was only thirteen, I spoke out against it to the guide. To my mother's great surprise, and of all the adults in the group, I said that I considered this form of existence not a blessing but a deprivation. For I saw boys my own age working in the new, gleaming, modernistic shops and factories—"only until three in the afternoon" we were told with pride, then they go to school until the evening—and I could not imagine the replacement: instead of absorbing impressions, thinking, reading, daydreaming—push-buttons, stop-watches, indicator lights, factory whistles. There was no question in my mind of misguidance and exploitation. True, the workers would eventually own the homes they lived in—dreadful those new homes, each a copy of the one on either side; true, the workers did not have to pay to go to the cinemas; all of the shops were owned by the company and they had some sort of share in the profits. But they were not free, or so it seemed to me. They were dominated by a money-making machine! Building after building seemed hospital-like and antiseptic. In the factories, each plant manager had his office inside a spacious elevator so he could move from floor to floor where he was needed and the workers did not have to waste time seeking him out: a push-button, a receiver lifted, and he was on his way to them! I saw this all as a severe, a monstrous intrusion upon my world, my cherished lands of the imagination where the grand edifices, the tones of my instruction awaited me. I was even then dead-opposed to utilitarianism, materialism as the absolute angle for a good life. I was indignant, as though some inner principle had been assaulted, and I railed against what we had been exposed to as we drove back across rolling hills, past low-roofed stone cottages and harvested fields which all seemed to me as permanent and consoling as the sunset falling upon them then.

►10

Another experience of the New World before my first direct confrontation with it the day we arrived on September 14, 1939, was deeply unsettling. A few days out on the *Statendam,* safe by then from torpedoes (since we had picked up survivors from sunk merchant vessels we knew that the Germans had complied with the laws of neutrality and had let us pass; the other passenger ship to have left directly after the outbreak of the war, the British liner *Athena,* had been sunk off the coast of Ireland) I sat on deck near some young Americans, eighteen- or twenty-years-old, I would say, who I supposed were students. The girl in the deck chair next to mine was reading and as she turned a page, a picture fell to the floor. I bent down to return it to her but as I picked it up I looked at it inadvertently. Tired, uncertain, hunted, haunted, disturbed by changes I could barely comprehend, I was holding in my hand a picture of the man responsible for my and the world's upheaval—here, on the Atlantic on my way to the free world, a photo of Hitler! "Why?" I mumbled as I gave it to her. "He's been very good for the Germans" she replied. She went on to explain that her parents were German-Americans from the Midwest and that she had been greatly impressed by the economic and social progress she had found in Germany. I was speechless. I felt like an outcast powerless to state my condition convincingly. I said nothing and returned to my own book (I was reading the plays of Oscar Wilde, I remember). So, they are over there too, I thought; America has Nazis. Maybe Herr Strutz was right. I recalled the day not long before we had left Vienna when he, an old and trusted business associate from Graz, one of my father's best friends, and his wife had come to dinner. Strutz, an old-time Nazi, hadn't even bothered to remove his swastika from his lapel—his had a special ribbon to it that indicated he had been an illegal Nazi under the Schuschnigg regime, a very marked distinction—and when he left he shook hands warmly with my father, and said, "Go, go to America; but remember, we'll follow you! We'll come there too, Germany will own the world!" And he repeated, as though in jest, the popular slogan: "*Heute gehört uns Deutschland, morgen die ganze Welt!*" (Today we own Germany, tomorrow the whole world!). Only a hidden recorder could have reproduced the avalanche of curses that poured from my mother the moment Herr and Frau Strutz closed the door. Who knows, I thought, as I looked across the grey vastness of the stormy Atlantic, maybe he knew what he was saying. Even in America!

But my mood improved later that afternoon during the daily tea-dance as I watched the young Americans dancing in a completely légère manner—a casualness that seemed to spring from some sort of unpretentiousness, a naturalness I so admired and had by then designated as being distinctly, and so pleasantly, American. The dancers did not hold each other in a tight clasp, as the Europeans did when doing a tango, a waltz, or even a fox-trot. These young women were dancing in low-heeled shoes, did not hold their partners tightly around the shoulder, but held them informally, only with one arm, the other falling by their side casually, as though they were not at a shipboard dance but out in the country for a leisurely walk. That was légère, and I was impressed.

Truth, forever elusive as the single principle at the root of words, hence beyond and outside statement, is nonetheless discernible when the expressions emanating from it are convincing, carry authority, and are received as genuine. Love loves love. The self delights in the self. Only the genuine receives the genuine. It is the power of the imagination to light up and make apprehensible the regions of imperturbable structures, of the heart's illumination, that lie beyond the limiting boundaries of personal ego-interests. Even at that young age, expressions that had behind them the authority that is beneficial to all found response in me, and rang through me like a gong in temple halls.

I believe this to be the condition of true receptivity for all children at an early age, but for some, for those who as they mature remain the child at heart, that condition remains unaltered. For, it seems to me now, that what I then perceived in these chance encounters with Americans—the group at the Hotel Excelsior, the delegate to the International Congress for Women, the young people dancing on the ship—was like the fragrance that emanates from a sure source in the earth. A noble concept, or concepts, and the agreeable qualities that flow from there: freedom, fairness, self-reliance. Qualities that did not characterize the cultural fabric that had shaped me and was about to be torn apart. It had given me other, equally authentic and valuable attributes, but the self-determination of the individual was not among them. That the culture that had bred me was in fact on a course toward that—ever since the Renaissance, and later, the French Revolution—and that the romantic movements and, more recently, the existentialists had proclaimed it, was of course outside the realm of my understanding at that time. Nonetheless, that form of self-assertiveness was not at the root of the world that had shaped me and it was—and is—at the root of the one I was about to enter. And I had sensed this from the conduct of the Americans I had observed. Man in relation to the Creation, to the Creator, and not man in relation to himself, lay at the root of the world I was coming from.

At thirteen and fourteen, America's commitment to freedom and fairmindedness had already communicated itself to me. Coupled with that had been its more readily demonstrable attribute of being entirely modern. These qualities had shone for me, had become visible in the lapels of some few people who were to me the most fortunate in all the world, during those days when I had taken Fifi on extended walks through the *Innere Stadt*. I, of course, had naked lapels. There was no flag that I could wear. The vast majority of the people I had passed wore swastikas; but occasionally I passed someone who displayed the American flag! And that symbol aroused in me all the envy I then possessed. There it was, a small flag, a beacon in my world overhung with the dread symbol of virulent antagonism and hatred. How I envied those casual foreigners who were not only immune to it but who belonged to a society firmly rooted in principles opposed to the vicious zeal and mass hysteria out to destroy me and the childhood world that I had cherished.

I was delighted to be reminded of this, of America's basic principles, its own ongoing tradition (that such exists I am quick to point out to my dubious European friends) and felt refreshed by its reality just the other day, more than forty years after my first contact with its suggested existence.

I was curious about an Austrian film, *Tales from the Vienna Woods,* directed by Maximillian Schell, and went to see it in a small, intimate theatre, downstairs at New York's Plaza Hotel. The film, based on the play *Die G'schichten aus dem Wienerwald* by Ödön von Horvath, takes place in Vienna in the mid-thirties, before the Anschluss. The film was marvelously acted. Stage-acting is obviously still first-rate in Vienna, and I am certain that the actors in the film were all from the stage, which was true of the Austrian films I had seen before 1938. But the atmosphere of this film was densely claustrophobic. It portrays the hopeless narrow-mindedness, the bigotry and cruelty of the impoverished Viennese lower-middle class of that time, and it has the vitality of a death-song. I relived the sense of the bigoted lethargy of the class that had embraced Nazism with whatever enthusiasm left in it, and the memory of it made me cringe. Drabness characterized their lives. The districts in which they lived were drab and poor, their spirit was drab, however much they might get drunk in Grinzing at the *Heurigen,* their emotions were nostalgic and sentimental, and worst of all, they were cruel, sadistic. (There was a sensational trial in Vienna around that time—this is not in the film—of a well-to-do woman, the wife of a piano manufacturer, who had tortured a maid to death with branding irons.) In the film, the supposedly pious fiancé, a butcher with high-toned moral attitudes toward his bride-to-be, bites her lip each time he gives her an innocent kiss. Cruelty and violence simmering beneath the placid surface. And, of course, the would-be bride, who does try to break away from this, hasn't a chance. Her "rescuer," a kind of gigolo, deserts her after she has given him a child. Her father declares her dead. Her baby is murdered by her lover's disapproving grandmother. The despair beneath the surface is unrelenting. Only one person shows some sympathy, the aging *Tabak* owner, who had previously been keeping the girl's lover and to whom, in the end, he returns; only she shows a measure of humanity. The rest were all fodder for the new hope: the Führer, *Grossdeutschland* (Greater Germany) and the sacking of the Jews.

I heaved a deep sigh of relief as I stepped out of the theatre onto New York's Central Park South.

JULIE

►1

Before September 1939, America's attractive attributes—liberty's beacon proclaiming to the tired, cynical world of Europe the individual's inalienable rights—had existed for me only abstractly, by means of suggestion. I had not yet confronted this as an expression of daily living, and when I did, the ideals receded in face of an alien reality, its external conditions disturbing and unsettling from the day I arrived. An inner shudder whose tremors did not subside for years and years.

On a wintry day, in 1959, pulling out of New York's Grand Central Station, on my way to Boston for a visit arranged by Theodore Holmes, a young poet whose work I admired, to stay at Harvard's Dunster House and make a recording for the Poetry Room at the University's Lamont Library, I felt suddenly as though something distressing in me had ceased. Seeing at first the wintry streets fly past, then the wintry landscapes, the wide, frozen river, white fields, farmhouses like saluting sentinels, grey sky and distance in an ever-expanding slumber inviting the soul to join the wintry sleep and expand in it, I felt, for the first time in twenty years, that assent that says: *yes, you are at home.* Was it that the imagination was beckoning once more? That there was, indeed, even here a truer, more expansive expression of man's fundamental connections, such as hastily put-up streets, industrial complexes built in the interest of economic expediency could not provide? Alas, this sense of at-homeness here was only an announcement of a possibility, not as yet an actuality.

► 2

Being at home is taken for granted, for it is a natural condition. "Something you somehow haven't to deserve," Mary says about *home* in Robert Frost's "Death Of a Hired Man." One's birthright. And Emily Dickinson makes the startling, radical observation, in a letter, that to *feel at home* is to know God. If the knowledge of that condition doesn't come to us by way of appreciation, it certainly does so by way of deprivation. Absence tells us of presence. And, before leaving Europe, I knew only intuitively, for it was too close at hand, what being at home meant.

An undisturbed rootedness, connectedness. I knew that it was there but couldn't objectify it, for that would mean creating a distance, disturbing its very closeness. We do not *know*—objectively know—happiness; enfolded by it, we are happy. And, indirectly, I knew this unbroken contentment: standing, in the days when I still went to school, in the front of the tramway where the conductor works the horizontal lever that controls the tram. To stand there and not be inside one of the cars only cost 10 groschen per zone as against 32 for an unlimited distance. To get to school I needed to take the tram for only one zone. Moreover, I preferred to stand outside for it gave me the sensation of flying horizontally along the familiar streets, past the trees of the Augarten, Maria Theresa's former palace on one side, the Nordwestbahnhof, a railway station no longer in public use, on the other; while hearing the conductor's occasional clanging and, on clear days, seeing the sun like an agile yellow creature leaping through the dense trees of the once royal, now public park. It was the familiarity that was so comforting, assuring, like a clear echo. It is through the deeply familiar that we come, by means of memory, to the source of joy. To be pulled away from it, as we often are on waking, irritates us and, for an instant, we are wary as an animal sniffing danger and sensing for the direction toward safety. The soul knows where its comfort lies. And I knew I was in it, when Julie would tickle me to get up and ready for school; and I knew I was not, when I sat that first day in America by the window and looked out on a suburban street.

➤ 3

Julie! She certainly contributed to that unstated, prevalent joy of my awakening adolescence. Julie was one among a constant influx of girls who came from the provinces to make their life in the capital. Those *Landmädchen* (country girls) were everywhere in evidence. They worked for bourgeois Vienna, the business and the professional class, as chambermaids, cooks or, most often, in combined capacities. They were healthy, robust, generally attractive, and always young. They had a hard life, most of them. They worked long hours for little pay—though they each had complete health insurance, which was important—slept in dark, makeshift rooms, or on a cot in the kitchen. They were off Sunday afternoons, some only every other week. Then they would make for the dance-halls in the suburbs or the Prater and were easy sexual conquests for the young and unmarried or the married but restless. There were endless jokes about these girls, especially among adolescent Gymnasium students. We knew they could be caught in amorous embraces in the bushes of the Prater, and groups of us embarked upon rowdy hunts, first spying a couple lying in the grass, then watching and, when the situation became too tense, jumping from our hiding places to jeer and laugh at the couple in its awkward position. They took these interruptions in their stride for they were common and to be detected was not really embarrassing.

I am reminded of an incident that illustrates the casual attitude of the Viennese populace to such encounters. One evening, about ten o'clock, I was walking home with my parents along a dimly lit street which was even dimmer than most because it had houses only along one side, the wall and the trees of the Augarten being on the other. In the doorway of one of the buildings— all entrance doors were locked by that hour—I noticed a couple in a deep embrace, the man pressing the woman against the door. A man, coming toward us, passing them, said, in the Viennese street dialect, "*Der da glaubt er's im Himmel, hoilt aber nur ihr'n Arsch*" (That one thinks he's in heaven, but all he's got is her ass).

Popular Viennese songs, Schnitzler's stories, and those of other local authors, are full of these casual encounters which often end badly for the girls. There was never any chance for them to marry into the families for whom they worked. That was entirely out of the question in those days. But the girls figured prominently in Vienna's sexual reality and if the man of the house could not make the maid his accepted mistress, he could make her his unaccepted one. Sexuality in Vienna was both promiscuous and controlled. It was not a separate, hidden part of existence. The Viennese were Catholic but not puritanical, and the nature of reality being felt to be ambivalent in all but the fact that nothing, but nothing is permanent—everything passes, nothing is as it appears—they consoled themselves by making pleasure an artful practice, and sex was certainly part of that pleasure. They sinned openly, but in good taste; the ladies of society atoning in the confessional during the day for their inappropriate passions of the night before. Sex was in the air and certainly on the minds of the Gymnasium boys. Julie was perfectly aware of this and teased me abundantly.

After she had come to us, late in 1936, she quickly became a pivotal part of our household. She was about twenty-five at the time and had not come directly from the country but from a previous post—*Posten,* as it was called—where she had worked for a few years in a standard situation. Not much money, hardly any time off, no more than a maid in the house. This was not her situation in our house, where it was very different, due to my mother, who had, and this is no exaggeration, the best of hearts, a pure, a childlike heart, and who had great sympathy for this young, attractive, intelligent woman who despite her poor education in an Austrian provincial town had a brisk sophistication, wit, good language, and a clear, crisp speaking voice. Everything about Julie was attractive. She was fairly tall, about my height when she came to us; she was slim, had good taste, and dressed with care. Her situation with us made her distinctly better off than most girls in household employ. My mother insisted that she be paid well, my brother and I were teenagers so there was no need for her to sleep in; she came in the morning and left at five; and she was off for the whole day every Sunday. She had a stable physical and emotional life as she was living with a young man in a rented room around the corner, in Fugbachgasse. Her boyfriend Poldi, a young Socialist of the Viennese proletariat, was half-Jewish. My mother knew this from Julie, but their friends didn't know, nor did the couple from whom they were renting their room. Poldi's was not an uncommon situation in Vienna. His father was Jewish, the mother not, the children had been brought up Catholic and the father had no Jewish connections, or had cut them off. There were many such mixed marriages in Vienna and the children from them were accepted as belonging to the faith in which they were raised. But there was a special irony in Poldi's situation at that time. When the Germans swept over Austria and overnight hundreds of thousands of hidden Nazis came out in the open and were accorded special privileges for having awaited redemption by the Führer in secret and danger, Julie's and Poldi's landlord was among them, and he became a prominent SS member in the neighborhood. Little did he suspect that he had a half-Jew living in his flat. Furthermore, when the infamous Kristallnacht was planned for November 10, 1938, he boasted about it to Poldi who promptly informed Julie who promptly risked coming to us late the night before to warn us not to open the door to anyone the next day except to her or Poldi. By ten o'clock the next day, when Jewish apartments all over Vienna were being ransacked, everything of value stolen, furniture thrown out from windows and Jewish males taken to prison, Poldi arrived at our apartment dressed as a Nazi party member pretending to arrest my father—I was only fourteen and not yet in danger—marched him down the street around the corner to his room and kept him there throughout the day until the rampage was over and it was safe for my father to return home. So my father had been hidden by a half-Jew pretending to be a Nazi in the apartment of a high SS official. What beautiful irony; and Julie wept over it with my mother, in joy.

It was also Julie who had stood in my parents' bedroom the morning of March 12, 1938, and wept; my parents, who had hardly slept and were still in bed, had to console her. "It won't be as bad as everyone thinks," my father, the political optimist said. But she had wept. She knew her life with us was over and probably with her friend. She also wept for Austria; she was Austrian through the bone and had no use for Germans then. (This changed, for she married a German during the war and went to live in Germany.) On that fateful day she was inconsolable. The entire city was bathed in swastikas, she told us. And indeed, immense Nazi flags flew from the roofs of all the buildings around us. How could this be? Had Vienna been that well prepared for the annexation while pretending to be against it? All through the night the mood had been entirely different. Severe, somber, the radio repeating over and over again the movement from the Haydn quartet containing the melody of the Austrian anthem. Had the great confidence that Schuschnigg would win in the referendum in which the Austrians were to vote for or against annexation that very Sunday been a pretense? All indications had been for a victory against Anschluss. But the very next day, that Saturday, following Schuschnigg's entrapment at Berchtesgaden, Vienna was on the march to welcome the Germans. It seemed that everyone was in the streets, running, shouting, waving flags. From behind our curtained windows we could hear the sounds of goosesteps, of tens of thousands of boots on the cobblestones. Austria was not overrun, annexed by force, as some claim. True, the referendum never took place, Hitler averted it, but anyone who was in Vienna on that day—and surely there are film-clips and photos to prove it—saw a populace greeting German troops not as conquerors but as victors in a triumphant entry. The flags were not only flying from the rooftops, children were waving them in their hands and grown-ups were wearing swastika armbands or buttons in their lapels. A few days later Hitler came to Vienna and addressed not a large crowd but a sea of faces in front of the *Rathaus* (City Hall), the vast square, parks, and streets surrounding it jammed with welcoming Viennese meeting his words with outbursts, salvos of hysterical joy . . . *Die Juden* . . . *die Juden* . . . *die Juden* . . . *die Juden* . . . and *Juda Verrecke* (Jews Perish) . . . *Juda Verrecke* . . . and *Heil, Heil, Heil, Heil* in endless response . . .

Hitler knew well how to bring his fellow Austrians to this pitch of unbounded enthusiasm. He knew how deep in them was the anti-Semitism instilled by emperors—the Empress Maria Theresa notorious among them, although their beloved Franz Joseph had opposed it—by politicians like Karl Lueger, the flamboyant mayor of Vienna toward the end of the last century, by Georg von Schönerer and, perhaps most insidious of all, by the clergy. There was an obscure priest in the provinces whom Hitler used to listen to as a youth who preached, and claimed to have mystical proof, that the Jews had daemonic powers, were in fact the devil; the devil's existence was to be seen in the reality of the Jews. This was extreme fanaticism but the guilt of the Jews as God-killers was inculcated in the minds and hearts of children by priests from peasant chapels to city churches. Certainly no edict went out from the Church forbidding such instilling of bias and hatred.

My mother told of an incident that illustrates this notion that

Jews had not only fallen from Divine Grace but were hence inhabited by daemons and devils, as caricatures of Jews often showed them to be. When she was pregnant with my brother she was advised by her doctor to seek pure mountain air, drink pure fresh milk, to rest in the midst of nature. My father found the perfect place for her, a village high in the mountains of Carinthia and my mother spent several months being nurtured by the freshness of the soil and the care of attending peasant women. She got on very well with the local people. I can imagine that her distinctly humane and liberal disposition must have soon dispelled the mistrust in which peasants were wont to hold city people and that she was accepted by them as though she were one of them. When, in the course of a conversation toward the end of her stay, she happened to mention that she was Jewish, their mouths dropped in disbelief. They conferred amongst themselves, then asked my mother if she would allow them to examine her. My mother agreed and two or three women put their hands over my mother's head, feeling her skull. Then they shook their heads and said: "No, you can't be Jewish. You have no horns, no stumps growing."

The Austrians hated the Jews en masse. To be anti-Semitic was part of what it meant to be Austrian; to be opposed to anti-Semitism meant being full of foreign ideas, of socialism, of cosmopolitanism. Of course there were those who, like Julie, not bred in a cosmopolitan atmosphere were, nonetheless, innately opposed to such prejudice because they were deeply human and had a liberal disposition. But the vast majority were bigoted and provincial. The Jews had achieved prominence in Vienna in the nineteenth century, and even during the century before that some Jews, financiers and textile manufacturers, had made great fortunes. The children of many of those converted and intermarried with the Austrian nobility; a number were ennobled upon their conversion. By the time of the rise of a powerful bourgeoisie under the reign of Franz Joseph, much of the banking, the railroads, and heavy industry was in Jewish hands. As need hardly be said again, Jews achieved great prominence in the professions, against equally great odds, and contributed powerfully to Vienna's intellectual and artistic life: Mahler, Werfel, Zweig, Schnitzler, Freud, Schoenberg, and many others. After World War I when the empire was decapitated and its head, Vienna, remained virtually without a body— a city of two million in a country of seven—the Jews managed somehow not to go under. Though there were poor Jews among them, the majority of Vienna's 200,000 Jews was well-off, at least by comparison to the largely impoverished population. Not only the professions, but a great many of the stores, the important department stores, and much of what was left of Austria's industry was in the hands of Jews. Proportionately at least, they continued to be a dominant force in Vienna's life. Despite the fact that many of the Jews considered themselves Viennese, they were not so regarded by most non-Jews. The Jews were intruders, not only the more recent arrivals who had come in large numbers from those Polish and Roumanian provinces that had been part of the Empire, but the old, long-established families as well. Moreover, the Jews had all the goods, their pedigree didn't matter. And, following the Anschluss, it didn't take long for the Viennese populace to consider Jewish property theirs for the taking. The very Monday after Germany's triumphal entry into Austria, long lines of people formed outside the banks waiting for them to open. They were not depositors but Viennese hopefuls come to collect the money of the Jews. They actually believed that Jewish money would be distributed the day after the Anschluss. Of course, it was confiscated, bank accounts taken over soon enough; but it didn't go into the pockets of an envious, heavily unemployed, poverty-tired populace.

Even on Sunday, the day before they lined up outside the banks, some members of local Nazi chapters began to harass Jews and to plunder where they could. Events of a hideous dream for me, those first days of Nazi rule, when what was happening had not yet penetrated, had not yet become real. It seemed to be occurring outside my mental capacity; it couldn't be true. It seemed in an odd way distant, as though I were merely *viewing* some horror. Mass-hatred has a strangely abstract aspect to it, you don't believe it, it isn't real. Even my first confrontation, meeting it in close proximity, seemed outside the realm of events that I had, until then, considered part of my life, hence real.

We had gone that Sunday to visit relatives in the neighborhood, the widow of the cousin who had owned the clothes shop on Kohlmessergasse, and as we entered the apartment we were grabbed by men in brown shirts—how quickly they had gotten their uniforms—and were told to join the others, our relative, her sons, visiting friends, lined up against a wall. Were we going to be shot? What did they want with us? What they wanted, it soon became apparent, was loot. Our relative was a well-to-do woman and she was known in the neighborhood. So the thugs came to rob what they could. The pretext was that they had received information that my cousin was hiding guns. While two of the men stood facing us and threatening us, the others turned the apartment upside down, finding no guns, of course, but jewelry, money, cameras, and other valuables which, they claimed, they had also been ordered to confiscate. Then they left, and we had had our first confrontation with things to come. "They won't get away with this," said my father. "The authorities won't permit this sort of thing. It's only now, in the turmoil, that they can do this on their own." This was met with infuriated looks from my mother and her cousin.

► 4

Julie was distressed when my mother told her the next day what had happened. My mother's cousin was one of the women who visited us frequently, of whom Julie had become quite fond, and whom she regarded, if not as her friend (that would not be seemly), as a friendly acquaintance. And as this woman had been almost a part of our household she had become that for Julie, by extension, part of her world. Moreover, there was a kinship between them: both had a rich, native intelligence and they knew, probably intuitively, that being women of independent spirit, they shared a common bond. It was that above all which I suspect had drawn Julie and my mother to each other as well.

Society and conventions had imposed restrictions upon each, though of different kinds and to differing degrees. My mother's possibilities for full development and expression of her many remarkable qualities—intelligence, intuition, striking good looks—were sharply restricted by the conventional bourgeois life she was expected to live, and lived. Likewise, Julie's chances for fulfilling the potential of her bright, vivacious personality were limited by her lack of education and provincial lower-class upbringing. Having accepted her situation, my mother, at forty still a beauty—people used to turn around to look after her, as I used to observe with pride; she resembled Pola Negri and was sometimes mistaken for her—had something of the tragedian about her. And Julie, fifteen years younger, seemed to sense the older woman's plight. There was no gloom about them but they seemed to have understood each other's feelings. They also loved to laugh and talk about their harmless flirtations. Evidently my mother had some admirers who pursued her but never succeeded in getting her on the telephone. Julie, who always answered during the day when the secret admirers would call, was instructed to say that my mother was not at home. But once, the two women contrived to trick their admirers. My mother did go to the telephone the next time her pursuer called, and made a rendezvous with him for the next afternoon at one of the corners that could be seen from our dining room windows. Julie also arranged to meet an admirer of hers at the same corner at the same time. The following day, at the appointed hour, the two women placed themselves behind the lace curtain and watched the two men waiting for them and getting increasingly impatient. Peals of laughter brought me out from my room. Of course, my mother wouldn't tell me that they were watching two disappointed men pacing back and forth, but Julie did the next day. I didn't think it very funny. At that age I had a particular sympathy for men in pursuit of amorous adventure, the sexual quest I was beginning to anticipate, and I didn't approve of this sort of teasing.

Another time Julie told me of a sight she and my mother happened upon one afternoon that aroused in me an early erotic curiosity. This was a case of exhibitionism and my first inkling of voyeurism. It also suggested secrecy and erotic mystery emerging from out of deep shadows and damp, old stones. The building directly opposite ours on Fugbachgasse was a conventional one of spacious apartments with high windows and stucco decorations on the lower floors, the entrance large enough to permit carriages into the courtyard—as in our building—and a smaller door in the entrance way for pedestrians which was the only one in use then, now that automobiles stood at the curb. There was a small shop, a *Drogerie* (perfumery) on the ground floor. It was a sleepy building, the windows of the lower floors hung with heavy drapes drawn only when the weather was warm. Julie knew, from other maids, I supposed, that the apartments were large and there was only one to each floor. Our apartment was one flight up and we used to get irate phone calls from a woman in the apartment in that building on the same level as ours about our radio being too loud. Even if it had been, and it never really was, it was difficult to understand how they could possibly have heard our radio across the street. She claimed they did, but I think that they were primarily objecting to us, to Jews living across from them; *they,* she made it quite clear from her speech and manner, were upper crust, old Viennese. So Julie had surmised. One day, when it was not yet warm, the drapery in one of the tall windows parted mysteriously and out came, placing himself on the inside windowsill, a young man fully naked, allowing himself to be viewed by the outside world, the old buildings facing him, the mansard roofs, the late winter sky, the stonelike greyness above. At that moment, Julie passed by, gasped, and called my mother; and from behind our dining room curtains the women viewed this specimen of naked aristocratic male beauty. Apparently, he displayed himself in this manner for quite a while for, according to Julie's account to me the next day, my mother withdrew, saying it was, after all, not decent to watch, but Julie didn't give it up until the display had ended and the drawn drapery shut in once more the dark, silent, mysterious interior world across from me.

And so in my early awakenings to the reality of sex, the mystery of the body, and in firing my fantasy and imagining its actuality, Julie had played as important a part as the boys in my class who had helped in this education and had taken me along on the hunts through the Prater bushes. She knew of course what was happening to me at that age and she liked to tease me. She would pull the covers off my bed to make me get up and would laugh at the condition she found me in. She told me all sorts of things, of the different classes of prostitutes—prostitution was rampant and legal in Vienna—of one she knew who didn't work the streets, even the best streets, but saw clients by appointment, had a chauffeur-driven car and a different dog for each of her many fur coats. Probably not all true, but she delighted in watching my intense curiosity. She told me about the famous actors at the Burgtheater who went for boys, of the aristocratic landowner in her village who had caused a scandal when he was found in the hay with one of his stable-boys, and warned me to be on guard against these *Warme*—as they were referred to there—for Vienna was full of them. And she told me about a couple who got stuck after intercourse, the woman had a spasm and couldn't release the man who was not her husband, expected home at any moment. At this point Julie's laughter started. What a dilemma. The police was called but couldn't help, the hospital was called, an ambulance came and the couple, covered in a huge sheet, was carried out on a stretcher to the jeers and uproar of the bystanders. Just as the couple was being pushed inside the ambulance, the husband arrived. Somebody in the building, some fat man had died, he was told by an acquaintance of his wife. Julie's portrayal of this scene was so vivid she ended it with tears of laughter.

In the spring, she took me along on outings with her Poldi to the *Alte Donau* (Old Danube), the arms of the Danube extending deep into reed-filled marshes, favorite spots with the Viennese poor populace for boating and bathing. And more, as I gathered from Julie's twinkle and from the scantily dressed bathers—especially the young men wearing nothing but a slim cloth on a string around their waists—dancing as though glued together, to music from a gramophone. We went rowing, Julie, Poldi, and I, and though this was not the world of Luhačovice but of a far less respectable, earthier order, I felt happy and secure despite my various bewilderments.

Not long after the fateful March 12, 1938, Julie had to leave us. An edict forbidding Aryans to be employed by Jews was soon issued, but as I have already mentioned, she kept a vigilant eye on us. In her features, short hair and dirndl, she was so typical of the young, pro-German Austrian that her friends and acquaintances who had become committed Nazis confided in her and told her what was up next for the Jews. Slogans on behalf of Schuschnigg in what turned out to be an aborted election had been painted all over the sidewalks of Vienna and the Nazis decided to put Jews to work to get rid of them. Only a few days after Anschluss men and women were dragged from their homes or picked off the streets and made to scrub the sidewalks to the loud jeerings of an hysterical mob. Thanks to Julie, my parents were spared this early indignity; she had warned us by telephone not to open the door to anyone, not to play the radio, not to answer the phone, to pretent we weren't at home. And so we had done; my parents did not scrub the sidewalk, but Julie did!

She had come upon some women surrounding a man, letting out upon his kneeling body, as he scrubbed the street, all the vulgarity they were capable of, and they were masterly at it. Julie felt sorry for the man, elderly, dignified, well dressed, and told the women to let him go, he had done enough. So they turned their wrath upon her. Anyone speaking up for the Jews was worse than they were, and the women told her the man could go if she would take his place. And she did. She scrubbed on her knees while the women insulted her. After a while, a brownshirt, a friend of Poldi's, came by and, thinking the women had made a mistake and thought her to be Jewish, led her away. The following day Julie told us how the women had tried to tell the young Nazi what she had done, but he had shrugged them off, saying they were just making excuses. As he left Julie, however, he turned to her and warned her never to help Jews again.

Which did not stop her from coming to us almost daily. My mother had been very popular with the people in the neighborhood and Julie was not afraid of them. It was careless of her, for there had been many betrayals, but she was never reported. There were others, non-Jews who had known my mother slightly but who came to her to unburden themselves of their dismay, something that would have been too risky with non-Jews. One afternoon the woman who owned the perfumery across the street sat in our living room and wept over what had befallen Vienna and more specifically over an incident she had just witnessed. She had been walking up Praterstrasse when she saw a burly young man, bedecked with swastikas, stop a young woman, a girl really, no more than eighteen. He questioned her and when he had made certain that she was not an Aryan, he took her face in his hands, forced her mouth open and spat into it.

Such were the things that were happening in the "good" days before the war and the holocaust, when men taken to concentration camps still returned alive if an exit permit and entry visa had been secured for them. But wholesale public extremity can be indicated by acts of relatively trivial consequence, like the one witnessed by the decent, middle-class shopkeeper from across the street and many, many others that occurred daily before war broke out. When at last we were in Zurich, in late August 1939, and went for a walk along the lakefront—my parents, my brother, and the family, our former neighbors, with whom he had fled to Switzerland—we were spotted by two Germans, some steps away from us. We were in a neutral country, we were free, we had escaped them, they had no rights over us, but the two Germans recognized us as the refugees we had just become by our language, the look we must have had of the hunted, humiliated, of those who are by force on the defensive. And seeing us as their victims, they were so pleased at this sight of human disarray and misery they were then causing, they pointed at us, at our apparently hilarious misfortune, and laughed and laughed; ridiculed us whom they had driven out.

We observed it, paid little attention, and walked on. But it has remained with me as a monstrous example of a nation's crime. For even in those days before the final solution—of which ordinary Germans probably had no direct knowledge—their government's program regarding Jewish rights and property and its general treatment of Jews, its pressure to drive them out, was declared publicly over and over again and was perfectly well known to all Germans and Austrians. There is absolutely no question about that. Government policy regarding the Jews was endorsed overwhelmingly by the masses, cheering on and on; every one of Hitler's speeches and of other high-ranking Nazis like Goebbels, Göring, Himmler, et al., was full of it. In addition, attacks on the Jews appeared daily in the newspapers. One weekly, *Der Streicher,* consisting *entirely* of vicious anti-Jewish lies and propaganda, was posted week after week in red boxes on streetcorners throughout German cities, which included Vienna by then. A traveling exhibition, *Der Ewige Jude* (the Eternal Jew), depicting Jewish atrocities through history—all lies, of course— were seen by millions throughout the new Greater Germany. So by the time hell broke loose, a few days later, on September 1, the morning after we had arrived in Paris, the Germans were well groomed for what was to come. The national propaganda of the preceding six years had worked. The incident in the lakefront park in neutral Switzerland was proof of that.

How did I react then to such events, to a brutality so extreme, an indictment of a nation, to attitudes and deeds outside the realm of possibility, outside the comprehension of a boy? What was happening around me before we left was like a shrill discordance I wanted turned off like a siren. I knew that was not possible unless we left, and from the time we received our American visa in Vienna in June of 1939 and until I took the train to Zurich almost three months later, I had that on my mind above all else. But in the early months after the Nazi takeover I had no clear view of things at all. The enthusiasm of the Viennese for the new order, the cheer of boys and girls my age marching, singing, carrying banners, the general atmosphere of hope and change had been catching in a way that the mood at any huge parade is. And for months, for the Viennese masses, life was one huge parade. I had to fight not to be caught up in it; more than once the celebrants tried to take me along. It was the custom then to drop a coin in collection boxes passed around by young volunteers wearing swastika armbands; every Sunday money was being collected for some patriotic cause or other. One such volunteer wouldn't let me go, held his arms around me, unless I dropped a coin in his box. Although I did not wear a swastika button, he evidently did not suspect that I was Jewish. I could have gotten out of this, he would have had to let me go, had I given him a coin. But I refused to do this. It would be cowardly; I said, instead: "*Bin kein Arier*" ("I'm not Aryan") though I risked being kicked or spat at. But a curious moment happened between us. He looked at me a while with depth in his eyes, a mixture of pity and affection; and he let me go.

I had been lucky then, and I had been throughout that year and a half under Nazi domination. I was never harmed physically; the only one in my family harmed had been my brother. We were fortunate because severe beatings of Jews had been a common occurrence. There were then, at that time, two major waves of events around me: the jubilation of the crowds and the rapidly encroaching fear among Jews. It created confusion in me and I often thought if I hadn't had cause to be afraid I might have also been one of the celebrants crowding the streets. But I had a distaste for the masses and probably wouldn't have joined under any circumstances. I suppose I envied them their joy. I was no realist, I was a kid of fourteen, and a dreamer. However, the euphoria subsided gradually and the atmosphere of fear increased. And when the oppression grew more intense, the regulations against Jews more severe, I lived, until I left, in a dual world: of my home, of deep belonging, of a rootedness as yet undisturbed, and of, to me, incomprehensible external events. Soon, after Julie and my father took me to the station and the following morning I crossed the border and saw not swastikas on the flags the train passed but the Swiss national symbol, the one was being cut, the at-homeness shattered; and, a few weeks later, when we arrived on the new continent, the other, the external world, not now threatening, had changed altogether.

. . . As I stood by the open window of the express train taking me to Zurich and freedom, freedom . . . ; as the fresh air gripped my face and I felt the enormity of the night, the depth of space, the rustling of the trees reaching deep into me, into my inner self equally endless, waiting to receive, to be filled: It seemed to me that is where my freedom was unimpaired, in my capacity to receive and absorb the impressions of the world, which alone seemed real. But were they, since they were flying past? It seemed incomprehensible to me that the home, the familiar streets and sounds I had just left, had ended. Yet, how vast the night, the stars that flew past through the trees . . . joy, an inner excitement I had always known, ran through me, flew across me like the night air . . . it was overwhelming to feel my freedom, to be on a train, to be scrubbed by rushing air . . .

. . . And it was also a melancholy, the incomprehensibility of

changes, I experienced, perhaps for the first time: a mysteriousness expressed by the water of the lake in front of me, the reflections of trees, of flower beds, of people lying in the grass or
walking by, of the bench on which I sat in Zurich's lakefront
park and looked at the sky inside the water. Which was
which? . . . Now that the fear had lifted like a beast that had
been crouching over me, something new was beginning . . . it
seemed to me a harmonious melody, welcome sounds were
about to descend, to invade my ready, waiting being . . . soon a
headiness came over me . . . I was in Zurich, with my brother;
my parents were due in a few days; we were to sail for America
on September 5; my father was to go ahead to London to settle
his business affairs; he was to join us on the ship at Southampton;
he had succeeded, had managed to rescue a great deal; we were
far from poor; we would arrive in America reasonably well-off;
my father had seen to that; and he had won . . . I blurted all this
out to my brother, insisting he take me to a good restaurant, for,
I said, we can afford it; we are rich! . . .

Julie had left my father at our door when they got back, having seen me off. My parents followed to Zurich about a week
later and with that Julie went out of our lives. The war made
correspondence impossible. We talked of her much and held her
up as an example of the brave, the truly decent people whom no
fanaticism could sway. We were fortunate to have known her, to
have had her help and support which were so critical to us during
those hideous months; and to have had as well the loyalty of a
few others who did not, like Herr Sturtz, mock a former friendship and gloat over our misfortune, but remained undeflected in
their direct humanity and decency. Poldi had risked his life for
my father, as had Herr Kellner, one of my father's former employees, a socialist through and through, the best example of the
one-time progressive Viennese proletariat. And there were
others. Decency did not die, however rampant the opportunism
out to ravage it. My father did see Herr Kellner again in Vienna
in 1948; and in 1945, when my brother was with the occupying

American army in Vienna, Julie, who had been living in Germany, sought him and found him. It was a joyous reunion and my mother wept when she read about it in a letter in New York. Soon she corresponded with Julie, sent her many packages of food and clothing, but they never met again. That part of the past was over.

►5

Contrary to my optimism in Zurich, my father's plans had in the end not worked out. The morning after we arrived in Paris Hitler attacked Poland and pandemonium broke out in the streets. Loudspeakers urged Parisians to leave, bombings were feared and the French were not prepared. During the months before we had left, there had been frequent air-raid drills in Vienna and signs pointing to air-raid shelters were all over the city. Not so in Paris. The city was in a panic. My father was to have flown to London that day to settle his affairs there; instead he and my brother took the Metro to the shipping office where, as part of the process of our emigration, my parents had sent a crate crammed with clothing, linens, and other goods to see us through the first years of our new life in America. Two other such crates had gone to Italy; these were, of course, lost during the war. The French were mobilizing, the men were being called up, going to the railroad stations, and it was impossible to get anywhere above or below ground. Late in the day my father and brother finally arrived back at the hotel, carrying the most valuable contents from the crate—mostly my mother's furs and other expensive items—in improvised, paper-wrapped bundles. Earlier in the day, as I was coming out of the elevator in the hotel, I saw two of my former Gymansium professors huddled around the radio in the lounge. They had fled to Paris and their expressions spoke very clearly of the danger and uncertainty that lay ahead once again. Despite the shrill confusion, I was thrilled to be in

Paris, fascinated by the extroverted Parisian street-life—at the cafés people faced toward the crowd rather than each other as was the custom in Vienna—the flirtatiousness I had heard so much of from family friends or older cousins who had visited there. An alertness, responsiveness to each other's physicalness which I found flattering and, as it was vaguely suggestive of future experiences, exciting. But these were quick moments, brief glimpses, soon overturned by the events around me. As Parisians had been urged to flee, we too decided to go directly to Boulogne-sur-Mer, where we were to embark on September 5, and not wait in Paris for the boat-train.

And so, my father did not get to London, we did not have on the ship the crate that had been sent ahead, we did not arrive in America, as had been my father's plan, in good financial condition, well equipped with personal belongings; we did not come to Newark to stay in a hotel for a few days and then, my father having met his obligation to his uncle and his uncle's family, settle in an apartment in New York. It had not worked out that way. We were penniless, my knowledge of English was our most helpful, pecuniary asset, we stayed in Newark for four years; when we arrived in Newark Fifi was, as already mentioned, our only token from our former life; my mother had worn the same dress on the crossing, it was the only one she had; for that reason she had hardly ever left her cabin, the steward bringing her her meals; and she also had some mild attacks of asthma which got worse after we arrived.

Nor had we boarded the ship in Boulogne-sur-Mer. The day after we had reached there, on a train jammed with soldiers, England and France had declared war on Germany. The panic we had seen in Paris had spread everywhere. There were repeated air-raid warnings in Boulogne and the clerk at the Holland-America Line office advised us to go on to Rotterdam where the ship was to leave at midnight on September 4. To get back to Paris for the boat-train to Rotterdam was out of the question. The only way to make the ship on time was to get there by taxi. On the morning of

September 4 we drove off from Boulogne hoping to reach Rotterdam by the evening. Again, despite the confusion, I was enthralled by what I saw. These were my first sights of the sea. For long stretches we drove up the coast of Normandy into Belgium and I had never before beheld such extensions of space, the ocean like an inverted sky, endless and tossing; I loved the craft in the harbors, their high masts and funnels, marveled at the wide and empty beaches, the steep dunes like walls of chalk. Fifi was carsick, I held her in my lap and tried to calm her but I couldn't take my eyes off the sea-scenery I was encountering for the first time. We had trouble at the Belgian border. Our travel documents were in order except for the fact that we did not have a Belgian visa. Jews fleeing Germany was not an uncommon occurrence to border guards; but we did have our American visa and ship accommodations, so the guard, after telephoning Brussels, let us through. Once more the seascapes, as we passed through Ostende, the northern beach-resort that looked deserted. Further up the coast, at Knokke, another resort, my father had an argument with the driver who insisted, suddenly, that he be paid double. My father refused, a crowd gathered, a policeman intervened; the driver was paid the agreed-on amount and we found another taxi which was to take us to Rotterdam. We drove through a tunnel under the Schjelde River; the walls were of bright, yellow tiles, the tunnel was illuminated by fluorescent lights; I had never driven beneath a river before; I felt I had already entered the new, modern world I was anticipating.

It was getting late. We had to hurry or we would miss the ship. There was trouble again, this time when we got close to the Dutch border and the car had to halt in front of a roadblock. Some defenses, mines, I believe, were being laid up ahead and we had to detour through a field. After a while we hit a large stone that caused a leak in the gas tank and we stood by helplessly as the gas leaked away and with it our hope of getting to America before the war entrapped us all. We saw a light ahead, a house in the field. To our great relief, it turned out to be the guardhouse at the Dutch border. It was midnight on the clock inside the office and we stood in the wooden room in a stupor of despair. But the guard told us of the sinking of the British ship, *Athena*—my stomach sank, my knees shook—and he thought that for that reason the departure of the *Statendam* had been delayed. He telephoned to Rotterdam and he was right. The ship would not leave until noon; spurred on by the danger, the crew had gone on strike for better pay and improved conditions. We were in luck. The guard arranged for another taxi and at daybreak we pulled up at the pier of the *Statendam*. We had to wait a few hours before we could go aboard. Exhausted, weary of the uncertainties of the last few days, we slept a while on the benches in the waiting room. Just before we were at last to board the ship we saw a train pulling in at the pier. Out poured the passengers who had waited in Paris and had been brought to Rotterdam by the Line at the company's expense! What troubles we could have been spared had we not panicked along with the Parisians. We checked in our bundles, which were all we had, and boarded. There was a great deal of confusion on the ship. Hundreds of Americans, desperate to leave Europe, were attempting to get aboard. The regular crew quarters were given over to this frantic crowd and the ship was jammed; people on all the decks, in the halls, and lounges; luggage everywhere. But a few days later when it had all been distributed to the cabins, our bundles were nowhere. In the chaos, they had been left behind on the pier. A few weeks later, when the Line's next ship docked at Hoboken we did get them, but on that crossing neither my mother nor the rest of us had anything to wear but what had been on our bodies.

►6

My father had accepted the inevitability of having to leave Vienna only after the destructions, plunderings, and mass arrests of November 10, 1938. By then his warehouses and bank accounts

JULIE → 77

had been confiscated and the Jews stripped of most of their rights as citizens. But he had clung to the hope as long as he could that the government was indulging the hoodlums for a while to insure its popularity but that its anti-Jewish bark was fiercer than its bite and that life would get back to normal in time. Seven months after the Anschluss he stopped saying; "The Germans aren't barbarians after all," and set about the business of getting out.

He was loath to leave his European life. Friends were departing daily for America, England, Palestine, Cuba, some even for Shanghai, but he wanted to remain on the Continent. He knew it intimately, had traveled extensively on business, and a change to another European country would by no means be as drastic as a move to the United States. He had planned to visit there during the World's Fair of 1938 but he was not inclined to go there as an immigrant. He had had business contacts in Yugoslavia where he used to ship large quantities of raw hides, and he decided therefore on Zagreb, or Agram as he referred to it and as it had been called when it was a provincial capital under the old Austro-Hungarian Empire. He knew it well and he could envision us living there. Yugoslav friends helped him, a senator secured a permit for us and by June 1939, when we were called to the American Embassy for the customary examination before being granted a visa, we could have chosen to move to Zagreb. However, by then it was clear even to my father that America was by far safer than any European country and he sent cables of gratitude to his family in Newark for having made our American visa possible.

Still, he resisted departure. First, he couldn't tear himself away from a city whose life had suited him, where he had done well, where, for twenty years, he had conducted even his important business transactions not from his office but his Stammcafé—the Café Fetzer—where every waiter had known him by name. Second, he was not going to be a penniless refugee, least of all in America. "If we are going to go to America," he would say frequently after June 1939, "I will not come there as a poor man."

And he meant it. He risked all, endangered his life to avoid this hideous prospect. When Hitler took Austria my father had several outstanding payments due him abroad. But the authorities would naturally not allow sums for exported goods to be kept in foreign banks. Therefore, any hope that my father would have considerable sums abroad soon vanished. One of my father's business associates had joined his daughter in England not long after the Anschluss and he became the anchor in a scheme of illegal, highly dangerous business maneuverings. The success of them depended largely on heavy bribes and the closed mouths of everyone involved; the consequences, should anyone participating in this smuggling network be discovered, meant concentration camp and death. With the exception of my father and his London associate none of the participants was Jewish; for that reason my father felt quite safe: no one could give him away without implicating himself on several counts. For my father the risk meant preventing the indignity of poverty on foreign soil. He felt it was worth the risk, but he also enjoyed it; for taking chances had always been part of his business life. What he did was to send to London huge shipments, enormous bales full of rabbit skins—the cheapest available raw hides—under the name of an Aryan firm sharing in the profit. Stuffed among the bloody, sticky skins were expensive Leica cameras that had flooded the Austrian shops after the Anschluss and could be bought cheaply because the supply far exceeded the demand. In London the reverse was true, taxes on imported cameras were high, and so these were sold at enormous profits. The skins were not sold but stored in a warehouse, and with the camera money returned illegally to my father, he bought more and more skins, sent more and more shipments, so that, by the time he would stop off in London on our way to America, sales of those skins, important in the manufacture of hats and other goods, and of the more expensive raw skins also smuggled in the bales, would bring him a very considerable sum—and he would arrive in America, if not as prosperous as he had once been, certainly not poor either.

By the time we received our American visa my father was deep in his "deals." He was doing too well to give it up, and since, American visa in his passport, he felt more secure and less in a hurry he kept on delaying our departure from Vienna because of the gamble of "one more, and then we'll go." By the middle of August I was too impatient to stay on and it was agreed that I would go ahead to join my brother in Zurich. This was at the time of the so-called peace treaty between Germany and the Soviet Union. Sheer delay tactics, the radio and newspapers called it in Zurich; war was certain, nonetheless, to break out any day, it was reported by commentators. I sent telegrams, telephoned my parents, urging them to come because "our uncle in Poland is very sick." (My mother's older brother was living in Poland.) My mother assured us they would come soon. We would receive a wire.

While my father was busy smuggling—or *preparing* as it must be called in fairness to his intentions—my mother had been busy shopping to prepare, in her way, for our exodus. The crates of personal belongings had already been shipped, but she was then getting ready the essentials for travel that she and my father would take in their luggage. This had so far been allowed without any papers, but toward the end of August the Nazi authorities suddenly decreed that nothing, no personal belongings were to be taken out of the country without official permission. This meant filling out applications, standing in long lines, and then waiting to receive the papers, which would take several weeks. The situation in Vienna was getting tense and my mother more and more irate. "Enough," she would scream to my father, "Enough! Let's go! Let's get out!" We had, after all, in our passports the most precious of possessions: an American visa for which millions would have given whatever they could still call their own! But my father wanted one more "shipment" and he had asked my mother to go to the Holland-America Line bureau to exchange our passage on the *Statendam* for one on the next ship out. "Only a matter of another week or so," my father had said.

This was toward the end of August while my brother and I were frantic in Zurich, listening to the news and waiting for the cable. When my mother, who had not succeeded in persuading my father to keep the *Statendam* bookings, went to the shipping line's office on the Opernring, it was so jammed she could hardly make her way to the counter. Everyone there was waiting for a cancellation, every single person there, Americans or others with American visas, hoping for a passage on the *Statendam*. When she realized that—that people were actually waiting for our tickets— she turned around, rushed home, stormed into our apartment, and shouted at my father, "Murderer! You want to stay, stay! I am leaving!" And she went straight to the post office and cabled us that they were taking the train the next day.

Unlike Vienna's railway stations, which all reflected the style of the nineteenth-century railway boom, Zurich's Bahnhof was modern. I got to know it well, for when my brother and I arrived there to meet the Vienna train, we were told the delay was so long they didn't know yet when it would get in. They did assure us, however, that the train had left and was on its way. All that morning we had listened to the radio and heard the news repeated again and again that Germany was closing its borders. It was August 29, 1939. We did not know if trains would leave Austria any longer. To think that we had had an American visa since June, and now our parents might have been cut off! This had gone through my head repeatedly as we got to the station.

And so I sat on bench after bench of Zurich's modern Bahnhof and looked at the blue of the sky at the end of the station. Again this contrast. As on the train, when I felt the calm of an unhurried order like a rustling touch on my face facing the night, the sounds of trees flying past, murmurs of an altogether different language finding accord in the depth of my being. Or, as when I sat for the first time near the lake and had watched the calm in the world's reflection as though the water had absorbed, had eliminated the events that had brought me there. So I now took in the sky's blue, its melodious, unchanged serenity as if it were the reverse of conflict; as if, on the other side of existence, a world about to erupt into war, a world in which my parents might be held back still at the border and might be kept from reaching us, had no reality; simply wasn't there . . .

My brother came running. The train was announced. When it pulled into the station and I ran past the cars, open windows filled with people being met by joyous family or friends, I was so anxious I ran past my parents. Didn't see them until, suddenly—Fifi—Fifi jumped into my arms. We were all crying. They had made it. We started to leave the station when I noticed that my parents had no luggage. "What about your luggage?" There was none. Our phone calls and telegrams, the crowd that day at the shipping office had convinced even my father. They had left in a hurry. There had not been time to obtain the required permit for personal belongings. They had brought with them Fifi wrapped in a black shawl.

III

APPRENTICE

►1

The first few days in Newark we floundered about the streets like shipwrecked travelers who had saved nothing but their skins. A cousin took us, my father, brother, and me, to a haberdasher's on Bergen Street and bought us socks and underwear. An old woman in the shop, being told that we had just arrived, exclaimed, "Ah, Greeneh . . ." (Greenhorns was the term for us from her immigrant world-view.) Hearing that we were from Vienna, she asked, "Vienneh? They have chimneys there?" I couldn't grasp this illogical question. On the dinner table in my great-uncle's house I saw an enormous bowl of chopped, raw vegetables and green leaves as though it were a floral ornament, but it was a salad; the bathroom facilities in the house included a toilet in each! All peculiar, all oddities to me who had been accustomed to sauteed vegetables, salads of cucumbers soaked in sour cream or vinegar with onions and paprika; to toilets in separate cubicles off the foyer and not fully exposed in bathrooms. Even the ordinary details of daily life were foreign. We were free but our joy in being so was soon crowded out by the differences in customs and external conditions confronting us. With a shock we found ourselves—as though we had not been saved but had lost the familiar sense of home ground beneath our feet—in an emotional state we had not expected: We were alien, and felt it.

I soon suffered an indignity that was not considered such here but was so for me. I had taken it as an insult to my ideas of an adolescent growing into life's romance and magic when I had seen boys my age on production lines in the factories at Zlin. I used to walk through my father's warehouse or sit at a rolltop desk in his office, papers piled up, the telephone ringing, workmen loading or unloading merchandise, my father sorting out skins, and I could simply not imagine a life of working and of business. While the romantic aspects awaiting me in the years ahead were compelling and beckoned me, promising a vague though grand fulfillment, the realistic part of the life ahead, of occupation, of giving one's time to impersonal facts and figures of business, descended before me like a wall of steel. I could not think of facing it. Yet here I was, not yet sixteen, and working as a delivery boy in a market in the neighborhood. The owners, acquaintances of our American relatives, wanted to help the newly arrived, destitute refugees so they took me on for six dollars a week delivering meats and vegetables and groceries. Insufferable, but it had to be done. I was proving to be my parents' best and only investment. I was the only one who talked the language, the only one who could help out. And of course I would not refuse to do so. I understood our predicament and was ready to help.

I was a poor cyclist, so I piled up the cartons on a large basket in front of the handlebars and pushed the bicycle through the streets. I soon became known among the customers as the little English gentleman. My accent was primarily British—I had, of course, been taught the language that way—and I was loaded with central European politeness. This made me the little English gentleman in the eyes of the middle-class, largely Jewish customers, mostly the children of "greenhorns," to whom I was an oddity. My parents were brave about this; outwardly they assumed the attitude of meeting life's necessities head-on with courage but, inwardly, their distress at seeing me not in school but pushing groceries on a bicycle caused my mother some bad breathing spells and my father, on one occasion, to wipe the tears from his eyes.

The customers I serviced all lived in the small one- or two-family homes I had had difficulty accepting as houses when my uncle Martin first took me on a walk through the neighborhood the day of our arrival. In each, a separate entrance led to the kitchen at the back of the house. Considering that I had just come from a society in which class distinctions, the divisions between the wealthy and the poor, between people served and those serving were part of one's upbringing and still strictly observed, to enter a house at what was to me the servants' entrance was, at first, entirely out of character for me. An insignificant dilemma, in retrospect, especially in view of other, much more drastic and unsettling adjustments; but I am not sure that I ever, during the month I worked at that store, overcame my humiliation when I made a delivery through the back door.

Once, on a delivery to the second-floor apartment of a two-family house, I had placed the heavy cartons on the kitchen floor not realizing that it had just been waxed. The woman had shouted something to me as I was coming up the back steps but I didn't catch what she had said and, afraid that I would drop the heavy parcels, I placed them not where she had directed me but, as soon as I had reached the kitchen, on the floor inside it. A barrage of insults flew from the angry woman and I felt so ashamed and humiliated that, rushing out and down the steps, leaving behind the dime tip on the table and saying that my parents would never have allowed this had they had any idea that such insults would be hurled at me, I peed in my pants as I ran away. I remember my agony, for this had never happened to me before, I had never even wet my bed; and now to feel urine running down my legs and clinging to my pants like blood was my life's worst experience yet.

Here was a pure, existential dilemma. A year or so later, I tried to incorporate this in a story. Hounded for over a year by anti-Jewish Nazi edicts, aware of monstrous events crowding in on us, I had, by comparison to what had just occurred, maintained nonetheless a distance toward those realities, as though they were threatening only in an abstract way. They had not crushed me; I had been spared experiencing them bodily. But here, free at last, I was reacting to what I considered an affront in a worse way, probably, than if I had been hit. For this was an attack on all my social conditioning; this was personal, not in the least abstract.

When I told my parents about the incident, my mother tried to shrug it off. I must not be so sensitive, she said. She knew it would not have helped me had she too broken down; she wanted to aid my courage not my dismay. But my father couldn't control himself. He said nothing but turned away and quickly blew his nose.

Existentialism was obviously not a philosophy I knew about in the fall of 1939. It wasn't for another six years that I first read Sartre and not for another ten, on my first return to Europe, that I heard discussions of it in the cafés and intellectual cabarets of Paris. But there is little doubt that our direct trauma, our existential confrontation occurred when we first felt in the depth of our beings that we were on alien soil, that what we had taken for granted in the background of our lives was simply not here; we had, until then, just never known what it would be like to live without that. Inwardly we were struggling, as though seeking a foothold in quicksand, and outwardly as well, with the necessities of daily existence.

Of the two, the outer struggle was by far more manageable. My parents and my brother immediately went to night school to study English. After a month, my brother took over my delivery job and I went to work as a beginning technician in a dental laboratory, again because the owner was a friend of a childhood friend of my father then living in Newark. I worked there for a year. My brother moved on to a sheet-metal shop—he had strong mechanical inclinations and later became an industrial engineer—and my father was soon setting up an operation of his own. With a Viennese business acquaintance—Herr Kohlmann, I recall him even now, slender, dark, looking more like an intense intellectual than a businessman—he established himself in the wholesale meat district of Newark, where they bought up the innards of cattle, dried the stomachs (the stink was unbearable—I used to work there on Saturdays when I was back in school), and sold them to sausage manufacturers abroad, I believe. Not precisely an occupation fit for a Café Fetzer habitué who used to dress like a dandy, but he didn't mind, he was once again on his own and he did well. After two years or so, some of his money reached him from London and, by the end of the war, when we were living in New York, he was dealing in leather skins and was part owner of a small manufacturing shop of leather novelties. Meanwhile, the struggle in Newark was very much uphill; those first few years were obviously the worst in the drama of our displacement.

➤ 2

Unease and inner disturbance kept gnawing at us, a bad dream, images of loss and emotional insecurity repeated all too frequently. Even Fifi felt it, her trembling grew worse—nervousness is a characteristic of Doberman pinschers—and she felt visibly lost. She certainly was on alien ground, sniffed everywhere, but to no avail; these were not the streets she knew, and she became evermore solicitous of our welfare. Our rooms during the first few months, following our initial stay on Lyons Avenue, were on the first floor, the windows only a few feet above ground. Whenever my mother would get up on the windowsill in order to clean the windows, Fifi would wail and wail, her front paws reaching as far up the wall as she could manage below where my mother was cleaning. She evidently must have remembered the height from our windows in Vienna to the street below and was fearful because of the danger. In Vienna she had been a friendly dog, allowing herself to be petted by strangers and even licking their hands. Not here, where she was often stopped because her breed is not common and people marveled at her size and gracefulness. But she was distrustful, would not allow anyone near her. And one cold evening, only about two months after our arrival, she was so eager to get back to our house when my father had taken her out and had let her off the leash in an empty lot, that she dashed across Lyons Avenue as soon as she was done and was instantly killed by a car. It hadn't even hit her, my distraught father told us, the car had come to a screeching halt, but her tiny heart must have snapped out of general confusion and fear. My father had brought her in, had laid her across his arms. "Here she is," he had murmured, "Here is our Fifi."

It was a dreadful loss, an added jolt in the all-too-frequent shocks of displacement. Our pain of exile lay there in the shape of motionless Fifi. I was disconsolate and began to sleep badly. It was during those weeks that I suffered the worst injuries. I could not fathom the depth of my uprootedness, from which came an ache that gripped me, sometimes paralyzing me so that I could barely speak. From there also sprang the early rhythms, as yet unformulated syllables and words that worked as a salve, a consolation badly needed, early urges toward expression through art. Walking to and from the dental laboratory on tree-lined streets of small wooden houses I would feel those rhythms, sounds of words surging upward; and the possibility of this, of formulations of feelings by means of language, a flow I could almost hear though not say, became a quiet consolation. Inwardly at least there was the possibility of a richness that could offset the poverty—of soul, of spirit—I sensed around me. Even then. Or, perhaps, significantly then. For there isn't any doubt that these experiences and hints shaped the direction I was to pursue later. The buildings beyond the narrow lawns seemed to me to lack life; certainly they lacked the qualities I had been accustomed to in the streets of European cities. It was not the buildings but the trees with which I did feel a connection, especially in the fall. My cherished, though here deprived, imagination was stirred by the leaves on the ground, the sounds they made underfoot, by seeing them whirled up in a gust of wind, by their smell when, piled in heaps, they were burned, by the empty, bare trees that stood like timeless witnesses, by the branches in their vulnerable nakedness. The buildings, however, which in Vienna had engaged me as if they were calling me when I passed them, as if they felt themselves, their secret beings, understood in me and mine enlarged in theirs, in them, in their human accumulations, their venerable age: their counterparts, the wooden dwellings here, stood like flat, paper-thin walls; and I felt nothing of what the others had contained in them. I did sense something from them, but it was a loneliness, not the fullness, the reaching-out I had received before. And so the melancholy had started; the syllables welling up from the chasm of my displacement.

► 3

Even fifteen years after this initial realization of irreparable loss, when its distress had become so acute, the split between where I was outside and where within so wide that a cure had to be found, a great journey to be embarked on, even after such a span of years I continued to be haunted by dreams, situations expressing the pain that had started at sixteen when I had to rise early on Mondays and face my new incomprehensible life as an apprentice in a dental laboratory.

During our last year in Vienna, when the Jews were trying to ready themselves for the hardships awaiting them in exile, a number of centers had opened to give young people a rudimentary training in a useful trade. I did not join these but my parents had apprenticed me to a dental technician whom they paid to train me. Although I was with him for no more than about three months, the minimal skills I had acquired had helped me get hired by the large laboratory on Newark's Clinton Avenue. I was earning only the minimum wage of twelve dollars a week but this was a real help to my parents then. My early indoctrination into American life had, therefore, not been by means of school and the company of my peers, but by working with adult men and by the rough, odd camaraderie existing among them. Most were much older, of course, and paid little attention to me. The manager had been particularly kind when he engaged me and he continued to treat me with parental thoughtfulness, even when after a year he had called me into his office to tell me how sorry he was that due to bad times he could no longer keep me. But there were two or three young men among the technicians, who had been only three or four years older than I, whose manner, language, and toughness were as incomprehensible to me as everything about me must have been to them—my language, my manner, my looks (thin, tall, pale), my general appearance referred to as "sensitive"! They were not unkind to me but they did often mock me in a sort of mixed rough and affectionate way. They were sympathetic to my condition and were curious about the life from which we had just escaped. At least one of them I remember as having been Jewish. The owners were of Russian Jewish background. But when my coworkers had had enough of the seriousness of world events represented by my person, they'd wipe away the attention they had given to matters they'd rather not have to face by making inane comments about me and my reports and, back on their home ground, would address me as they did each other with an assortment of four-letter words I was then beginning to learn. Except that in my case the endearment was preceded by "Viennese," so that I became the Viennese so-and-so, etc. I was not offended by these appellations for they did not disguise the good-naturedness that underlay them—one of these teasing fellow workers became a friend of mine who employed me part-time when he opened his own laboratory and I had gone back to school—but I felt assaulted by the strangeness of this realistic world of grown-ups into which I had been thrust too soon. I managed it somehow through the week, by the long walks to and from the laboratory and my growing introspection, the trees along the way, the schoolchildren being led across the street by volunteer guards, and other sights that touched me as though whispering of something I longed for. But weekends, when I found my own rhythms again and lived in them without interruption, were the worst, for I dreaded the return to my enforced realism, and Sunday nights were often sleepless. Once, I felt my entire being cry out; I needed rescue, urgency possessed me, my hand reaching up to be grasped. But there was only darkness, the first grey of daybreak floating on the ceiling like an eerie shape wisplike, haunted and without hope. Soon it would be day, I would be back in the routine of alien occurrences, and I had not yet slept. I could hear my parents' breathing in the next room. I crept into their bed, my mother grumbling but tolerating me beside her. How was she to comfort me, a youth of sixteen needing to be held as though years did not matter, only the child's urgent need for assurance, the consolation of love?

▶ 4

If there existed an instrument for recording the anguish at the loss of the familiar, the deepest attachments, how many times, how many millions of times would such acute disturbances in the sleep of new immigrants have been registered? If there were a way to view these disorders as on an X-ray, would it reveal the harm they have done, the insoluble mass they have caused in the individual's inner life, and the generations that followed? I could not have known then, and it would hardly have eased my pain, that I was feeling what millions must have suffered before me in crowded immigrant slums or even in comfortable lodgings. The immigration I was part of did not live in conditions common for the great waves that had come decades earlier. But regardless of outer circumstances, the inner turmoil had to have been the same.

Would it have mattered, would this trauma have been much different had we arrived in the fairly prosperous circumstances my father had risked his life for? Granted, I would have been spared some of the unexpected indignities, but the difficulties of adjustment could not have been much different. As immigrants had done before us, we too sought out our old friends or even people we didn't know but who were also refugees from Austria or Germany. My parents met them at night school and we attended social functions sponsored by a growing number of refugee associations. There were dinners, dances, lectures, excursions to Washington and other important historic places of our new home. These activities, bringing together people with whom one shared a common language of more than words but of similar backgrounds and experiences, helped soothe the fresh wounds of alienation.

For a while I attended the dances; I was not then, and am not now, a joiner of clubs or groups, but I liked to dance and I used to go often on Saturday nights to the Essex House or other hotels where these functions were held. But soon, I developed a horror for the term "function"—affairs of forced cheerfulness—and I stopped going. I did, however, seek out my former friends and I frequently took the Hudson Tube to New York to visit them. The Kemplers, who had preceded us here, were living in the Bronx and Fred—as my brother is now called—and I went to see them almost immediately after we had arrived. Fred was nineteen, Gertie seventeen, and the flirtation, which had gone on in full force two years ago, had simmered down into a playful interest in one another. Fred had had a serious and, for someone his age, long love affair with a Danish girl during the year he had lived in Switzerland, and he was then busy discovering American girls. After the war, when we were living in New York, I introduced him to one soon after he had returned from the army, Rhoda Serot, then a coworker of mine, whom he married in

1946. But in 1939, despite his active interests elsewhere, Gertie still had her eye on him and he would often spend weekends with the Kemplers. They had been rich in Vienna, had lived in a large apartment in a building they had owned. Here, Fred slept in a tiny room off the long hallway in their "railroad" flat in a Bronx tenement. Gertie's father had opened a small drygoods store and Gertie, always spoilt, did nothing, neither went to school nor worked. But she had made many friends in the neighborhood and introduced us to them.

From the first time I went to New York—the owner of the market where both Fred and I had worked took us by car one Sunday—I was astonished by the multitudes in the streets and on the subways and by the behavior of the people I observed on the trains. The overriding impression was that they were much freer than the people I used to observe in public places in Vienna. The casual clothes, the chewing of gum, the way they conversed with each other in a group, the loudness, shouting, frequent laughter, the slapping of others on the shoulder, the storming down the stairs of the elevated, yelling to friends across the street, above the traffic—all these were immediate indications to me that people here were not conforming to conventions I had been raised in. What theirs were, where the restrictions lay that shaped their directions, I could not guess; it was clear to me only that they were free—freer outwardly than I had ever been.

Over the years I am reminded of this quality, having taken it for granted, when I return from my almost yearly trips to Europe or when friends visiting from London or Paris remark on the free openness and friendliness they meet here everywhere. Looking back on my first encounters with this attractive outgoingness, I can certainly understand their enthusiasm; for it is definitely not a European quality. On my early trips into New York, on the elevated to the Bronx or in the subway to Brooklyn to visit Willie or Eugen—Willie had preceded me, Eugen came soon after—I sensed among the people I watched a generosity, an openness toward others I had not seen expressed publicly in Europe. No doubt this was the democratic spirit, a basic attitude in a nation's character that I responded to with zest. I sensed then that living in its atmosphere would, with my help, alter me in time. For it was obvious to me that where these people felt free I felt restricted. What they had acquired by birth I would have to acquire by a willed change. As long as I met this welcome quality of freedom and openness in public I felt enthusiastic about it and comfortable in it; in private, however, face to face with someone brought up in a completely different framework from mine, I didn't quite know how to respond. People I was introduced to, whether or not I was likely to see them again, were extraordinarily friendly. In the world I had just left it would have taken years of patient care, of building up to a cordial intimacy between two people before such free and open friendliness could have been arrived at, if indeed it ever could. Here, it was instantaneous and I didn't know how to react. I was embarrassed to be treated by someone I barely knew as though we had been inseparable childhood chums. Nevertheless, it was this quality of friendly openness expressed impersonally by the masses that I had found so attractive.

An incident a few years later, when we were living in New York in Washington Heights, in which I witnessed a seemingly unrestricted, affectionate friendship expressed freely and without any regard to the fact that we were on a crowded subway car, is vivid in my mind. Its effect on me was similar to that of the event in front of the Hotel Excelsior in Vienna in 1938. Like then, this confrontation brought forth possibilities in human behavior that had been constricted for me, freedom where I had known rigidity, and what this chance encounter also suggested was immensely appealing. The two young men, who were just "horsing around," were about my age (I was twenty-one at the time). Again, their casualness of manner and dress attracted me. I felt stiff, in my hat, which I knew did not become me, in my overcoat, really not necessary for a man my age, in my business suit, white shirt, and tie. And seeing these two friends, in their zipper-jackets, open necks, unpressed trousers, saddle shoes, their gestures of affectionate friendship which they expressed so exuberantly, so freely—one forcing the other to give him his seat, the other now standing tormenting the first until he was once again seated, the other standing holding on to a strap—I felt that my appearance was entirely unimaginative, that a hopeless stiffness still controlled me, that I was encased in outmoded attitudes which, moreover, belonged to a world now in ruins, and that the statue that had been bred in me had to be broken, cracked apart. I wanted the freedom I witnessed. I wanted the ease of "horsing around." I envied the friends their lighthearted, easy affection, and I was determined to achieve the same. To free myself, to cast off the bonds for which there no longer existed any actuality. For, by citizenship I had become an American; I swore to become one in spirit and habits as well. It proved a difficult, if not impossible task.

If I was no more than a sapling by the time we had fled Europe, my parents were certainly fully formed by then, molded by the only world they ever really understood. Fond as my mother became of America (it so suited her innate liberal disposition), the American way of life was not hers, could never have been. My father's connection with this country also remained only on the surface, it could never have been made at a deeper level. He was nearly fifty when we came here and he had been too accustomed to his former way of life. Almost directly after the war he reestablished his European business ties and until the middle fifties my parents shuttled back and forth. They were well aware that my situation, of someone who had to make his way into mature life here, was different from theirs. Nevertheless, how could they accept in me any other development but in forms that they understood, had taken for granted, and expected of me? How this was to come about here, where conditions were so different from those in which they had been raised, was never clear to them. The main difficulty of people who, like my parents, came here as adults was this: They were fully formed personalities living in a world that did not shape them. The attitudes that had shaped them, their entire cultural and social fabric, were distinctly different from the ones instilled in people born and bred here. When I saw the two young men in the subway, I swore that I would achieve a manner as free as theirs. The fact that that was not possible in someone transplanted, even when no more than a sapling, I might have sensed dimly, but I would not admit it. Against all odds I was going to be as American as they. And for the next ten years—until, disappointed, disillusioned, still struggling for the anchor I knew I had to have, I set out on a journey to India—I pursued this goal as far and as best as I could.

► 5

Along with this freedom in behavior so different from the politeness and codified formality that had been instilled in me, I was also impressed by expressions of public generosity in place of the suspicious, bureaucratic atmosphere I had been reared in. On the radio the range of public sentiments and group identifications went from Father Coughlin's anti-Semitic rantings to the Andrews Sisters singing "*Bei Mir Bist De Schen.*" I had never before heard Yiddish programs on a public radio and turning the dial was like choosing stations on a shortwave apparatus in Europe; for although we were in an English-speaking country I was amazed to find nearly every language transmitted over the airwaves. And it amused and astonished me to hear women I considered of venerable age address each other by their first names, and even more so when I heard this from younger people who would refer to them as "girls." Unthinkable in Vienna, where only family members and the most intimate of friends would have this privilege and everyone else would say, stiffly: Frau Doktor, Frau Ingenieur, Frau Geheimrat; thereby addressing the woman by her husband's profession and title. To me, the signs of freedom I met here, the expressions of equal rights, came across as a fundamental sense of tolerance, an underlying assent to human life that I had not yet experienced.

Still, what was so appealing in public was, again, often a trial in private; how were we to act in view of such an atmosphere of ease and casualness? People were kind, full of advice, even overly solicitous, but we did not want charity and if we did not accept what others offered, pursue what others suggested, those who offered felt offended and thought us ungrateful and arrogant. They did not understand us any better than we understood them. Acquaintances we had made, or friends of theirs, came to my father suggesting jobs as dishwasher or gas-station attendant, or "a candy-store, a corner candy-store, that's what you should do." My father thanked them politely but didn't follow through. Some women in the market where I had worked were astonished to see my mother get on the bus one day smartly dressed and wearing two silverfoxes—they had been among the contents rescued from the Paris crate that had reached us by then. "Who do they think they are?" I overhead them say; "We lived in a cellar and worked in sweatshops! But look at them! They are not greenhorns, *they* are *refugees*! They walk around in furs, want big apartments, nothing's good enough for them."

Of course these women knew nothing of our world. They had come here probably directly from an eastern European ghettolike shtetl. But even those who hadn't, who were born and raised here, were understandably put off by our foreignness, which they often mistook as snobbishness. Whereas by rejecting suggestions of charity, we were merely struggling to maintain our standards. In fact, what took place during these early days of our immigration was a split, one which undoubtedly had happened to every immigrant; the behavior of people here did not conform to the conditioning we had lived by; for the first time in our lives the outer world contradicted our cultural habits, and in private encounters a response was expected from us which we simply could not enact.

Inwardly this split was never resolved, and couldn't be; outwardly we tried our best not to reveal it but to comply with conditions that prevailed here. For us, the good will of people, despite the petty observations, by far exceeded any embarrassment it might inadvertently have caused. Adjusting to an atmosphere of freedom was, after all, far less grave a hardship than being deprived of it. And on the whole people were thoughtful and considerate, like the owner of the market where my brother and I had worked in the beginning. He, himself an immigrant from Poland, had only been here for fifteen years. No doubt it was the memory of his own experience and the fact that a good deal of his family had remained in Europe, their fate then uncertain, that had made him so generous to our plight and eager to be of help. We felt from him and from other former immigrants that, yes, it's tough; America's streets are not paved with gold, no bed of roses; but you can make the most of what you've got, of what you are; we've all been through it; now it's your turn, and we sympathize.

►6

Soon after our arrival, my father's American cousin Kay, a spirited, lively schoolteacher who had come to Vienna one summer when we were in Luhačovice (only my father had met her then), went to visit friends in Brooklyn; I wanted to see Willie, who was living there then with relatives, and she took me along. First we took the Hudson Tube and then the subway that went across one of the bridges in lower Manhattan. New York harbor seemed even livelier and the skyline rounding the tip of Manhattan and extending up the East River more imposing than on my first sight when the ship had pulled into the Hudson. Crossing the bridge slowly, I responded differently this time to the industrial "landscape." As I looked around me, at the river below the grid work, the water grey, I thought, like the color of heavy labor, its surface beaten as though worn-out from all the tug-boats, ships, long oil-tankers plowing through it; and to my right, through the black cables strung upward like strings in a giant instrument, at the sweep of tall buildings beyond the East Side Drive where streams of cars flowed in two directions; and on the other side, along the Brooklyn waterfront, seeing tall warehouses, huge signs of company names, billboards advertising products; and below me, trucks loading and unloading bales and crates of merchandise: I felt the rhythms, the expression of labor like the network of a giant machinery. Energy was throbbing all around me. This was power of the *moment,* not slipping by but caught, worked, sung, I thought, and it was thrilling, a totally new sensation. Many years later I found the exuberant expression of this, the potential it represented, in the poetry of Walt Whitman, Hart Crane, and William Carlos Williams, but it was new to me then, a wave of the power of energy, the joy of the moment transformed by work.

Cousin Kay was pointing out the sights to me but I listened only politely. In the midst of the confusion that had beset us since coming here, this view was like the sudden onrush of powerful orchestral passages and, for as long as the train was still overlooking this impressive vastness of action, I felt elated. Kay was singing me different praises. She wouldn't live in New York. She had traveled all over the world, she said—this was true if one considered the world as consisting of Europe, Mexico, and Palestine, where she had been on her summer vacations—but despite all that she had seen, all the great cities she had toured, there was no place in the world for her like Newark. I couldn't grasp this and took what she had said either to be apologetic—for I had already developed a total dislike for that, to me, nontown—or sheer chauvinism. Newark had everything, Kay sang on, good shopping, quiet, languid residential areas (this was 1939!) even its own Mosque Theatre with its first-rate concerts and operas; in short, all one needed without having to buck the noise, the crowds, the tremendous distances, hour-long subway rides in New York. I demurred quietly. From my few visits there, I knew by then that New York was a true city, a magnificent conglomerate of industry, business, culture, and residential neighborhoods. I had sensed this from my trips to Radio City, rides to the Bronx, and especially a day spent on the grounds of the World's Fair, which, I had thought, in its displays, its visualization of and readiness for the future, represented the spirit of New York. It was not Vienna, it was not a European city, the buildings did not reach out toward me as they had done there, but it was a city, a vibrant, great city, and the buildings, the street life, the lights blinking magically from the roofs and tops of towers, the cars traveling on miles of low roller-coaster ribbons surrounding the island, or forming a noisy denseness in the cross streets and long, long avenues where I saw shine a luminous sky of a radiant blue I had not seen in any European city: All this told me clearly that it was a great place with a character all its own and that I wanted to live in it—had by then determined to live there as soon as we possibly could. I knew it was the right place for me, I had to explore it, to know it, for it had roused something in me the way the weekly hour of jazz on Saturday mornings had done in Vienna: It had talked to me of something I perceived vaguely to be the power, the reality of *now*.

Kay can have her Newark, I thought as we stepped down from the elevated subway station where the Brighton Express had let us off. And she can have this, as well. For we were once again in a neighborhood very much like the one in Newark where Kay and, for the moment, we lived. Small houses, mostly wooden, with lawns in front, yards in back, kids on bicycles; though when we turned into the street where Willie's relatives lived, I saw buildings I had not yet come across. Blocks of them, attached so that it was a wall of low buildings, each absolutely identical to the next, small, red brick one-family *townhouses,* steps leading up to a small porch that led to the front door. Below was a large garage door, drawn up or open, a car inside or in the driveway. Perhaps the car came with the house, I thought. The uniformity of this, though it seemed very modern, did not appeal to me. It reminded of the houses in which the workers had lived in Zlin. Soon I was greeted by Willie and his American relatives—an aunt, uncle, and two girl-cousins around my age. Kay left to go to her friends and a meeting for the evening and our return to Newark was arranged.

Again, everything here was novel. It neither.attracted nor appalled me, it was just different. The same warmth, outpourings of friendliness . . . *isn't it nice,* said again and again and again. I had read about such visits in a book shortly before coming here. It was a story by and about a young Hungarian who had come to stay with relatives in Brooklyn and who had felt miserably out of place amidst the effusions of *niceness.* I felt the same just then though these were close relatives of one of my dearest friends. But how different the surroundings in which our friendship had flourished! Still, I felt, not from the depth of me but rather out of necessity, that I had now to be in tune with this reality and I was astonished, or pretended to be, to hear from his lively cousins, typical high school girls (as I was to discover a year later when I went back to school—and how different they were from Gertie, their age when we had been in Luhačovice) that Willie was morose, went to school but didn't join with any of the school *gangs,* sat at home alone in his room when others were out playing ball or were taking girls to the movies, and never, never listened to jazz on the radio or the gramophone but only to Mozart, Mozart, Mozart.

Much to my surprise, and more to Willie's, I am sure, I joined his cousins in their tauntings. Give it up, give up the Old World! Yes, we had gone together one Saturday afternoon and heard Helletsgruber as Donna Anna; true, the boys used to exchange opera libretti during school recess in the yard the way they trade girlie magazines here. But that's all over now. A world at war, a city of willing Nazis, a world dead for us. Now join your new life. Follow the times. Go with your uncle to baseball games. (I couldn't believe I was saying all this. Obviously, half in an attempt to show the girls and his American aunt and uncle that, unlike their cousin and nephew, *I was with it;* I was of *their* world, no longer of his; a vain attempt of a sixteen-year-old to sound realistic and grown-up. But I had already been to a baseball game. A week or so after we had arrived, my father's cousin Sam tried to indoctrinate my brother and me in the most American of all American pastimes. The game had made no sense to me whatsoever, nor the peculiar, noisy camaraderie all around us that it engendered; yet, here I was chiding Willie for not joining in!) I don't listen to Mozart any longer, not ever; jazz, only jazz; only the popular hit songs.

So ended my first visit in America with a friend I had loved so dearly as a boy, of whom Julie used to say, "Your god is on the telephone." Now, I did not want to sympathize with his condition of uprootedness and confusion. His parents were not yet here (they did come within a year), he was alone with a family representing nothing but the *new* way. He was withdrawing into himself and I had sided with his family when they complained about this! How could I have? Why did I not offer—and I was the only one who could have then—the solace, the understanding he needed. A Viennese boy alone in a Brooklyn high school! Why did I not sit with him and listen to his beloved Mozart? Our fabric of life having been torn apart, we were each torn apart, each in his own way, though we were too young, too confused, to have understood this. How to adapt ourselves, how to become one with this new way of life, confused us all then, and in my case, for years to come. The split within had happened but, as with some injuries, did not make itself felt for some time.

I did not see Willie often. Not only because while still in Newark we lived two hours of traveling time apart. After his parents and sister and younger brother arrived, they had moved to religious Williamsburg. His parents had been observing Jews in Vienna but they became more so, strictly orthodox, once they had escaped the flames of Europe. Willie conformed to this piety.

The common interests and artistic expressions, the world we had shared as boys, no longer sustained us. My parents and I did visit his family in the early forties and we were distressed to learn some years later from Willie that his sister had died. Our relationship had receded from the passionate intensity it had had for me in Vienna at thirteen to occasional phone calls in New York by the time I was twenty. Eventually, even these stopped.

From time to time, however, during the many years that have passed since, I have dreamed of Willie, and of Eugen, though it is not together that they appear. Each time, they come before me, move across the screen of a submerged reality, my sphere of undisturbed harmony, as emissaries of a loyalty, of shared, innocent affections which not age, not a world wherein our lives have shaped themselves so differently, has marred or altered.

►7

When Eugen came with his parents from Belgium in 1940 and I visited him in their apartment in Brooklyn near Eastern Parkway, there was no split response in me at our reunion. If the windows of their apartment did not look out on Schwedenplatz, the Danube Canal, and the surrounding elegant streets of the *Innere Stadt* where they had lived in Vienna, they were at least not in a building of new, connected homes, and the family atmosphere within the apartment was not disturbed by acute cultural differences. Here, the deprivations of a refugee family like mine, the Kemplers, and about a dozen others who became our circle of friends during those early years, were evident from the impoverished furnishings, the small rooms, and, in general, the absence of a style of life that our former bourgeois homes had clearly indicated. The faces of our parents showed the stress of (for them) unprecedented upheavals and economic uncertainties and we, still teenagers, alternated between states of excitement and apprehension. At Eugen's I found conditions similar to ours;

the sense of alienation so powerful for us in the outside world was appeased within our homes by friends and family members who shared the same predicament. But it was for even more personal reasons that spending weekends with Eugen at his family's was an occasion I looked forward to at first with anticipation, later with some misgivings.

Again, as with Willie before him, the affection I had had for Eugen as a boy in Vienna had been strongly influenced by the surroundings which had nourished our friendship to no small degree. Throughout my boyhood I was possessed of a fierce ardor for a closeness with a friend which would make the nostalgic yearning I had sensed all around me somewhat tangible. I had absorbed this not only from the old streets, to me of a dreamlike character, from the formal, often deserted parks, friends or lovers walking arm in arm in the dust and dusk of tree-shaded lanes, from the monuments spaced at equal intervals, the statues, each indrawn as though in revery and thought, but also from my father resting in his fauteuil on a lazy Sunday afternoon and humming a melody he had sung as a boy in his Russian village—a wistful, longing melody in which he was sometimes joined by a friend who had come from the same village and who hummed along with him in her deep, melodious voice of lasting, unperturbed memory. In the same way, I had been affected by the chant in *Madama Butterfly*—I had gone to see the opera by myself one Saturday afternoon when I was eleven—the chant of waiting and Butterfly's aria of waiting which had stirred me so deeply each time I heard it, my receptivity to feelings so strong it was fragile, that, touched by this melody, I broke into tears I was not ashamed of. They were tears of an overwhelming response that gave me the gratified sense of having reached into something I could not name but was well familiar with and felt elated by; though these emotional enthusiasms were—understandably—disturbing to my mother.

At fourteen, my affection for Eugen when he came into my class at the Gymnasium was as melodious as my father's chant of a Russian folktune and as the suggestions of romance, of loss, of time heaped upon time that rose from Vienna's panorama, its revery at sunset. Through him, through this new friend, and with him on walks through the city and its wooded surroundings, or arranging to meet him in the park of the Lichtenstein Palais, this emotion would be shared and lived. But here now, in America, the background against which this friendship had to be continued, was, of course, totally different. Neither of us was accustomed to it, neither of us understood it and our new surroundings became the exploration for us by which our friendship would have to be sustained if any of the joy and intensity I had derived from it was to continue. It didn't. The forces that had promoted the bond between us, their romantic background, were dead; it now had to be supported within a totally different framework.

Our friendship continued for a time but without any of the strength and ardor it had had for me in the past. The change of environment was certainly not the sole reason for its decline. Our early adolescence was over, the time when such first romantic friendships flare up; at sixteen our interests and temperaments were beginning to shape themselves, and their directions did not coincide. When, some years later, I talked to Eugen of art and poetry and, with great excitement, showed him my first published poems, we were no longer on the same track. Though he responded politely I knew that my endeavors and, moreover, uncompromising ambition in the realm of art, made him ill at ease. Whatever the reasons, this continuity was also broken.

When I used to go out for weekends with him in Brooklyn in 1940, we would always take trips into Manhattan and often went to Radio City Music Hall. On each of these visits to New York I saw another aspect or elaboration of a way of life whose surface expressions, whose vibrancy fascinated me. The traffic patterns, the glamor of some of the people on Fifth or Madison avenues, the large proportions of many of the buildings, the bulk of such older structures as the 42nd Street Library, Grand Central and Pennsylvania stations, the Morgan Library, the sedateness of the clubs on Fifth and Park avenues, the small, red-brick buildings on Sixth and Third avenues, a dark, dingy bar in nearly every one of them, the glamor of the shops on Fifty-seventh Street, and so on. The city and most of its buildings seemed gigantic, larger than human life. I was especially impressed that Radio City Music Hall was the biggest cinema in the world; probably ten Tegetthoff Kinos could have fit into it. Walking though its immense lobby with dark marble columns, down the wide staircase to the spacious lounges as though one were entering the first-class accommodations of an immense luxury liner; then, at the beginning of the show, entering the auditorium probably higher than Vienna's *Hochhaus,* the giant organ on one side of the gigantic stage (everything gigantic!), the hundred or so girls kicking their legs in absolute uniform motion, the spotlights, the announcer's voice amplified so that it was like an echo speaking out of a Greek amphitheatre, all of this made me feel that we were not inside a movie house but actually within a glamorous Hollywood film. And then, when the film came on, on a screen suitable for the size Grecian or Biblical heroes had taken on over the centuries, what wonderland! what bigger-than-life dramas and emotions! what dreams of great love and happiness projected as though out of the minds of the audience, of the public's daydreaming and fantasy! And always glamor, always enlargements, whether a film depicted squalor and horror, or the world of Fred Astaire and his glittering partners. I remember, in particular, *The Little Foxes* with Bette Davis and Herbert Marshall. The enthrallment with which I had watched films at the Tegetthoff Kino was here repeated a hundredfold. The screen of the Vienna cinema had been only a small corner of this one and the films I had watched there had originated in the world in which I was now viewing this spectacle of a tempestuous family life in bygone days. The selfishness of Regina, the illness and disadvantaged position of her husband, her shy, timid sister-in-law, the manner in which this web of pitched emotions was handled with a mixture of fierceness and polish, this display of expertise in externalizing emotions—all this held me spellbound.

Needless to say, it is only now that I can discern the cause of my fascination at that time, the brand of sophistication that attracted me. It too was new and unfamiliar. It was the realization, the visualization of my cinema-going fantasies in Vienna. The manner in which people of social distinction had comported themselves in the world I had left behind was vastly different from what I was now observing, in films and life alike. The American style of appearance was continuing to cast a powerful spell over me.

After the movie, we would explore the neighborhood east of Radio City. The facades were impressive, the height and power of the buildings comprising Rockefeller Center, the revolving doors, the spacious lobbies, the escalators, the Promenade with long, rectangular flower beds, the skating rink, the windows of Saks Fifth Avenue, the high, imposing lower part of the store: each, in appropriate style, expressing great wealth. We observed how the rich lived, the doormen on Park Avenue, the women being helped from cars usually dressed strikingly, in a sort of sumptuous restraint, the men in white silk scarves and black coats; the tall apartment houses looking as solid as their occupants. Unlike the apartment buildings of the wealthy in Vienna where the first floor windows (second floor here) were considerably taller than those of the floors above, and were also distinguished by stucco decorations, these windows were uniform from first to top floor, and from many of them we could see the sparkle of chandeliers behind parted draperies. Here was the power and style of a wealth that had become legendary in Europe. It gave off an effect of such confidence in the world that the result was both attractive and intimidating.

Eugen and I observed these things and talked about them. Though what we saw was a by far more exaggerated materialistic style than we had lived in or even observed in Europe, we felt nonetheless closer to it than the manner of life that then surrounded us in Brooklyn or Newark. And so we speculated on what it would be like to live in one of those buildings, and if we ever would. At sixteen, the possibilities that lie ahead for one, the directions to take, seem so vague, the desire for the marvelous life that surely awaits one so strong (yet not any the clearer for all its intensity), that two friends pondering these still-adolescent matters can only walk, observe from the outside, the time when these destinies begin to take shape at a great distance still, can only guess, dream, speculate.

But, for all these joint explorations, for me the real depth that had existed in this friendship was not there. Was it because we were older or because the external aspects of our new world that we were witnessing were cold, impersonal, however grandiose, imposing rather than inviting? They could not unite us at the depth where friendship can flourish; they were of the world, not of the soul; they could not fire the imagination whereby one perceives as a feeling the hidden sameness that joins us. They stood as a worldly challenge rather than as the great wrought-iron gate to the splendors of our legacy.

I have obviously no way of knowing how or if our friendship would have grown had world events not interfered with its natural development. But the crack of displacement—irreparable, as I have learned—also affects our most personal relationships, often shapes or destroys them. It makes our need for them so urgent—for who but the object of one's love can soothe this rift?—and this urgency works against them. In exile, friendships or loves are not lived within the patterns, the movements of the daily life in which the exiles remain outsiders. Thus, intense relationships, not part of a larger social web, are sustained, if at all, against great odds. For, regardless of the extent of adjustment, even if outwardly the adaptation has been successful, alienation continues at a deeper level, at which the needed foothold cannot be regained; the absolute fact of birth on foreign soil has made that impossible. Outwardly, spirited explorations; inwardly, the continued loss of heart connections. The anguish of this rift is not appeased. It invades one like a wandering sorrow from an ancestral past. At best, one has learned to live with it.

Eugen and I continued to see each other—our fathers even became business partners for a time—but gradually our interests diverged and our friendship became perfunctory. We met our obligations as our upbringing had trained us to do, he attended my college graduation in 1945, I his wedding in 1946. Occasionally I met him and his wife, at their home for dinner, or at a restaurant; and in the fall of 1947 I invited them to a private exhibition of Hanna's paintings in a brownstone on West 11th Street.

►8

Hanna, my great friend Hannelore Axmann, now von Rezzori, who, after so many years, stands for me, and evermore, as the firm, sculpted idea behind feelings, ornamented facade of an innerness where even anguish comes to rest—in whose home in St. Firmin sur Loire I have spent, for some years now, many happy weeks of summer. In her, in this complex, extraordinary woman, the residue of perhaps the greatest culture man has ever shaped, evident in its best creations and felt to this day in the soil, is vibrant still. The effect her astonishing beauty and human qualities had on me and others who formed her circle of devoted friends in 1946 when she came here from Munich, having spent the last year of the war in hiding, remains unforgettable.

Though thoroughly German on her father's side and educated at a convent school in Switzerland, her mother, a Catholic convert, was Jewish by birth and Hanna had in consequence been in danger of being sent to a concentration camp. There is now a well-described incident in Gregor von Rezzori's (her former husband's) splendid book, *Memoirs Of an Anti-Semite,* of Hanna being saved from the Gestapo by, not surprising to anyone who knew her then when she was very young, her beauty, which was, and is, not only of a perfection of features but of a subtle, mesmerizing mysteriousness. One of the ways in which Hanna hid for a while was to stay in mountain inns in obscure villages her Aryan friends had reconnoitered for her and designated as safe. One morning, while staying in such an inn, she was awakened by a great deal of noise, maneuverings inside and outside. To her horror she saw from behind her window a group of about fifty SS officers in their black uniforms and high black boots standing near or sitting in army vehicles. Later on she found out from the landlady that these men were not only high-ranking officers but were part of the elite corps serving as Hitler's bodyguards. Evidently, they had stopped at this inn for a respite from their duties. Hanna had stayed in her room all day but in the evening the innkeeper's wife entreated her to go downstairs and join the men. Earlier, the woman had boasted to some of them that she had staying at the inn one of the great beauties and the leader had sent her to Hanna to invite her to join them. Obviously, Hanna had no alternative. The landlady argued with her that she had to go, she could not let down Hitler's Elite Corps, and Hanna agreed. How could she not have obeyed? Frightened though she was, the power of her presence was nonetheless such that at first an exclamation of amazement and then a hush rippled across the room. The men related to her as though a collective symbol of perfection, what they had thought of as the German ideal, stood before them—they said as much to her later on. Instinctively, they no doubt also sensed the social sphere that had bred her—the distinctions of upbringing of the daughter of a wealthy industrialist were easily apparent. What they did not know, of course, was that Hanna's father had relinquished his holdings rather than divorce his Jewish wife, the alternative the Nazis had presented to him, and that her mother had been in hiding, along with an Aryan friend to protect her, in a peasant hut high up in the Bavarian Alps and that she wore around her neck a vial of poison she planned to take, and her family knew this, if caught. Hanna feared of course that the SS corps would find this out should they discover who she really was. She had to get away. Meanwhile, she knew she must not let them down in the vision they had of her. So she talked with them, danced with them, even sang for them—though untrained she had the talent of an actress and in later years appeared in a number of Hollywood and postwar German films—and when it was late enough, and safe enough to do so, excused herself, saying that she had not been well, had been resting at the inn, but she would not have missed the opportunity to be with the men who were serving her country in the most strategic and privileged of ways. Before they let her go, however, the leader of the group begged her to get up on top of a table. She did, and pointing to her, he said: "Cheers to this symbol of Aryan womanhood" and the entire room responded with shouts and applause. The next morning, when the maid knocked on Hanna's door to bring her breakfast, her room was empty. She had fled at daybreak.

If Hanna had in this manner affected the SS group by concealment and with caution, how much more powerful, more total, her capture of those of us who became her close, intimate friends, with whom she shared her hopes, the scars of her plight, her former and present torments? Among many happy memories, hours spent stimulated by her encouragements and her sadness—she supported my fervor toward artistic discovery and creation with her own fervor—the following incident stands out not only because it illustrates again the power of her appearance, but also because it recreates some of the cultural atmosphere of which I so very much wanted to be part in 1947.

Not surprisingly, my exclusive preference for jazz was short-lived. I soon discovered WQXR, which reached us even in Newark, went to the opera at the Mosque Theatre, to outdoor summer concerts in Newark, eventually to the Met where I used to stand behind the Family Circle at the top, and, after we moved to New York in March 1944, regularly frequented Carnegie

Hall, the City Center, the theatres, movie houses specializing in foreign films, etc. While still living in Newark, I had come into New York one day to see *Salome* at the Met (with Lily Djanel, as I recall, in the title role). In those days *Salome* was given on a double bill with another short opera or one act from an opera. I recall seeing it along with *La Serva Padrona* (with Bidu Sayao, the now legendary singer, and Salvatore Baccalone), with *Cavaleria Rusticana,* and once, with the second act of *Traviata. Salome* so gripped me, I saw every single performance first at the Met and later, in 1947 I believe, at the New York City Center where the title role was sung by Brenda Lewis.

At nineteen, when I had seen it for the first time, it had evoked in me, as both the play and the opera were indeed meant to, the darkest fascination. The susceptibility, no, the corruption, of innocence turned by unbounded desire and privilege to perversity, the unrelenting intensity of the dramatic score, the doom foretold the moment the curtain rises, even the Dance of the Seven Veils (which I found corny before long), the great climax of Salome's last scene when, at last, she kisses the prophet's decapitated head, all lured me to see the work again and again. I suppose the aestheticism and decadence of the opera suited my then-emerging rebelliousness and separation from conventional morality. Incidentally, I kept on going to new performances whenever they were given; I even saw the, by now, historic one with Ljuba Welitsch in the early fifties. But that was the last time. By then the only part of the opera I still wanted to hear, and still do, was the great last scene of Salome's triumph and doom.

The second time the opera was given at the City Center I had asked Hanna to go with me, but the party grew. One of the friends in Hanna's circle was a bright, tall, very attractive young woman, Eleanor Kask, who, then in her mid-twenties, was already a publishing executive. (A few years later, she married the publisher Donald Friede and today she is herself the publisher of Eleanor Friede Books. For a few years, during the sixties, we were colleagues in the trade department of Macmillan; today we are colleagues in our affection and continued friendship with Hanna.) At the time Eleanor was living with an eccentric, red-bearded painter, Joachim Probst, who painted only Christs and Madonnas and for whom, because he felt himself too good for any of the Madison Avenue galleries, Eleanor a year or so later bought a small townhouse on West 12th Street which was to serve as his year-round gallery. This never happened. They were married but he turned out to be so deeply disturbed that Eleanor feared for her life and divorced him. Today, some of his paintings still hang in the top-floor studio of her house. But in 1947, he was a handsome and impressive bohemian figure. Eleanor, who was then what was called a "career girl," always dressed in the latest fashions, and she and Hanna—always elegant and stared at wherever she appeared—wore what was then called the *New Look:* full skirts falling in rich folds just above the ankles, high-heeled, old-fashioned looking boots, the new style so romantic and ample after the severe war austerities. Probst was in corduroys, and I (no longer the conventional specimen I swore to cast off in the brief illumination of rebellion in the subway train a few years earlier) was well dressed, but with a certain flair that set me apart from the conventional style; with Eleanor and Hanna, each of us tall, young, looking assured and daring, we moved through the City Center lobby and into the auditorium as though we were the living advertisement for the overly romantic atmosphere of the opera about to follow. All eyes, I felt, were on us then and when we left. And it suited me; not the attention—which is of course gratifying especially to the young—but to move with ease among, and startle because of our looks and style, the artistic world of which I was eager to become a part.

Around that time, Hanna's close friends decided to have a private showing of her paintings in the brownstone of friends of mine, Fran and Earl Coleman, where Hanna was then living. (Hanna went to Hollywood in 1948 but this did not stop her development and she has become a distinguished painter, awarded the City of Munich Prize and exhibited widely; she has also written a family-novel,

Keine Zeit Für Engel, published by the old Hamburg firm, Hoffman und Campe, in 1982.) At the time of Hanna's private exhibition, my feeling that I should belong to the artistic milieu of that period was justified by publications and acceptances of a number of my poems in leading literary journals. *The Saturday Review of Literature, Poetry* (Chicago), *The Yale Poetry Review, The Tiger's Eye, Accent, The Quarterly Review of Literature, Contemporary Poetry,* and others. (This was not at all bad for someone twenty-three, who had arrived here with nothing but English only eight years before.) Writers and painters gathered almost nightly in Hanna's room, some well known, others just starting out. They all came to the private showing on a Saturday and Sunday afternoon, and some of my old friends came as well, Eugen and his wife among them. It was our last meeting of that period.

A few months before my mother's death in May of 1965, as I was sitting in a movie theatre on 57th Street waiting for the film to start—the dim lights were still on and I was talking with two friends, Jean Garrigue, the poet and great, close friend of mine, and Joyce Ray, wife of the painter Rudolph Ray with whom I had stayed twice in Mexico, once in their home in Cuernavaca and once in Tepotztlan—someone tapped me on the shoulder. I turned around. I did not recognize him at first, a large, heavy man. It was Eugen. He had spotted me from the back. He looked now like his father had to me when I had first met him in the salon of their apartment above the Schwedenplatz. His father had died, Eugen told me, but his mother was living with him and his family in northern California, where they had moved some years back and where he was now the owner of an elec-tronic products manufacturing plant. He was very sorry to hear that my mother was in the last stages of cancer; he gave me his card and asked me to be sure to get in touch with him should I ever come out to California. Seven years later I did spend an academic year as Visiting Professor at California State Univer-sity's Hayward campus across the bay from Palo Alto where he lived. But I did not look him up.

ADAPTATIONS

► 1

In New York during the early forties there were certain sections where Austrian, German, and other refugees lived and could be seen with each other in the streets, cafés, and restaurants. Just as the two Germans in Zurich soon knew who we were then they had seen us huddled together in a group along the lakefront park, it was not at all difficult for local residents to spot the refugees. The stress of persecution hung about them still like invisible placards. Before they had managed a reasonable adjustment, outwardly at least, a foreign air surrounded them as they moved, in groups, on sidewalks of the Upper West Side or sat around tables at Rumpelmayer's, the Café Arnold on Central Park South, at Eclair's on West 72nd Street, or Neugröschel's Restaurant on 81st Street, later on 72nd Street. When out walking, they had a habit of stopping, gesturing while in heated discussions, the men usually walking apart from the women, the children hanging about one or the other or running between them. At tables in public places (the Automat on 57th Street was another favorite rendezvous spot) they were always talking intensely, leaning closely to the person they were addressing. Wherever they were, even in the subways, they seemed to be huddled together, and my mother would touch me with her elbow to indicate a group with a nod of her head. They—and we, of course, as well—were then like the fragments, torn and frayed, of a once tightly knit cultural and social fabric, now adrift and not yet reattached or, in some measure at least, integrated. In the years that followed, some managed this, as far as it was possible; others, like my Aunt Greta and Uncle Martin, continued their lives with the most tenuous of connections to the new cultural framework. But the split that had occurred in us the day we arrived here was the same regardless of the extent to which one succeeded in outward adaptation. Each had to grapple with this in one manner or other and some—a few in our immediate circle of family and friends—succumbed altogether.

In recent years, since the middle seventies, each time I come across a group of newly arrived Russian-Jewish immigrants, I relive these sights of families wrenched from the familiar cast of their former existence. Parents with their children, pointing out to each other the buildings and shops, walking on timidly, uncertain and wary of the sudden strangeness. I have seen them looking with great care at items in the supermarket, exclaiming what I assume to be the Russian equivalent of foods packaged differently here. Once or twice I have seen boys the same age that I was when I first encountered the same strangeness more than forty years ago; they have that pure, red flush of adolescence, of shyness that is evidently still characteristic of early youth in a European background where childhood is a world apart and where, on the verge of leaving it, one looks toward adulthood with timidity and bashfulness. The boys holding a younger sibling by the hand, turning and talking to their parents with deference. What will happen to the imagination of these children and adolescents set along one course and deprived now of its growth and continuity? Is it wise to leave, I ask myself, unless it is a question of life and death as it was for us? I would like to warn them, to say to them: It is painful to have lost your home; I know that you will not replace it. And I am reminded of Dante's yearning for Florence, of Akhmatova's refusal to leave the Russian soil she loved, of that woman's great spirit, in whom and through whom the soil became transformed into human invisibleness, as that other great poet of the spirit, Rilke, called it: "*Ist es dein Traum nicht einmal unsichtbar zu sein?—Erde! unsichtbar!*" (Is it not your dream to be invisible once?—earth! invisible!).

And sensing the uncertainty I know these boys must feel at having been forced into a world not only adult but foreign as well, I am also reminded, seeing them, of Hart Crane's moving warning in these lines from *Voyages:*

> O brilliant kids, frisk with your dog,
> Fondle your shells and sticks, bleached
> By time and the elements; but there is a line
> You must not cross nor ever trust beyond it
> . . . .
> The bottom of the sea is cruel.

Over the years following the war, the foreign air the refugees projected, the distinct marks, were minimized, perhaps they finally even dissolved. The surfaces were replaced, mannerisms adjusted. But there were casualties—an anguish hung on, continued as a troublesome reminder of an alienation some could not put to rest.

►2

One Sunday, in the early forties, my parents and I were on the IRT subway when, as the door opened and people were getting off and others pushing in, my mother suddenly yelled out: *Anna!* and pulled at the sleeve of a woman about to leave the train. *Anna! It can't be!* I tried to restrain my mother in the split second in which all this happened. She is in Shanghai! But it was Anna, not Anna Lust who had stayed behind in Vienna, but Anna Thaler, my mother's oldest girlhood friend who had been part of our family and whom my brother and I used to call Tante Anna. She was with a companion, a tall, handsome naval officer, and we got off the train with them. A joyous reunion. She had arrived here not long ago from Shanghai to where she had emigrated in 1938, and for my mother finding her here again was one more step in reassembling her full family.

Anna, who was my father's age, five years older than my mother, around fifty by the time they found each other again, had always been a very independent woman. She had never married and that was unusual for a woman of her background in Vienna. She had come from a very religious, distinguished home in Poland—her grandfather, in whose house she was raised, had been a rabbi—and had gone to school in Vienna where she remained and started to work in women's fashions. It was during these early employments that she and my mother had met. Eventually she became the manager of a fashionable dress shop that specialized in making jersey suits and dresses. She lived in the *Innere Stadt* on Petersplatz—a round "square" with the baroque Peterskirche in its center—and as a boy I used to love to go to her home, which was furnished in a completely modern way, had a stall shower and other "American" appliances. She had an extremely good figure, which was always commented upon by my mother's friends, as it was not matched—and this was added quickly—by her face. But her overall appearance was splendid; she was always very well dressed, as not only her social world but her professional life demanded; she had many foreign customers and talked English quite well. She used to spoil my brother and me; we were, in a way, here surrogate children; she used to take us out sometimes on Sunday afternoons to a museum, the zoo, *Schönbrunn* (the summer palace), *Kobenzl* in the Vienna Woods, always ending up, regardless of the object of the expedition, at *Demel's* or the *Aida Konditorei* for some of the best pastries in Vienna. And we could always count on her for fine presents on our birthdays, certain holidays, and often on just some of her regular visits.

She never married because—so I had heard my mother tell a relative or a friend—she had been engaged to and deeply in love with a soldier who fell on the front. Born in Poland, she had had no hope in 1938 of getting to the United States for years, the Polish quota was the most crowded of all, and so she had decided to go to Shanghai where, as we soon learned, she had opened her own, and very successful, dress shop. The situation in China during the Japanese-Chinese war and after the outbreak of World War II being very uncertain and dangerous for foreigners, she left and came to the United States as soon as the quota permitted it. Here, she was employed almost at once and had a good position in the garment district on Seventh Avenue. She lived in a brownstone on West 92nd Street off Central Park and was, at the time we met her again, having a liaison with the naval officer, a Yugoslav, who, when his ship was in port, often accompanied her to our house. One day she came alone, visibly in deep distress. Her friend's ship had been sunk, he was lost at sea; she was now alone.

Her sorrow did not ease. For some years she managed to maintain some form of equilibrium but by the early fifties a slow process of deterioration began to set in. Outwardly, her interests were such that she managed to carry on—she took trips, went to concerts, the opera, etc., and continued to do well in her job. But in a more meaningful way her life had turned empty and as the years went on that emptiness must have become unbearable. Her relationship to the world around her was finally only superficial. She talked of the fact that she would never have a real home again. She began to be irritable even with my mother who—at least in what she said openly—lay the blame of her deterioration on the fact that she was too alone. My mother had a horror of that, what she considered unnatural condition. Man was not meant to be alone, and she would add in German: "*Allein soll sein ein Stein*" ("Only a stone can be alone").

However, I don't believe that it was entirely due to her aloneness that she had developed the paranoia that became so acute she had to have shock treatments in a mental hospital. After all, she had been alone and independent all her adult life. But in Vienna she had participated on all levels in the reality of its existence, the obvious surface as well as that of the underlying cultural accumulations which must have given her, though she had not been born there, that needed sense of home. An assuredness that expressed itself in all sorts of ways but mostly in an intimacy of place, of the cares and concerns for the details of daily life. To buy rolls in a bakery in Vienna was to experience an ordinary occasion as an agreeable, cozy, *gemütlich* human reality. The way one was greeted on entering the shop, the variety of rolls available, the odors of freshly baked dough, the way in which the rolls were wrapped in tissue paper into a parcel—it all contributed to this *cozy* at-homeness.

I have no use whatsoever for the extent to which the Viennese took the importance of their cherished *Gemütlichkeit,* but there is no denying the fact that it provided a very agreeable ingredient to civilized living. Had Anna been entirely alone in Vienna, she could not have suffered the sense of neglect she must have experienced here as someone without immediate family ties. There was no soul-feeding (how else to call it?), no simple expressions of assurance, no implied communication, an understanding of things that need not be talked of, in the world in which she now conducted her daily life. With the exception of my mother, the communication she now had—and especially after her Yugoslav friend had been lost at sea—was on the surface and superficial. No doubt that amorous relationship had helped allay, had postponed the terror of emptiness gnawing at her. But she was in her fifties when he went out of her life and, as far as we knew, no friend ever replaced him.

Anna did have some relatives here but she had had little contact with them. Most east-European Jewish immigrants came here directly from their little towns and villages; they bypassed entirely, knew next to nothing of the middle- or west-European way of life. Anna had had a cousin here who was dead when she arrived; his wife and grown children living in the Bronx were good people who took an interest in her but there was no real contact between them, there could not have been. I am reminded of the immigrant woman in Newark who had asked me if there were chimneys in Vienna. Granted, this ignorance was extreme, but her question does indicate the gap that existed between many a refugee and his or her immigrant relatives who were generally responsible for the affidavits without which an American visa was—and is—not possible. No, considering Anna's earlier life it is not unrealistic to assume that she was a casualty, that her persecution complex in her late fifties was nurtured by emptiness and alienation. She tried living in Israel, but that also failed. She returned here after a few months and died of cancer, my faithful mother by her bedside.

► 3

From the very start, my brother appeared to make a good adjustment; he had liked it here right off and had, as I have mentioned, a succession of American girl friends before he was drafted in 1941. His male friends, his *pals,* however, were Viennese. He was especially close to one somewhat younger than he was, which means that his friend Bob was eighteen at the time they met. Like my friend Willie in Brooklyn, Bob was living with an American aunt, uncle, and cousins in Newark. Unlike Willie, however, Bob seemed to have determined from the start that he was going to be one of *them.* He was very quickly "Americanized" and but for his gentleness, his refined, almost delicate features—not a bit uncommon in a Viennese youth, on the contrary a mark of quality and good breeding—and his European politeness, he appeared American. He tried, in fact, to disguise those European characteristics that were likely to be misunderstood and interpreted as *soft,* as *sissyish,* by his American peers. But try though he did, he could of course not succeed, and so when he and my brother met and he felt understood and not threatened, they became fast friends and remained so for the duration of his life.

Like Anna, Bob's parents and sister had had no alternative but to emigrate to Shanghai, which had been open to refugees, and they too came here eventually. Although Bob would have wished to eradicate his past—for example, he refused to talk German unless his innate cordiality required this of him with newly arrived refugees—we knew of course at once something of his background from his refinement and from his German which, in the very beginning, he would talk to my parents. He had already been here for about a year when we arrived. We learned, gradually, some of the facts of his background. His family had lived in the *Cottage*—one of the English words the Viennese pronounced as though it were French (*Cotège*)—the fashionable villa district on Vienna's outskirts. His father had been either a banker or a textile manufacturer, I can't remember which; in short, they had belonged to the wealthy Viennese bourgeoisie and had lived accordingly—summers along the Adriatic, winter sports in the Alps, theatre, concerts, maids, etc., . . . a way of life his looks, manners, and speech reflected and he had wanted so badly to wipe off. He was by no means an intellectual; in fact, eventually I found him unimaginative, very conformist and dull. Conformist he certainly was! Any sign of rebelliousness, so common at that age, of spirited disdain for the simplistic conventionality that surrounded him and me in Newark and against which I soon railed in however diffuse and fumbling a way—an attitude that might have been mistaken for arrogance at that time—he shrugged off, would take no part in, would ridicule. He had no use whatsoever for youthful dissension, either aesthetic or political, and I soon gave up talking to him seriously.

Like the rest of us, Bob had to support himself, and he did. Still, he could nevertheless have gone to college, at least at night, but the mental discipline he could not have escaped in schools over there he gladly did without here. Intellectual curiosity was not expected of him in his Americanization; he simply wanted to be one of the crowd, an ordinary American interested in a good job, girl friends and, finally, a good, that is to say, advantageous marriage. He had taken on the social ambitions prevalent in the society with which he now identified; he wanted to marry well, and did: the daughter of a well-to-do manufacturer living in a large, rambling house with extensive grounds in South Orange, then a wealthy community. His new in-laws were thoroughly American, they had even anglicized their name. Bob and his wife also lived in one of the Oranges in New Jersey, had two children, and led the sort of life he must have envisioned for himself: executive positions, cars, country clubs, Florida trips, etc.

Bob's father had died in Shanghai, but his mother and sister arrived here after the war. Eventually they too integrated within the life of the Jersey suburbs, Bob's mother living in a new apartment complex near his home. One day, entirely without any warning or previous indications of severe disturbance—so his wife has stated repeatedly—following an outing or a weekend at one of the Jersey lakes, on the pretext that he wanted to visit his, by then, old mother, he took the elevator in her building to the roof and jumped off.

This was in 1964 or 1965, I am not sure. I know we made certain to keep the news from my mother, who was gravely ill by then, and she died in May 1965. Bob left behind two teenagers, a son and a daughter. His wife has remarried and the daughter too is married by now, but his son suffered from severe emotional disorders that, I have no doubt, will never be entirely healed. Sorrows are transmitted as are genes; they continue, are more pronounced in some than in others. The Greeks say, and so do the great religions, that only by intercession—by a shaft of light, of knowledge and love, or of both—are the Furies dissolved. Apollo's intercession laid Orestes' plight to rest. More often, they are appeased. The individual who engages and overcomes them has heroic inclinations; can such be expected from a boy whose father shunned his torments until they overpowered him? Was Bob's anguish the result of inherited disorders, of the split that perhaps unleashed them, gave them their opportunity (for they thrive on disturbance and turmoil) the split he too must have suffered—unexpectedly, in all innocence, without the least comprehension, when he entered into a new world that had to have been as alien to him as it had been to me? We will never know; only that he was pursued by inner monsters he evidently could not face, and had to escape.

▶ 4

Another calamity that befell someone my family knew well—and that erupted here after the afflicted woman had lived in New York for seven years—was not as tragic as Bob's, for the woman survived and has lived on into her eighties. But it was a grievous disturbance which I believe must have been aggravated if not caused by the trauma of emigration and attempted integration in middle life.

Betty's mother-in-law had been one of the few women my grandmother had deigned to talk to when she had come to live with us in Vienna in the mid-twenties. This was my paternal grandmother—I never knew my mother's parents—smuggled across the Russian border by my mother's enterprising sister Genie once it had been decided by her two sons living in Vienna that she should join them, although two of her other sons had remained in Russia. At this writing, one of them, now eighty-five, is still living near Moscow. Widowed for some years, my grandmother lived with us until she died, at the age of sixty-nine, in 1933. She had belonged to one of the leading Jewish families of the small town, or village really, where her ancestors had settled many generations before. Her maiden name was Yawitz—no doubt from Yahweh—and the large family had lived like a clan in the surrounding villages and towns, where they had become prosperous. When, at seventeen, the time had come for my grandmother to be married, a suitable bridegroom was selected; that he come from a rabbini-

The author's paternal grandparents, Yerichem Fischel Goldenberg (c. 1900) and Sarah Gele Yawitz (c. 1930). The grandmother's picture was taken in Vienna's Augarten near our home.

The author's parents and older brother in Vienna in 1921.

The author (in the middle) at age four with his brother and Uncle Martin.

The author, his brother and mother in the Czech resort Lazne Luhačovice in 1929.

The following summer in the same resort with his brother.

On an Alte Donau *outing with Julie in 1937.*

By a Nazi decree in 1938 Jews had to carry identification cards with photographs taken at an angle to show the subject with one ear exposed. The author and his mother are seen here in these poses.

These two contrasting photographs illustrate the drastic changes in the author's life between 1938 and 1945; from the boy on one of his "educational" walks after Jews were barred from school in Vienna to the young "radical" in America (second from right) with coworkers of the Electronic Corporation of America on a day's outing along the Hudson. The young woman on the extreme left, Rhoda Serot, became the author's sister-in-law a year later.

The author in 1947 at age twenty-three on a tennis court in the Canadian Laurentian mountains.

The author talking to friends (c. 1950) at a Greenwich Village private exhibition of the paintings of Hannelore Axmann seen here in the center.

Left: *With Hanna (Hannelore Axmann) in New York in 1951.* Right: *Hanna (now Hanna Axmann-Rezzori) with her beloved dog Elfe in a recent photograph.*

The author's parents, Benjamin and Regine Goldenberg, on the occasion of their thirty-first wedding anniversary in a picture taken in Vienna in 1950.

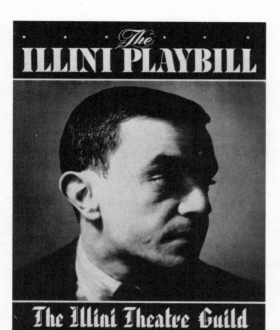

The author appears on the playbill for
"Fire!" produced by the Illini Theatre
Guild at the University of Illinois,
Urbana, as its contribution to the uni-
versity's Festival of Contemporary
Arts in 1952.

A scene from the play. The stage set
and costumes were designed by the
New York artist, Sari Dienes.

The author, on his first return to Vienna in 1949, strolling through the "Innere Stadt" and lunching on the "Leopoldsberg" in the Vienna Woods.

The author (at right) at one of his frequent cocktail parties in his New York apartment in 1953. The woman with the cigarette is the painter, Nina Balaban.

Left Top: *The balcony at "Par-vathi Vilasom" in Trivandrum, South India.*

Left Bottom: *Front view of "Vidyuth" in Karamana, Trivan-drum where the author stayed dur-ing the early part of 1955.*

Above: *Snake catchers—"profes-sional deceivers"—on the Vidyuth compound.*

Left: *The author with Mme. Denise Bagues, also a devotee of Sri Atman-anda, on her departure at the Trivan-drum airport, 1955.*

The author at his desk at Indus-trial Design magazine, 1958.

The poet, Jean Garrigue, around the time of the Capri excursion in 1958.

Backstage at Town Hall in November 1958, the author is greeted by Rosalyn Tureck following her triumphant "return" recital. Bottom: Marianne Moore at a party given by William and Roslyn Targ in 1967; the author is next to Miss Moore.

Above: *With literary agent, Roslyn Targ, at a Gotham Book Mart party in 1968.* Right: *The author appears on the jacket of his book,* A Bed By the Sea, *published by Doubleday, 1970.*

On the campus of the California State University at Hayward where the author was visiting professor during 1972–1973.

cal house was obligatory for the daughter of a prominent home. Her father chose a rabbinical student, a trained *shochet* (ritual slaughterer) whose brother was a rabbi in a small town in Galicia that Yerichem Fischel Goldenberg, my grandfather, left in order to marry the rich man's daughter in the nearby Ukraine. Although a gentle, scholarly type, he did not practice the sacred profession he was trained for but was set up by his father-in-law in an export business of livestock, poultry, even pond-bred crabs. My grandmother, therefore, carried with her all the attributes of social distinction of the then still strictly observed hierarchy in east-European Jewish community life, and though living in Vienna did not relinquish her social habits. She was quiet and withdrawn, very gentle; I don't ever remember hearing her raise her voice. What I remember most is seeing her sitting in front of her window with her small prayer book and reading in it for what seemed to me an endless time. And I also remember going with her to the nearby park, sitting with her on a bench where she again read in her book or occasionally talked to a few, highly select ladies. When one of these women, in silk skirts down to their boots and wearing *sheitls,* as did my grandmother—the indispensible wig of Jewish orthodoxy—sat down beside her, I would run off to play and would come back only once the formidable old lady had risen again and I felt my grandmother couldn't do without my companionship, or if an ice cream vendor passed and I needed ten groschen—which she always gave me without putting me through the ordeal my parents inflicted on me years later when I asked for one schilling for the movies. One of the few ladies my grandmother deigned to converse with—they had to be *rebbezins* (the wives of rabbis) or to have belonged to her own former social stratum—was, as I said, Betty's mother-in-law. Returning home from one of those still afternoons in the park—an extraordinary stillness, a languid timelessness prevailed along those gravel paths and what seemed to me endless allées of enormous trees, a denseness of leaves through which rustled the sound of winds as if it came from distant waters—I recall on one such return the delight with which my grandmother had told my mother how polite I had been. It seems that as soon as one of those grave-looking women had approached, I had immediately risen to my three-year-old height and, although there was plenty of room on the bench, had said—not in German but in Yiddish, of which I must have picked up a few words, for I never spoke it, but must have known that the women conversed in it—"*Setzt 'ach, Frau Czaczkes!*" (The German would have been: "*Setzen Sie sich, Frau . . .*") The friendship these two ladies had—actually they were acquaintances, they never visited each other's homes—was at that time not duplicated by their daughters-in-law, Betty and my mother, who knew one another, but that was all. Here, however, under totally different circumstances, they became very close friends, formed a deep, intimate tie that ended only at my mother's death.

The adaptation of Betty's family to a new life was really quite standard for middle-class Europeans who had been deprived of whatever their means may have been and had come here with little more than their rescued bodies. They applied whatever skills they possessed to making a living, either by starting modest businesses or finding employment. Betty's family managed by getting jobs, her husband as an upholsterer, she as a saleslady, and by having everyone in the household earning salaries from part- or full-time jobs. In addition to their daughter a niece lived with them; the girls, around twenty then, also worked and so the family was able to reestablish itself, economically at least, little by little.

When we met them in the early forties they were living in a three-room apartment on Riverside Drive in Washington Heights, another of the refugee bastions in New York where we also lived when at last we moved from Newark in 1944. As in the other sections where refugees tended to settle, one could easily distinguish them from the other, mostly Jewish or Irish middle-class residents. Some of the local shops—groceries, butchers, bakeries, nuts and chocolates, and even apparel and appliance stores—had been taken over or established by the recent immigrants and they not only frequented each other's homes, went walking together but patronized each other's businesses. In that way, the neighborhood was quite characteristic of other such in New York where, by clustering together for the first few years at least, ethnic groups tried to hold on to their former ways and habits. To me, this separation, this retreat into a self-imposed ghettolike existence became a stifling, unacceptable externalization of the refugee's inner split. I saw it as a restriction that only limited one's understanding of the world to which one had now to become accustomed.

Though I feel certain that this separation could not have contributed to one's well-being but had only been taken as a path of least resistance in the face of adversity, I have no way of knowing whether this false sense of security—an insecurity really—was behind Betty's breakdown and attempted suicides. Nor do I know whether or not her change of life had occurred then, which might have further aggravated her fragile psychic state. At any rate, one afternoon in 1946, my mother walked into Betty's apartment to find her looking crazed and literally foaming at the mouth. At once my mother called an emergency ambulance—Betty had admitted to her that she had taken something—and she was rushed to the hospital. The paramedics had tried to get her to bring up whatever was inside her and in the hospital they succeeded in cleaning her out. She had indeed taken poison.

There can be no doubt that Betty, like the rest of us, had in those early years of emigration lived in a condition of cultural estrangement. The shock of emptiness, of absence I had suffered the very day I arrived must have been felt by her also, however unconsciously, in some form or other. She must have found it more than difficult, beyond her own conditioned attitudes to cope with an extroverted worldliness and moral framework at odds with that of a society for centuries strongly influenced by religious and spiritual values. How adapt to this much more relaxed morality, especially as there were two young women under her care? And Betty's daughter, a strikingly attractive, dark-eyed beauty, had in addition to her own adjustment also to contend with her mother's clinical uneasiness regarding her and her future. She soon married, also a Viennese refugee; whenever I saw her she seemed to me to be controlled but very high-strung and nervous. Her mother's second suicide attempt was also foiled, but fifteen years or so later, tragedy struck again and this time with full force. One day her teenage daughter succeeded where her mother had failed. Locked inside her father's car, the girl had left the motor running and had died of carbon monoxide poisoning.

► 5

Of course, these were extreme cases of neuroses and maladjustment. There was another such in our family, the young sister-in-law of a cousin of mine, ten years my senior, a Viennese woman who in her mid-twenties or so had to be hospitalized in a mental institution where she died some years later. But a far greater number of our refugee relatives and friends did not collapse mentally and made adjustments to the best of their abilities. Many were successful in business like Eugen or one of the sons of my mother's cousin (who had owned the clothes shop on Kohlmessergasse), who became a millionaire and a leading figure in Jewish community life in St. Louis where he had settled in 1940. Others in our immediate circle of relatives and friends have had successful careers in the professions, as doctors or lawyers or, like my brother, as executives in industry.

With the exception of my brother and the aunt and uncle I shall talk of in a little while, I have had very little continued contact with this early circle of refugee friends and even family— why this is so will, I trust, become apparent as this spiral-like progression of memories unfolds—and I cannot, therefore, know how deeply they have struggled with the effects of their displacement or to what extent they have recognized and learned to cope with the symptoms of estrangement. That these exist in their lives, that the secure hold in home soil, the firm root of the fundamental, supporting pillar is missing—of that I feel certain.

Outward success is measured by ambition, ability, perseverance. Some had the stamina to meet the challenge, others didn't. The striking successes—in big business, the arts, politics—are probably even rarer than the extreme failures. Most have made their "meek adjustments"—to borrow a term from Hart Crane—and for the forty or so years that they have lived here have had very little of the heart-warming satisfactions a cultural environment can, and should, provide.

Who, in the long run, can fulfill all of his needs by himself or even with the aid of one other person, and his family? No one, I feel convinced. Perhaps only the mad are self-sufficient in their minds. The saints went into the wilderness—actually or figuratively—to find union with the whole of existence by utter material deprivation. The soul cannot live without its extensions; the individual must feel himself connected, and few, very few, have the ability to accomplish this on their own; for most the culture must provide the essential connections. If not, the effects of deprivation can, at worst, be tragic or, more commonly, paralyzing in one form or another.

► 6

A year ago, my Aunt Greta—she was called Grete in Vienna and it was because of that that we had changed our dog's name to Fifi—had an operation and I went to visit her in a hospital in Newark. Of all our relatives who had lived there at some time, my Aunt Greta and Uncle Martin never left Newark or its vicinity; they moved to nearby Irvington about fifteen years ago, probably among the last migrants in an exodus from what had been a predominantly Jewish neighborhood but had become almost entirely black and badly run down. My aunt and uncle had held on to the last. Resettling had traumatic implications for them. They had established a niche for themselves—like the two hares I loved to watch from a distance that wouldn't threaten them, on the large grounds of the Karolyi Foundation in Vence, in the south of France, where I spent much of the summer of 1980; like these charming creatures, my aunt and uncle have always been innocent and, in their environment, on guard and insecure. Their continued existence in a three-room apartment on Newark's Clinton Place for more than a quarter of a century gave them a semblance of the security they needed, and they had resisted leaving until it actually became dangerous for them to continue living there; crime had become rampant.

In this connection, I am reminded of a number of people who for different reasons fought leaving their old neighborhoods until, at last, they had to. Marianne Moore, then the last surviving poet in America of the generation of great ones that included Robert Frost, Wallace Stevens, T. S. Eliot, and William Carlos Williams, had refused to leave the section in Brooklyn where she and her mother had lived for decades but where living alone (her mother was deceased by then), as well as the necessary subway rides to and fro, had become too hazardous. Her friends insisting that she move, she finally did, to West 9th Street in Manhattan where during and after 1967 I had the great privilege of visiting her often; but of that later.

Likewise, my mother refused to leave her neighborhood, where she had lived for twenty years and to whose streets, though deteriorating, and changed population, largely Hispanic and black, she had become accustomed. My brother and I kept urging our parents to move. My mother pacified us by saying, yes, they would, in time. When she died, in a hospital in 1965, they were still living there. My father did move shortly after that but my mother had not wanted to because she had established meaningful connections with her environment that she had cherished. She told me, with great feeling, how it had touched her when, on returning from one of her frequent stays in the hospital, one of the children she had befriended had jumped up and down when from across the street he had spotted her near her window: "Look," he had shouted to his mother, "she is back. She is back!" The apartment house in which my parents had lived on Upper Broadway was a large corner building with a great many windows. Yet one pigeon found its way to the window of my mother's kitchen where it came each morning at eleven to be fed. My mother had always been capable of the outgoingness Emerson writes of when he says: "The heart refuses to be imprisoned; in its first and narrowest pulses it already tends outward with a vast force and to immense and innumerable extensions." Such is the need of the truly liberal heart, and my mother possessed that in great measure. Affection for place, even when aesthetically seemingly inappropriate, is the result of this ongoing, silent communication. She saw no reason why she should give this up simply because the neighborhood had changed for the worse. I suspect these women knew in their souls the absolute need of nurturing and its supremacy over conventional standards. Of course, not one of them resisted leaving once safety and expediency demanded it. Had my mother lived, she would likewise have taken the necessary action.

It cannot be surprising that the works and lives of poets come to mind when attempting to comprehend human motivations, the soul's need for the soil, the soil's sad neglect when not so needed. Louise Bogan and Jean Garrigue, two of the best lyric poets this country has produced, who each believed in exercizing her trust in essentials, lived for many years in simple flats— Louise in upper Washington Heights, Jean on Jones Street in the Village—to whose atmosphere and details they had become devoted in a manner not very different from the devotion to place and things that I had been reared in. And how critical they were of their society for the severity of this neglect. W. H. Auden believed a man should own two suits at the most, should live in these as long as possible. He too had resided, until he left America for good, in a modest apartment in a modest neighborhood. All his long life Robert Frost was a firm believer in man not only living on but with his soil. For the soul, and this the poets know—and the poetic sense in each and every human being must know—is only at home when and where the comfort of place is pervasive, even in one's dreams, and the care for essentials, a harmonizing order, is never neglected.

►7

To get back to my Aunt Greta in a hospital room in Newark two years ago. For as long as I can remember her, ever since my Uncle Martin had first brought her to our house before they were married in December 1933, when I was ten, she has had unusually well-kept hands, long, slender fingers, long, markedly curved nails that looked always as though they had just been lifted from a manicurist's pillow. In her hospital bed, in her mid-seventies then, hard of hearing and with very poor eyesight, she made certain that her fingers looked as though nothing at all had changed, as though the person to whom they belonged had given them the same care they had had when I first marveled at their civilized grace. An unchanged emblem, like a coat of arms, of my aunt's hereditary social status and habits. Since 1938, when she and her husband first set foot here, her life has not in the remotest way resembled her former pattern of existence, but she has clung tenaciously to its precepts and to certain mannerisms; and so, the beautifully maintained hands rested on her bedsheet like a pampered memento.

We are, all of us, a combination of inbred cultural attitudes and innate character traits. In most, the former control or absorb the latter; in some, the gifted ones, the latter govern and achieve expression in terms of the former. My Aunt Greta belongs to the first category, her personality having to a very great degree been dominated by the cultural characteristics that have shaped her. I am not now thinking of the artistic and intellectual accomplishments of that culture, of which my aunt has only the scantest knowledge, but of its ethics, aesthetics, and morality: in other words, the way in which one lived one's daily life within it. In short, my aunt as an individual is almost totally the product of the world that had formed her. Nothing extraordinary about her background: Her father died when she was quite young; I don't even know what his business or profession was. For years, until her mother died, and that was long before my aunt came into our family, her mother had run Vienna's *Film Klub;* the family appears to have been in the film business until the Anschluss. My aunt's uncle was a film distributor and, before her marriage, my aunt had worked for Germany's famed film studio UFA in its Viennese branch. Again, it was not what her people did that had influenced and shaped her, but *how* they had lived: in that unique, middle-European, especially Viennese, intimate way of easy formality and *gemütlich* conventions. Cozily furnished apartments where very little was altered over the years, the sun barely penetrating the rooms too overhung and overlaid with damask, plush, and lace; families visiting in established patterns on a rotating basis; telephone calls to one another daily at the same hour; Saturday afternoons at the *Stammcafé* (the Café Babenberg, in their case, or was it the Casa Piccolo? I can't be sure); summers at the Corinthian lakes; occasional trips abroad and, of course, attending the Opera to hear Selma Kurz or Maria Jeritza whose fabulous high notes and long breaths were talked of with pitched astonishment over *Kaffee mit Schlagobers* and delicate pastries. And so on, and so on. (It was precisely this stifling, overly conventionalized, densely superficial, highly mannered bourgeois life which artists and the intelligentsia attacked, often savagely, and which would have driven me from Vienna, I am quite certain of that, even if world events had not forced me to leave.)

My Uncle Martin's background does not parallel my aunt's but he too fit too snugly into the mold of Viennese life, which had suited him so well that he gave up his youthful Zionist fervor for it and stayed on there rather than return to Palestine, where he had gone from Russia as a young *Chaluz* (pioneer settler) around 1920 and from where, in 1925, he went to Vienna to be cured of malaria; he had caught it working in the Palestinian swamps. By that time his mother was living in Vienna, his eldest brother and my father. And he stayed on until he left for the United States in 1938. Vienna had evidently met his needs better than his life in Palestine. He was about ten when his father died, fifteen at the time of the Bolshevik Revolution, and, whether or not it was due to these events or other hereditary traits and early conditionings, he developed neurotic tendencies that expressed themselves in a visible nervousness and, at times, uncontrollable outbursts of anger and fear. When walking he had a habit of pushing his coat or jacket up and thrusting his neck forward in a regularly repeated motion like a nervous tic and when I was about ten I saw him once to my horror literally trying like a monkey to climb a wall in his dining room.

It says something about the insular sense of security the Viennese derived from, or invested in, their habitual existence that they paid scant attention to such disturbances, attributed them to nothing but bad temper and being too high-strung, and wouldn't allow them to upset their regular living habits whose order, they felt convinced, would somehow restore the seemingly afflicted back to psychic health. Even my uncle, something of a maverick in his youth and who in Vienna enjoyed a dual aspect of its life—its easy *Gemütlichkeit* and its agitated political and artistic milieu—wouldn't think of consulting the doctor on Berggasse of whom, in his circle, he surely must have heard by then. For by the time my uncle's outbursts became more frequent and almost violent, Sigmund Freud was eighty and psychiatry a field that attracted many doctoral students at the University's highly lauded medical school. I know this from a cousin who took his doctorate there in the mid-thirties. At any rate, nothing was done, no one took his symptoms very seriously, not his mother, not his brothers who called him *meshugge* and let it go at that.

Such irregularities in personality were somehow considered normal by the placid Viennese, as a necessary and not really worrisome part of life. And evidently this atmosphere suited my uncle for he took part with gusto in its bittersweet pleasures. He frequented the intellectuals' cafés, the Zionists' cafés, and joined various claques in the theatres which interested him more than the Opera. He made a decent living in the fur trade in which his two brothers had helped him get established. He had a long, on-again, off-again love affair and engagement which very noticeably increased his nervousness, and when the girl jilted him and married someone else, he promptly married also, Grete Nichtenhauser, my Aunt Greta, who in 1933 was about thirty years old. Within six months he was off to Palestine once more. By then the country was growing rapidly, Jews were settling there from Germany and Poland, and as a returned pioneer and a man of ability and keen intelligence he should do well there. And he did; he found a good administrative position, and his new wife was to join him soon. But he delayed this; after his enjoyable years in Vienna he found it difficult to adjust to the by far rougher Tel Aviv frontier life. Vienna lured him back, drew him like a siren's enchantments, and he returned there after a year, saying, to appease something in himself, that he would eventually go back to Palestine and settle there. He never did. When the Nazis marched into Vienna, anxiety and fear befell him—he walked around with shoelaces untied, his fly-buttons open, and he lost things, once even a briefcase containing his precious passport and his by far more precious American visa—and he continued in this agitated state until he and his wife left for the United States. They were both in their mid-thirties at that time.

They collapsed here at first, from the ordeal, from the transition, from the experience of estrangement; but even after more than forty years they have never truly recovered, have hardly integrated, have only tenuously adapted their life to the American way of life. To them the new world was so alien they retreated. Its facades, its vigorous externalized vitality, the aggressiveness of self-assertion intrinsic in its trust in freedom, its boisterousness, all of what I had, at first, found so novel and appealing was to them a fearful intimidation that they lacked the impulse to overcome. Their participation in local life has only been in the ways needed to survive—jobs, concerns for security and health—but they have never been able to accustom themselves to its habits. They are childless and have lived their years within a small and ever-shrinking circle of family and very few friends. There has been very little here to nourish their deeper needs as their European environment appeared to have done. They have never again felt as they had on their own turf and they have suffered for it and, considering this severe deprivation, have managed nobly. For they have maintained their sense of dignity—as my aunt's well-kept fingernails, even in the hospital, indicate—and have managed an economic independence of which they have good reason to be proud. To the best of their ability they have carried on within the only ethical and moral precepts they have known. But the emptiness they endured for more than four decades is gnawing at them, especially at my aunt. My uncle's intellectual curiosity keeps him occupied but my aunt never had it and for the last years she hasn't been able to see well enough to cook, which she had enjoyed and had done very well in the past, having learned a great many recipes during the days when her mother had managed Vienna's *Film Klub*. Nearing the end of her life she is overcome by an anxiety more severe, more crippling than her husband's had ever been. In a matter of years she will die, and for more than forty years she has not lived.

► 8

My father, eleven years his youngest brother's (my uncle Martin) senior, was not intimidated by the circumstances he had found here. It was not his habit to be so, as he surely demonstrated when he had smuggled a small fortune from under the noses of the Nazis. My father was a born businessman. All his considerable talents of mind and ingenuity went into his love for *handeln* (dealing). His business successes and failures had been closely linked to the mercurial conditions of the Vienna *Börse* (Exchange). He never played cards, roulette, or the horses but he relished the gamble of the business game. He was not a gambler but a shrewd businessman who loved to take his chances; and this was true no matter where he was, Europe—first in Germany, then Austria—or here.

His talents appear to have been detected early on by his father. Once in 1907 when my father was sixteen, my grandfather needed a trusted emissary to conclude an important and delicate business transaction in Kattowitz, then part of Eastern Germany and now of Poland. A large shipment of one of his export products had gone there and he entrusted the mission not to his two older sons but to my father, whose age had to be advanced by two years so that he could obtain a passport. Not only did the success of this venture earn him his father's esteem, which had meant a lot to him for he was very devoted to his father, it had set the course of his life: It had given him his first glimpse of the outside world and his lasting love for it. In a family that still teetered between religious orthodoxy and worldly interests, he became—as his two older brothers had already become—a confirmed secularist. To be trite about it, the world, almost at once, became his oyster and he threw himself into the expanding horizons with zest and gusto.

He soon settled in Kattowitz, where he did well not only for his father but in his own independent business ventures. When World War I broke out he moved on to Vienna, where, for reasons that were never clear to me, he had gone to enlist in the Austrian army. He became a Russian censor and remained stationed there throughout the war. There, one day in the house of his brother, he had met my mother who had become a friend of his sister-in-law's younger sister—the same woman who with her husband haunted one of my recurrent dreams, many years later after both had perished in a concentration camp. As I mentioned earlier in connection with the Café Fetzer, where my parents' wedding reception was held—I have pictures of them in an open carriage, my mother in a veil deep on her brow, my father holding his top hat on his lap—they were married in the summer of 1919. Not long after that my father became an Austrian citizen and the Fetzer his business headquarters.

My mother had come to Vienna in 1912, when she was sixteen, from a strict, orthodox home (her father, a grain merchant, never missed celebrating the important holidays at the Court of the Belser *Ruf* [Great Rabbi] a great distance away) into the far more relaxed, more worldly, though still religious, home of her Viennese aunt—who, however, no longer wore a *sheitl*. One of my mother's sisters also had lived in Vienna at that time and there was a certain amount of back and forth travel between their small home town, or village, in Galicia and the capital. Contrary to the conception current here, of there being nothing but abject poverty and severe deprivations in *shtetl* life—which certainly existed—there was a small, fairly well-to-do layer within Jewish *shtetl* (I never knew that term until we came here) society that was quite cosmopolitan and, unfortunately, continued to live there until the Nazi liquidation. My mother's brother who, though a Talmudist also belonging to the Belser Court, later ran the family business, frequently traveled abroad; and my mother's sister, who had married in Vienna, eventually returned to the family home. And I remember, when I was a child, relatives from Poland stopping off in Vienna on their way for a health cure to Bad Gastein in the Austrian mountains or the northern Italian resort of Meran.

My father was very fond of music. He had a good voice, a light tenor—I mentioned earlier how his humming a nostalgic melody had affected me as a boy—and he had had a passion for the violin when he was himself a boy. He used to tell us how one night his father had stormed into his room and had broken his little violin in two after having discovered that my father and another boy had secretly taken violin lessons, a transgression my grandfather would not tolerate. It was not fitting, he had told the heartbroken child, for a son of his to become a *klesmer*—a musician who entertained at Jewish weddings and other festivities. His own boyhood dream shattered, my father had made me and my brother take up the violin when we were six or seven. I did miserably at it. One of the torments of my otherwise joyous childhood was having to go, each Monday afternoon, to the house of a first-rate violinist—a friend of my parents and a member of the highly esteemed Vienna Philharmonic and later of the Metropolitan Opera Orchestra—who, as a teacher, was a sadist and a madman. Even more nervous in his mannerisms than my neurotic uncle, he would, each and every Monday fall into a fit of despair over my poor fingerings and would curse my musical ear; for I could play a melody better by ear than I could follow notes. My playing was atrocious and never improved. I should have studied the piano, which is the instrument I have always loved, but not so my father. How he could have derived pleasure from the hideous sounds my brother and I made when practicing is hard to understand. It proves that daydreaming can flourish despite a screeching reality.

This ambition thwarted in his childhood—and, alas, never fulfilled through his sons—my father's probably more pronounced talent for business became the stuff of his life. The two were one, in fact; there never was a separation between them—his business, his "deals" were his life almost to the very end. This often caused severe consternation and annoyance to my mother. For one, he was absent from our home too often due to extensive travels, and this was put ahead of certain family obligations; and also he needed to have his business so close to him that he was in the habit of keeping some choice pelts such as bundles of raw martens or minks in our apartment in a small room whose window was nearly always open. For these pelts were uncured and they stank. My mother was furious but my father always prevailed. He would show them off to visitors who understood the value of such things, or would visit the isolated room by himself, as one does a pet or an artist's studio, and would stroke the silken furs and blow on them so that the skin could be revealed, for that is—so ran his indoctrination—how one tells their true value. To overcome the odors that surrounded him in his warehouse or his private "showroom" he always carried in his pocket, in a small silver flask with a turquoise button whose oval shape I remember distinctly, a powerful cologne with which he sprayed himself all the time. Annoying though this habit of keeping some choice items always nearby may have been to my mother, it helped us, for he packed those he had had at home at the time into the crate of personal belongings that had gone to Paris. When the rescued bundles finally reached us in New York, some of those pelts were consequently in them, and this helped my father get started again here.

He was undaunted. He met the new circumstances he found here with the by then toughened will of someone determined to be his own man, and not only didn't resist, as my Uncle Martin had done, but felt himself aided by the atmosphere of self-assertion that prevails here. As I mentioned before, he did well. As it was not possible to export and import the merchandise he had dealt in before the war, he dealt in related products during the war, mostly in leather which, I believe, he imported from South America. By 1945 he had an office on Nassau Street near City Hall Park and was a partner in a manufacturing firm of certain leather goods on lower Broadway. Nonetheless, as soon as the war was over, his mind was set on Europe once more. His holdings and belongings had been confiscated by the Nazis—warehouses full of skins, bank accounts, etc.; he wanted reparations. Some of the illegally exported merchandise had been lost in the fires of London; his partner had received insurance compensation but had not yet settled with him; these were some of the reasons why, he said, he needed to get back. But he also missed his Café Fetzer life. The large, noisy cafeteria on Seventh Avenue in New York's fur district which he frequented, because it was where the dealers gathered, was no match for his Stammcafé. But the most compelling draw of all was that he "smelled" new opportunities.

Early one morning, a few months after he had sailed for Europe in the summer of 1948, we were awakened by a telephone call from my father's business associate here. According to a front-page report in that morning's *New York Times* my father had been arrested in Vienna. I rushed down to get the paper and read: *"American Businessman Held In Austria."* The irony, I thought right off! They didn't catch him under the Nazis and they are holding him now! The news item was brief and gave little information but we learned more by telephoning his contacts in Vienna. He was under police surveillance, not in custody, while a claim lodged by competitors (by no means pleased to see him back!) that he had declared his imported merchandise at too low a value was under investigation. The government had confiscated a portion of the shipment until the situation could be settled—it was, after a few months, and not in my father's favor. He had no doubt that the incident had been instigated by local dealers to intimidate him—which goaded him on all the more. He remained there, reestablished his former connections, and, for the next ten years or so, did a brisk business between Vienna and New York. Then, the shuttling back and forth over, he returned to Europe only for occasional visits, the last one all by himself in 1975 when he was eighty-four and still active in business here. He died at eighty-seven.

My father's adjustment here had then not only been conditioned by business opportunities but by his capacity for challenge and adventure. Though he was nearly fifty when he had come here, he learned the language well, took an interest in current affairs and, after the death of my mother, continued on his own, or with a new woman companion, to go to the opera, to Carnegie Hall—he had loved the building—to Lincoln Center, and to try new restaurants. Though he would have preferred to live again in Europe—he had proposed Switzerland—it had been the pattern of his life to assert himself, to enrich his independence, no matter where he was. I have observed in the lives of people of marked assertiveness and forthright character that it is the unfaltering idealism of their early adulthood that forms their life's path and development. That thrust, like an arrow spearheading a person's growth, does not change. Almost to his end—he had slipped into a mild senility during his last years—my father's gusto for life's possibilities, his love for exploration and taking his chances, were intact in him. It was as if the experience of the journey when, as an enthusiastic youth of sixteen, his father sent him out of Russia and the world had opened up before him, had never left him. His discovered secularism, by which he had expressed the ethical precepts of his religious background, his considerateness, his dignity, his value in life had sustained him.

►9

My mother's eventual adaptation to her new environment could no longer stem from the challenges it offered her talents—she was forty-three at the time of our emigration—but came from her profound appreciation of the opportunities it provided. Once the initial struggle for economic security was over—and it was after about a year when I was able to go back to school—she settled in to discover her new world. She appeared to have been less afflicted by the consequences of the split that had occurred in the rest of us. I think the main reason was that she responded at once and with never-flagging enthusiasm to the freedom she found here. Perhaps she had never yet realized how needlessly restricted her European life had been by those conventions that had given her a certain secure comfort on the one hand, but no real chance for self-development on the other. In her time, girls of her background received whatever little education was deemed right for them at home, were married off young, and from then on followed the prescriptions laid out for bourgeois Jewish matrons. The pattern was loosened for her somewhat by having left her very strict orthodox home at sixteen, but for a girl as striking and beautiful as my mother had been, to have stepped from that milieu into the sophisticated, cosmopolitan, and licentious atmosphere of Vienna before World War I must have had its shocks and problems. Though she had worked for a few years before she got married, it had been either for a brother-in-law or some other relation; a career, for which she would have been eminently suited, in business or in a profession, was out of the question.

My mother was not only beautiful—she possessed a beauty of a kind one retains all of one's life—she had a keen intelligence, an intuitive grasp of people and of situations that had given her a continuing curiosity, a good sense of humor, and the ability to mock narrow conventions. She could mock them, but she would not break them. Apparently she had fallen in love, when she was about eighteen, with a station-master in a small town somewhere in one of the provinces of the Austro-Hungarian Empire. She used to talk of him for years. All throughout my childhood I would hear her tell how handsome he had been, how he had courted her but how the thought that were she to break all taboos and marry him—a non-Jew and a station-master!—he might one day in anger call her a dirty Jew, prevented her from entertaining any such notion seriously. When she married my father she stepped into a life all outlined for her: a marriage approved of by both families, who traveled a great distance to meet each other before the wedding, a place consigned to her in the home, where she ruled, but not in my father's world of business. He used to discuss many of his "deals" with her but he never listened to her if she felt that he was taking a wrong course. *"Was verstehst Du?"* (What do you know of such things?) was always the pitch of the heated argument.

Other than reading, my mother simply had no outlet for her considerable intellectual powers. Whatever the exact reasons were—perhaps it had a great deal to do with the fact that she had not married her station-master—I know that she was not happy, though she never spoke of it. She had too much consideration for those she loved to burden them with her plight. But once she became familiar with life here, she felt that her own could have run a very different and more gratifying course. She used to say she wished she had come here as a young girl. As far as she could still do it, she corrected those social and conventional obligations which she now considered meaningless and superfluous. She strove toward simplicity, living with essentials; she must have imbibed the Yankee strain by osmosis. She continued to regard the home as a place of sanctity and lit her Friday night candles, but its trappings as a showcase she abhorred. The physical glamor of the home—right furniture, right china, right location—no longer interested her. She wanted none of it, now often to my dismay, for I felt—as I was making my way in the world—I couldn't bring my friends into her house; it not only lacked distinction, it lacked attention. It was clean, of course, nor was it shabby; it simply didn't interest her—who, when I was a boy, didn't let me sit down in our dining room if I wore my shiny lederhosen! She knew that it was too late for her to establish another way of life, one that would more closely approximate her abilities as a feeling and thinking woman, and this was a deep frustration from which she suffered, but she was not going to pour her attention into matters which no longer seemed important to her. And the bourgeois home was one of them. In this society, where people are free to set their life's course along the pursuit of personal, not merely social, fulfillment, her own lack of this became acute and the realization of this deeply troubling. She felt, and rightly so, that life's opportunities had passed her by.

But, of course, she continued to care passionately about her human obligations and, curiously, even more toward strangers who became friends than her family, not that she was ever neglectful toward any of us. As she had been in Vienna, she was popular with the people around her—the superintendent, the cleaning woman, the shopkeepers, and later with some of her

Hispanic neighbors. She was, in the deepest sense, a born demo-
crat. And so, she appreciated this country, couldn't see why I
was off to Europe every chance I had, and wouldn't hear of
settling there again as my father would have preferred. As it was,
she could barely get herself to go with him during those ten
years or so when he did business from and with Vienna. She
spent a year in Israel in 1950, where she had most of her own
family, a sister, a brother, and so on. She became its passionate
supporter and went there again, with my father this time, for six
months in 1963 following her operation (it was for cancer,
though neither knew the nature of her disease). When they returned to New York, my mother looking astonishingly well; she
said to me on the dock as we were waiting for their trunks that
they had decided to return to Israel eventually, to live out their
lives there. "There," she said, "there, yes!" She died here, a year
or so later.

In the lives of the friends and family members I have talked of,
the removal of the cultural and social framework in which most
had grown to maturity released their own deep insecurities,
fears, frustrations, talents, and hopes, and a combination of
these. I mentioned at the beginning an intimation of an absence,
and a despair because of it, that came up in me like a haunting
shadow the first day of our arrival. Was this the anguish of a
sapling torn from its soil? At fifteen, it was not the excitement,
the opportunities afforded here by personal freedom that seized
me—that came later—but the shock of loss. Proceeding from
that, how did I adapt to the new conditions within which I had
to struggle to find and maintain my needed connections and
extensions now that the soil was gone?

IV

FORECASTS

►1

When I returned to school after a year, at the end of 1940, my integration within my peer group was hardly more successful than it had been with the technicians at the dental laboratory. My fellow schoolmates did not refer to me as "Viennese horseshit," at least not in front of me, but they were, understandably, put off by my foreign ways, especially my mostly English accent, and my behavior in general, so different from theirs. Even then I had a great fondness for ideas and abstract thought which endeared me to the teachers and this, in turn, made me suspect in the eyes of the students. By the time I joined high school, in my senior year, they had known one another for three years, groups had been formed, and of course I belonged to none of these—nor did I wish to. I was polite to the girls in a way that the boys weren't, and that too contributed to the distance between us.

When, to my immense relief, the manager of the dental laboratory had told me that there was no longer any place for me there and (urged on by my brother, who was working by then and who has always, over all these many years, been a staunch supporter in my struggles toward independent development) my parents had agreed that it was time I went back to school, there was only one month left to the school term. The principal of Weequahic High School—Newark's newest then as well as best—gave me permission to sit in on classes during the final month before joining the senior class at the beginning of the following term. Among others, I attended the Latin and English literature classes. It soon became apparent to the Latin teacher that I could hold my own in Latin Four—as I mentioned earlier, at the Chajesrealgymnasium I had nearly failed my third year in Latin—and she allowed me to take the final exam along with the rest of the class; I passed and was given credit for two years of Latin. In English literature, the term assignment had been a paper on a Shakespeare play. I did mine on *The Merchant of Venice*. When the papers were returned, there were two top grades, one A and one A− in a class of perhaps thirty students. The A went to a French refugee girl and the A− to me. These were seen as scholarly stunts by my fellow male students who, at least outwardly, projected the easily recognizable characteristics of athletics and a swagger acquired to attract and chase after girls, and to whom, in consequence, I appeared as even more of a foreign oddity. The girls were friendlier, invited me to their parties—Saturday evening dancing, smoking, drinking, and necking parties where I, most definitely, did not fit in. So the invitations stopped, to my relief, saving me from hours of embarrassment. It suited me to stay on the periphery.

The newness of high school life—the scholastic ease, the groupings of the students, the male-versus-female strategies, the looks and the dress of both sexes, the sweaters with the large *W* worn by both, the long plaid skirts, bobby socks and saddle shoes, the beaver coats which were the highest status symbol among the girls (there was one higher, the highest, and that was to be picked up by a chauffer-driven limousine, as a few of the girls were)—the red convertibles signifying the highest status among the boys—the physical qualities of the school itself, the locker system, the lunchrooms, the vast gymnasium—all of these were enough for my gradual adjustment. I had no desire at first to penetrate more deeply and certainly no wish to become part of one of the cliques.

Compared to the strictness and stiff requirements of the Cha-jesrealgymnasium—where we used to stand at attention every time a professor entered the class and where, more than once, the director swooped down upon me like a predator (and not to take a bite out of my mouth but to hit me across it) if he had seen me, from his fifth-floor lookout perch, enter the school gate five or ten minutes late—schooling at Weequahic High was a pleasant, easy game. Moreover, I was delighted to be free of the, to me then, highly unrealistic world of the dental laboratory. I enjoyed being a student once more, especially in this new, free style. What a delight not to have to lug a heavy case full of books but to carry them under one's arms or in them, and to keep those one doesn't need in one's locker. And despite my aloofness, partly forced partly by choice, a general sense of friendliness toward me and of good will prevailed which more than restored, lifted my youthful spirit that had been burdened and constrained for a year.

► 2

It was during that senior year that my interest in poetry began to come into focus. I don't remember what we read in class—no doubt the English Romantic poets—but I do remember Miss Wyckoff, the teacher who had, which is not common among high school teachers of English, a high regard for poetry and who encouraged me in my first efforts. A few years later, in May of 1949 when I made my first return trip to Europe abroad the SS *Nieuw Amsterdam,* I thought with delight one morning as I entered one of the lounges that I had spotted Miss Wyckoff reading at a table; I rushed over to the woman, all eagerness to tell her that her instincts had been right, that her interest in me had not been in vain; I had already published poems in some of our best journals; but when she turned to me full-face, it was not

Miss Wyckoff. I had been mistaken and it saddened me for I had wanted to talk to her about modern American poetry, which she had never taught us.

I had stumbled upon modern poetry by myself, in one of those mammoth anthologies that cover everything from Beowulf to the present, when I was a sophomore in college. As I majored in engineering and had few courses in the humanities, we never reached the twentieth-century portion of the book in class. I had read that on my own. T. S. Eliot's "The Love Song of J. Alfred Prufrock"—it was an earthquake in me when I read it at nineteen. Nothing I had read had ever affected me like it. I felt as though the rhythms and word sounds that had begun rising within me as perhaps a transformation of my sense of loss into a consolation through art when I used to wander through the empty Newark streets had here been given voice and resonance. Oracular utterances could not have affected me more powerfully. The poem's impact upon me was not due to its literal meanings but its groundswell of feelings. I felt comforted, understood, uplifted: The solace that only great art provides, as I began to think then, for I had already embarked upon my student-days standing-room career at the Metropolitan Opera. I read the poem so often, I knew portions of it by heart. When I recited it, or read it, to some of my fellow students, the response was always "but what does it mean?" I couldn't deal with that question then; I didn't know, I only knew what the poem did to me.

I have no recollection of what I wrote during that senior year. It was a busy time. The New Jersey school board did not give me credit for my tortuous years at the Vienna Gymnasium. I had to take make-up exams in all the courses I needed in order to graduate; I took them in addition to attending the regular classes. I passed them all and graduated in January of 1942. Though crowded with studies it had been a free year for me, free in that I was able to engage my mind and allow the imagination to expand before me without restriction, to marvel at its own musical, majestic, though as yet obscure and hidden structures. The outside world too was expanding for me, free days and no timecard clocks, but it was to the inner that I turned for its consolations; I felt then still very raw in my new environment.

I am sure what I wrote must have been dreadful. I remember staying home from school for some days with the flu and writing reams of the stuff. It was in the fall, the colors were blazing, the leaves were being raked and burned, their smells like the odor of memory capturing my mood. "I see you now, stony New York . . ." I recall this opening line of one of those horrors and that I read it, sitting on the porch that faced a leaf-covered lawn, to my mother and the upstairs neighbor. I even sent one to "Coronet," the only magazine I had come across then that printed "filler" poems. Needless to report, it came back with a printed rejection slip. I remember many long-lined quatrains and Miss Wyckoff reading them out loud in class. Consequently, when I graduated, the prediction for the future, the forecast the editors of the Yearbook for January 1942 had written for me was that ten years hence my first book of poems would appear and receive favorable reviews. They were off by two years—it appeared in 1954.

► 3

On my last ride through the streets of Vienna, across the *Innere Stadt* and up Mariahilferstrasse to the Westbahnhof accompanied by my father and Julie, or later that night, standing by an open window on the express train feeling the reality of trees flying past, of the star-filled night, of the air brushing my skin as though communicating something to me, as though night and time and nature were a language and had something to say to me; or a few days later sitting at the Zurich lakeside absorbed in the mysteries of reflection, of the clouds in the water, of the trails made by ducks and swans and dissolved in the lake's calm surface, and of my face held between my hands staring at the deception of appearances: What had I known, at fifteen, of the culture that had nourished me along so far? One doesn't have to bother to understand the things one has taken for granted, but even if I had, even if I had tried, I was too young, too much of a dreamer imbibing with eagerness impressions that had enriched and formed me. Nevertheless, I sensed something of purpose, of a principle or principles, of ideals that underlay continuity, the history that had lived for me in buildings, statues, museum galleries, in faces caught by music, their expressions of introspection or yearning like those that had stared back at me from many a painting. I felt, naively perhaps, but felt almost without thinking, that there was a noble purpose, and sensed that there had in consequence to be an appropriate style for one's life.

As I reached adulthood and the time for the spirited idealism of men and women in their early twenties, I had assumed that I would find such a style among the artistic temperaments active and prominent then, or just starting out as I was. But, as I made my way into their world and touched on their lives, I did not at first encounter the purpose, the artistic direction that my world had led me to expect. I found, instead, among people of my own age an almost exclusive preoccupation with personal matters. The only voiced exception to this was a political interest which at war's end was common among young artists and intellectuals. We were Russia's allies and to be what was called "progressive" was the prevailing style.

►4

To be rebellious in 1945 or 1946, to join other young people in taking a stand against mediocrity and stultifying conventions meant then not drugs or love-ins but to be part of the revived leftist milieu. A number of postwar causes for domestic reform and world unity were espoused at frequent rallies, marches, at adult camps, in newspapers such as *PM,* and by a number of radio commentators, all arguing for greater liberalization and firmer ties with our new ally. It was all quite vague to me; I had no deep interest in politics but as the full horror of the Nazi years was only then becoming evident, the documentation in newsreels and newspapers every day presenting further proof of atrocities such as no one could have ever thought possible—and it was a ghastly realization of the actuality of monstrosities—I felt drawn to join the trend and sought to express my indignation in some tangible way. But I also, frankly, needed to meet people; I was twenty-one, and no loner. Set on the course of developing my talents, I knew I would not sharpen my perceptions without participation in the activities that characterized the period, and I desired ardently to expand my human contacts. I already sensed then a reality within American life that has been confirmed for me more and more over the years, namely, that in the absence of a cultural framework that can contain and supply it, the only possibility for spiritual recognition and strengthening exists within the personal orbit. Here, it is only through interpersonal relationships that the essential wellspring is touched (Robert Frost deals with this magnificently in his poem "All Revelation"). Alas, that achieving this is severely blocked by ego-centered interests and hence a mutual nurturing of it rarely sustained, I discovered, painfully, in the ensuing years.

My first "progressive" alliance was with the Jefferson School, then on Sixth Avenue and Sixteenth Street, where I enrolled for a poetry workshop in the fall 1945 semester with Louise Mally, a poet and novelist. At college, then called the Newark College of Engineering, now the New Jersey Institute of Technology, no such workshops existed and I doubt that they did at that time even at the liberal arts colleges (it was long before the creative-writing workshops explosion on campuses). After my Prufrock earthquake, it was not surprising that I was doing little more than imitate Eliot. Nevertheless, Miss Mally almost at once singled me out from the rest—a doctrinaire bunch on the whole, more interested in message than meter (a line by one of the students has remained with me for its banality and unintentional humor: "In the subways of humanity, I lost my identity")—each week read a poem of mine out loud to the class, invited me to her home for dinner, and advised me to put a collection together and circulate it among publishers. Fortunately, I didn't. I was certainly not ready. She also directed me to a group called Contemporary Writers, whose members organized workshops, readings, and lectures by famous and budding writers. The club was very *left* and probably a front for the Communist Party. Arthur Miller, known then not only as an emerging playwright but as a young novelist as well, read from his novel, *Focus,* an attack on anti-Semitism in America; Howard Fast read, I don't recall from which book, and so did a number of others, always from works dealing with social injustice. That was essential: the cause, the message, the social significance—style and aesthetics were labeled the hobbyhorse of decadents, reactionaries, and revisionists.

I wrote constantly at that time. While still at college—engineering had been my choice not because of a strong inclination for it, though I did like mathematics, but because it was a popular field of study during the war years and guaranteed one a decent living—I had met at the house of Cousin Serge (by then a prominent corporate lawyer) the owner of the Electronic Corporation of America, a strongly progressive company which had sponsored one of the very liberal news-commentators on the air, and was therefore known to me. The owner (whose name escapes me), as it turned out, was a cousin of my sister-in-law to be, who had also worked for him then; he asked me to come and see him before graduation; I did, and he hired me. Indeed, the company did have a most "progressive" atmosphere: constant discussions of political matters, time-off for important rallies, black (then still called Negro) employees even among the engineers. A socialite with communist leanings was one of my co-workers—she was only part-time, didn't need the money—and it was she who had suggested to me that I take the workshop at the Jefferson School. At any rate, by 1946, when I had worked there for only a few months, the heyday for liberal manufacturers was over and we were all laid off. To my great delight. I was still living with my parents, I could get by without working for a while, and I didn't for an entire year. I helped my father somewhat in his office on Nassau Street and manufacturing shop on Broadway near Canal Street, but most of the time I spent walking through New York—I was still exploring my new environment—and poured my feelings into my writing. Some of this I read at Contemporary Writers' workshops or open readings, and I soon became treated there as the principal young talent. Before long, the editor of the *New Masses,* a very appealing, civilized man, asked me for poems and at the age of twenty-two I found myself featured in the centerfold of America's communist literary organ. One poem, two printed pages long, for which the editor had commissioned illustrations, dealt with the recent atrocities— the scene, an imagined exhibition of drawings depicting them, and the Poet's reactions to them. Others had as their subject certain memories of our Nazi experience and escape. They were, obviously, very early poems and I never included them in any of my books. But it was exhilarating to be included in a magazine available at newstands all over the city and I took pleasure in buying copies at subway stations. It was also tormenting, for I felt very uncertain about my precise artistic direction. I was very sure though, soon enough, that it did not lie within the political precincts of Contemporary Writers.

Within a few months, the break came. I had, at that time, and I am not clear now in just what connection, some contact with the Committee of Emigré Writers and Scholars whose office was on lower Fifth Avenue. Certainly, I was not on the roster of its distinguished members. One of its officers, its President, I believe, was Marion Canby, the wife of Henry Seidel Canby, and a friend of William Rose Benet, then the poetry editor of the *Saturday Review of Literature.* Mrs. Canby had asked to see some of my poems; they pleased her well enough to send them on to Mr. Benet. He took one, and it appeared within a few months.

My bonds with my radical friends were loosening. They complained during our workshop sessions that I was becoming one of the bourgeois decadents who believed in and practiced art for art's sake—a sloganlike phrase which no one ever bothered to debate—and that I was being too influenced by the overly decorative, hermetic, self-indulgent style favored by the elitists' literary magazines. I considered this party talk, paid no attention and went on writing in my—to them—ornate fashion.

One day, early in 1947, my mother telephoned me at work—one of the engineers I had gotten to know in my previous job had become chief engineer of a transformer company and had hired me as an assistant—to tell me that I had a letter from *Poetry* magazine in Chicago. I asked her to open it. I had submitted two poems and they had been accepted. I was delirious. For the past few years I had read each monthly issue of the magazine, then the best, most highly esteemed poetry journal in the English-speaking world. To break into it had been my most cherished prospect. And I had! At twenty-three! For days, I was in a stupor of excitement. But when I read these poems to the literati of the radical left, I had gotten a chilling response: brilliant but decadent! I was, they warned me, sliding into a sickening nostalgia for a culture that had pampered the few and oppressed the masses. (More boring party talk!) I had read around that time, in *Partisan Review,* a translation of a powerful one-act play by Hugo von Hofmannsthal, a dialogue between two hetaerae, in which one recounts to the other the uninhibited lovemaking of a primitive tribe a sailor had described to her all through the previous night, and bewails the fact that civilization had deprived her forever of such elemental joys. When I then read to the zealous group a short play I had constructed in a similar fashion, a dialogue between two young men, dense with a sometimes lush symbolism, I was accused by one woman, especially vocal in her defense of social causes, of indecent self-indulgence.

Next to poetry, history had been my favorite reading, intrigued as I then was by the power of yearning and the extremities this has resulted in in human behavior. Robert Graves' *I Claudius* had fitted that mood to perfection and a mélange of juxtaposed historic images and incidents—referred to by one critic when my first book appeared as "perverse, historic fictions"—turned up in my poems. The tone was nostalgic but also sharply ironic; I was also then under the influence of Pound and the early Eliot. *Continued Departure,* the short play, is a dialogue between a rich, world-weary young man—I made him twenty-eight, which actually seemed old to me at that time—burdened with too much history and tradition and a yearning nothing satisfied, and a local youth of twenty-two whose naturalness and ease with the elements (he is an expert deep-sea hunter) is untouched by time and man's corruption. At the play's end, the frustration of the world-weary man remains uneased, and the youth's innocence and basic joy untainted. When I mailed it off to *Accent* some time later, one of the finest literary magazines of that period, where I had read works by Thomas Mann, André Gide, and by the important as well as upcoming poets, and where some of my poems had also appeared, I received back a thick envelope which I felt sure contained the returned manuscript; but it didn't. The editors had rushed the play into print and these were my proofs; it appeared in the next issue. Many years later, Maurice Edwards gave it two fine productions at the Cubiculo Theatre, in the late sixties one of New York's best experimental theatres.

But the play and most of my work of that time had clearly dismayed the political sensibilities of Contemporary Writers and my attendance there, less and less frequent, soon stopped altogether. A few years later, the political climate having changed, the group was disbanded. When, in the summer of 1955, I returned from India after a six-month trip, I was visited in my apartment on Second Avenue and Fifty-eighth Street by two men from the FBI. A routine check, they assured me, to inquire whether I had been approached by Russian agents in India or Egypt, where I had stopped off for a week on my way back to

Europe. I hadn't been, of course, and after I told the men why I had made the journey, to study religious philosophy with a Vedantic Master, they left; I never heard from the FBI again. But I suspect I owed that visit to my Contemporary Writers affiliation and to my endorsed support of various causes during the liberal epoch following World War II.

►5

My participation, however limited, in political action and attitudes had not been a flirtation with radical liberalism but an early attraction to expressions of a liberalizing force—which, as I have since discovered, has run behind the traditions of the Occidental culture I have come to cherish—and to the radical posture that has kept it alive. That, in our age, this is not accomplished in political but existential terms, I must have grasped even then. But that such a stance must promote principles that transcend the age and cannot be on behalf of personal ambition, I knew, and often expressed, with arrogant certainty. And I was very critical of writers and artists I met whose work and lives did not reflect the heroic, the noble dimension. Therein then lay *my* clash of the old, the ongoing, versus the new and fragmented; of means directed toward ideals versus those employed for personal gains. This was *my* refugee dilemma! What I had imbibed unconsciously, I now felt urged to express consciously; ideals on the one hand of timeless character but on the other essential in, and applicable to, one's life of action. While I found little reinforcement of this among my own contemporaries—certainly not among the radical left nor among the proponents of the current hermetic aestheticism, of what I came to call "the cult of the personal life"—I did find at least aspects of the struggle in the literature of postwar France that was reaching us then. In the plays, novels, and essays of Sartre and Camus, even in Genet's *Notre-Dame des Fleurs,* which

confused me but whose extreme posture and underlying intel-
lectuality appealed to me. All these works were frankly serious,
of course, and seriousness, I discovered with unease, was ana-
thema among the young literati I met. Even if it existed—and it
did in the work of some and certainly of the major poets still
alive then—it was not displayed. What counted among my contemporaries was, on the surface at least, cleverness not seriousness; small talk but no intellectual passion—the only such acceptable had to be political. In time, this changed for me, for I
was fortunate to have eventually among my friends writers and
others whose intellectual acuity gave excitement and sparkle to
many a dinner-table talk. But discussions of spiritual exploration and assertiveness as a cultural ingredient were shunned and
remained rare. Pragmatism and a reliance on observed and ob-
servable fact, dominated. I found little support in the radical
cultural posture I espoused.

➤ 6

I assumed it in the things I wrote. In "Octavian Shooting Tar-
gets"—which became the title poem of my first book—the pro-
tagonist is a ruined figure, a best-selling author done in by society's superficial ambitions he did not expose but lived out, a
conflict which landed him in the madhouse. This critical view is
taken in a few other poems in that volume. I felt aided in my
commitment not only by an instinctual grasp of the extent of the
human potential—instilled in me by the memory contained in
my childhood environment—but by the works of the masters I
took as my models. The compassionate heart, a luminous, un-
changing edifice in the music of the composers I loved, amongst
whom Bach's assumed the firmest instruction. The recognition
of something that has always existed, the wellspring of love, I
was certain these were contained there. In the sounds of the
phrase, of each note, reverberated the pattern, the undeniable

grandeur of the whole. In the works of contemporary poets I discerned this strongly in Wallace Stevens. Everything he wrote seemed to me to proceed from a supreme center where the poet stood and whose representative, voiced authority, he was. These were my inspirations, and as their power has not lessened, I may assume that I did not attribute such things to them but that illumination did indeed radiate from them.

It gave me audacity and a haughty attitude, which I set about to correct, for I had to break down the statue within me to inherit its content and make the pose genuine, and mine. A photograph taken of me at that time—and used, to my immense delight along with my first appearance in *Poetry* magazine in its first picture insert, which also included, and how significant for me, one of Eliot—shows a young man of twenty-three, all too certain of his purpose, with a mocking disdain for some invisible, inferior apparition. This was an attitude that had not yet been tested, and I knew it. But it seems to me that I must be grateful to have had it, for however annoying and out of place it may have been, it did help me along and gave me the confidence to reject trends that seemed to me to be a refutation of the concepts I treasured. *Action* was the key word in my struggle for the proper strategy; action in order to affirm; the conscious breaking down of limiting restrictions. Just what it was for which this action had to be taken was not all that clear to me; an independence—but toward what? Some area of sacred feelings. The strongest experience of that in those days was for me the creative act, sudden moments of a joyous reaching forward, a reaching into that it gave me. How become centered there? How be rooted in that of which the soil is only symbolic, namely in unchanged authority? The essence in the soil as much as in him who tends it?

I attempted to work out my belief in existential action in a full-length play. In a history of Rome I had come across the data of a naval calamity that occurred around 256 B.C., during the first of the Punic Wars: 284 Roman vessels smashed to bits in a horrendous storm in which 80,000 soldiers and sailors drowned. I also came upon a reference to the Carthaginian custom of human sacrifice. Using these, I constructed a conflict between a ruthless upstart ruler and his oppressed, aristocratic wife who defies his decree of a human sacrifice, which was to include their only daughter, to thank the gods for the vanquished fleet. With the aid of her daughter's nurse, the lady, forced at last to face up to her husband's brutal opportunism, smuggles the child to safety in Greece. Learning of this, her husband orders her to take their daughter's place at the sacrifice. The high priestess, a partner in the ruler's corrupt power play, brought to remorse by the lady's action and pending death, incites the populace against the ruler who cannot now face them and chooses not to escape the fire his wife has started at the palace shrine. The play was called *Fire!* Operatic, yes. But its theme was action, the rallying of the self in the face of annihilating opportunism; the inevitable triumph of the indestructible! The idealism of an uprooted middle-European of twenty-five.

The play received various professional readings in New York, including one at the Piscator Theatre Workshop, and was finally produced after various revisions by the Illini Theatre Guild at the University of Illinois' annual Festival of Contemporary Arts, in April 1952. The Festival committee had decided for that year to sponsor a national competition for a new play by an American author, and the editor of *Accent* had sent me the announcement. The play won First Prize, which consisted of a full production and my consultation in its preparation. I was flown out to Urbana at Christmas, 1951, and again two weeks before opening to be on hand during rehearsals. Needless to say, it was a significant experience. Not only to see the play come alive but to spend time on a midwestern campus, to walk through the elm-lined streets with spacious lawns and large old-fashioned houses with wide, pillared porches, to get to know an indigenous aspect of the country whose citizen I had become but did not as yet know well, of whose connection, with its past, streets, towns, and landscapes reflecting it, I had had very limited experience. I learned something of this country's intimacy, of its atmosphere when removed from the pressures of the big city, when commercialization did not dominate quite as much, and I welcomed the subtlety for human values, the genuine friendliness and sensitivity in human affairs I encountered there in abundance. It was important for me and enriching. Even my parents traveled out to Urbana. They had been in Europe but rushed back to be present at the first performance. In the statement about the author in the playbill, I was quoted as having said, concerning *Fire!* "The struggle of the individual to maintain or attain his individuality (the most pertinent problem in the life of the individual today) is what I seek to express . . ."

Almost twenty years later, I returned to Urbana to give a poetry reading and I was saddened to see the changes on campus and in the town. The great elm trees, which had stood like sentinels of a former age, were gone, as were most of the Victorian houses, replaced by much smaller split-level homes, one looking exactly like the next. The university had expanded, its plant enormously enlarged. The intimacy suggesting a less hurried time, farmlands, country churches, the horse-and-buggy era, and a closeness to the soil, the possibility for a lived, an established oneness, was gone.

FIRST RETURN

➤ 1

On a sunny day in May 1949, a friend, Doris, drove me down the West Side Highway, through the tunnel across to Hoboken and to the Holland-America Line pier where, almost ten years after my debarkation there, I was to embark on the SS *Nieuw Amsterdam*. The drive in Doris' open convertible, at first through crowded midtown, where we picked up her friend Marcy who came along for the farewell party, then through the tunnel, and for a while up the Jersey side of the Hudson from where Manhattan sparkled in the sunshine and its clear, deep shadows; then, finally the drinks at first in my cabin and later on one of the decks where my faithful brother had joined us to see me off; and, of course, the fact that I was actually to be in Europe again—it all had a most welcome, though ambiguous reality for me. For I was immensely eager to go, but did not know what to expect. My parents had been in Europe for about a year and I had decided, on the spur of the moment one morning, to join them in Vienna. I called the Line, made a reservation (my passport had been ready), arranged for time off from work, and here I was, a few days later, about to sail. A band playing, an atmosphere of cheer as in so many films just before a luxury ship's departure, dancing, drinks, and toasts and then the whistles telling visitors it was time to get off. Very movielike, indeed. The girls and my brother left, and I waved from the deck as the ship departed.

I had met the girls the summer before in New Mexico, where under dramatic skies, amid the unlimited views from the Taos plateau, the sparse desert vegetation, white adobe huts, unpaved side roads, stray dogs, poultry gaggling in every yard, and among its odd mixture of immensely cosmopolitan and local, primitive population, I had spent three happy and productive months. The first time, in fact, since leaving Europe that I had known again more than the tentative connection with the physical surroundings of my immigrant years; and now I was on my way to an environment with which I had had such a powerful identity during the first fifteen years of my life.

Standing on deck during boat drill soon after leaving, looking back at the New York skyline now far in the distance, out across the ocean at the opposite horizon joined to the sky, an anticipation arose within me as though dream images of desires were about to become realized, a joyous, suspended state, as between sleep and waking, there, between coast and coast.

Despite successes in my literary endeavors, I had not yet felt locked in within the framework of my new world, had not yet found the hold in the soil I had lost. Almost without thinking, I had thought constantly during that past decade of my childhood background, of an at-homeness I had missed each moment of the day, a belonging that had been a constant, unrestrained sadness, often heart-breaking and melodious through the nights.

My favorite place during the crossing was an open deck, and I sat there watching the sky and water joinings, the cloud and wave formations, the sun like beaten brass surfaces radiating a blinding brightness from the sea, the wind driving the brilliance onward and often away, occasionally the backs of whales and from time to time a chill and a deep greyness descending. I sat in a deck chair musing on these elemental changes and on the main challenge I faced in my disrupted life.

►2

It was my work. It would not proceed very far, could not become a structure unless, as I knew the poets I admired did, I too stood rooted at my center. I sensed vaguely that, though I was returning to what had once been my anchor, it could now be nowhere but within myself. But I was twenty-five and eager for the experience of the world, for intimacy with the force that lives: a need so powerful only abstract ideals are a match for its unabashed willingness. I yearned for a world still, not just for secure innerness, a world that, reflecting my needs, would aid them in coming to fruition. Naively, much as plantlife strives toward light, I strove toward the condition in life that helps one's potential toward fulfillment. Little did I realize then, as I dreamed on in the open sea air, that I was hoping for nothing less than an enlightened cultural framework, a time of harmony in history, its golden epochs, crests of human intelligence and illumination, a social and cultural network that certainly no longer existed anywhere, and hadn't for centuries. If it doesn't exist, I thought, if I won't find it now, I have to strive toward such structured reality nonetheless. That much I can do. To strive toward it!

I had been aided in this commitment not only by the examples of others but by my dreams. As long as I can remember, they have been indicators of discoveries, of a melodious assent awaiting me somewhere, one that had been but still is, a harmony such as Gluck gave to Orpheus as he steps unto the Elysian Fields, of the oneness in whose supremacy and glory the poets have created their monuments. Not only have I not ignored these dreams, I have been alert to their symbols, cryptic instructions, as prophecies of deeply desired events, and I will record them here as they form part of the story.

Around the time of that trip—my first return as I have said, but there have been about twenty since—in a dream in which a feeling of happiness, the joy of achievement was pervasive, I was holding a book of poems, a thick volume through which I leafed. The lines were long, the poems even had a familiar look on the page, for the book was mine; my volume of *Selected Poems*. As I was savoring this joy of holding my own book, my accomplishment, in my hands, there was a sudden jolt as though something moving at great speed had come to a sudden halt, or as though an earthquake were shaking a building. Wherever it is I was in the dream, I was up high and as I looked outside to see what had caused this jolt, I saw, far far below me, vehicles, tiny because of the distance, racing back and forth along roads like ants or bugs. I asked: "What is it? What has happened?" "The earth has finally conquered the moon," was the answer, and I awoke.

Years later, I wrote long poems with long lines. In the summer of 1969, about two decades after that dream, I was in Dubrovnik on the Adriatic coast with Jean Garrigue when the earth conquered the moon and we both watched on a giant screen set up in the town's main square, as the astronauts stepped from their vehicle. Two years after that, my *Selected Poems* appeared.

When Doubleday & Co., where four of my books have been published, first considered a manuscript in 1966—*Figure in The Door* which appeared in 1968—I dreamed that Ken McCormick, then its legendary chief editor, had telephoned me to say that the book had been accepted. A few days later, my secretary at The Macmillan Company, where I was then a senior editor, turned to me as I was standing at her desk and said that Mr. McCormick was on the line. He had called to tell me of Doubleday's offer to publish the manuscript.

More recently, when I had given the manuscript of my collection *Embodiment and Other Poems* to Stanley Moss—an old friend (we had met reading our poems at Comtemporary Writers), fine poet, art dealer, and publisher of The Sheep Meadow Press—I dreamed that the contract for the book was among my mail. The very next day, it was.

I am not mentioning these as examples of prognostication or

forms of extrasensory perception—I put no emphasis on such communication—but only to illustrate what a determining principle in my life's direction my work had been from the start. When, in my early twenties, I would browse through the books on the poetry table at Brentano's, which used to be the first display table right off the Fifth Avenue entrance, the possibility of one day finding there one of mine had about it all the enchantment, all the lure of a much desired destiny. Again, many years later, when my *Selected Poems* had a favorable review in the daily book column of the *New York Times,* stacks of the book were on display there.

Having a cup of coffee at a coffee shop counter in the fall of 1947, on my way to a poetry workshop I was taking with Horace Gregory at the 92nd Street "Y" Poetry Center, I found myself caught as in a trance of prophecy; another dimension of time had come over me for perhaps no more than an actual split second, and I experienced something of a realization, a fulfillment of the voices I had first sensed rising within me on my solitary walks in Newark, a joined chorus of the rhythms and phrases that had struggled in me toward accomplishment. And so I had sat in my deck chair musing and recollecting, taking notes and wondering all the time what this next, necessary and, I knew, decisive step would bring.

➤3

There were interesting people on the ship: Gore Vidal carrying under his arm a copy of his book *The City and the Pillar* which had just been published; the dancer, Leon Danelian, whom I used to see in *Péricole* with the Ballet Russe de Monte Carlo and who, along with other dancers from, I believe, the newly formed American Ballet Theatre, was on his way to European engagements. When I was not daydreaming in my chair, I watched them rehearsing or practicing on the inside portion of one of the upper decks. I was seated near them in the dining room, their table, always full of flowers, clearly, though subtly, the object of everyone's attention and curiosity. When the boat train from Southampton pulled in, at Victoria Station I believe it was, the group was met by other dancers, including the choreographer Frederick Ashton. The ballerinas were greeted with bouquets of roses and they were all driven off in tall black London taxis. All very glamorous in postwar London, where the damages were still very evident.

On the ship, during the afternoons of my musings, when we were served tea or hot bouillon, and before the cocktail dance which I never missed, for I loved to dance and to drink Dutch gin—I recall the tune that was played repeatedly, *Ay Ay Maria, Maria de Bahia* . . .—I used to chat sometimes with the woman who occupied the deck chair next to mine. I told her my destination and that I would stop off in London and Paris on the way. The lady was English, had been living in the United States during the war, and upon inquiring from me why I was going to London, seemed interested to hear that I meant to see if I could do anything with a play I had just finished. This was *Fire* in its earliest form. One afternoon, she asked me if I knew Cecil Beaton. No, I didn't, but of course knew who he was. She was his aunt, she told me—I was amazed to discover this, for she was rather plain looking and very tweedy, and suggested none of the glamor I had associated with the famous photographer-designer; her name was Lady Moore, I believe, and she seemed to think her nephew might be of use to me; would I like an introduction? I thanked her, and she gave me a letter the morning of our debarkation at Southampton. A few days later I telephoned Cecil Beaton and he asked me for cocktails the following day.

His house on Pelham Square had none of London's shabby postwar look, neither outside nor inside. It was small, charmingly furnished in mostly white and gold; he, around fifty, I thought, was lean, elegant, and most gracious. He offered, after we had talked a while, to recommend me to his agent, for which

I expressed my gratitude. His sister and brother-in-law came in; we were introduced and he mixed martinis in a cocktail shaker. I wished he had talked of Greta Garbo, with whom he had been linked romantically, or of the royal family with whom, as was commonly known, he was on the closest of terms (it had even been rumored that he was the illegitimate son of the present king's father, George V) but he spent nearly all his time praising Truman Capote. *Other Voices, Other Rooms* had just appeared with Beaton's much-talked-of photograph on the back of the jacket. When I left in the early evening, he saw me to the door and as he opened it and shook hands with me never took his eyes off two young men in evening clothes who had just emerged from a house across and were getting into a taxi. It was the end of May, there was a clear sunset; although rationing and other postwar regulations were still in effect, a new mood was setting in, hope about to be refreshed—that was the impression I had had that afternoon and especially as I looked back and he waved at me while still watching the taxi driving off into the evening. When I went to see his agent, I was received at once. Evidently Mr. Beaton had telephoned. The agent promised to do what he could. I think he actually sent the play out to one or two provincial theatres but nothing came of it.

►4

I spent the next month in Paris. The fact that the war had ended only four years ago was evident everywhere. Unlike in London, there were no signs here of heavy destruction but the looks of the people in the streets, subdued and without the confidence, pride, and *joie de vivre* customarily associated with Parisians, suggested that the city had not yet recovered from the indignity of occupation and revealed collaboration. As though the cinders, though out of sight, were smoldering still. People were poorly dressed, restaurants half empty, traffic was light.

But it was also spring. The flowers in the Tuilleries, Palais Royal, and Luxembourg gardens were in full bloom, trees dense with leaves, white blossoms, and webs of sun; children were playing around the edges of the ponds, benches, and chairs full of people reading, chatting, knitting, resting, or watching the children. From the mansard room of the Hotel Stella on rue Monsieur le Prince, I looked out on church bell towers, mansard roofs, trees in the backyards, their clear shadows in the spring sun; bells chimed, not booming, overpowering but rather inviting, an intimate announcement and summoning; from an open window across the yard the sounds of a piano, a Scarlatti sonata, and images suggested by it of steps across canals, of water in the sun—all habits, angles, shadings, and sounds, memory reverberations of the home I had known, had had, and had missed for ten years. For I was surrounded on all sides once again by the European city persona, the result of centuries of intentions to make human life human; and it didn't matter that this was Paris and not Vienna.

In European cities the stress on life as a human affair, on human rather than physical comforts—as I discovered it to have been in America—is very much the same. In Paris it was not structures of corporate wealth and power like the Chrysler Building and Rockefeller Center in New York that stood out with prominence—a contrast I saw then for the first time—but the cathedrals, the parks, the palaces and museums, the broad tree-lined avenues, the open markets in the winding, narrow streets—the human extensions and not the towering buildings of business energy. That spring, Paris was full of young Americans, students who discovered the nurturing power and charm of this collective human attitude for the first time, and they reveled in its atmosphere. Among them were many young veterans who had sensed this cultural background even as they were occupying towns and villages in France, Italy, and Germany and had come back to explore and enjoy it under more promising circumstances. Some were enrolled at art schools, others at the Sorbonne, still others were just traveling and living freely before settling into jobs back home. They crowded the cafés, bars, and night clubs along Boulevard St. Germain and other popular arteries in the Latin quarter. Their enjoyment, enthusiasm, and openness—it was also incredibly cheap in Paris then—was infectious and it helped lighten the drab mood of the Parisians. They had cheered the Americans when the Allies had liberated them only a few years before, and they now took kindly—something they haven't always done—to those boisterous, good-natured young people who had brought with them a bright freshness and new hope; and the Parisians took to them even if they couldn't speak French, or spoke it badly.

▶5

Joyous as it was for me to be there, it was also acutely painful. This was the atmosphere of what I understood to be *home*, as mine had once been, but where was that now? People in the streets shopping, strolling in the parks, stopping to talk to friends or relatives: They were the existing fabric of life, it was they who continued it. They lived where they belonged, had their homes there, their professional lives, their friends and families. What they had, had been torn apart for me. Though I felt completely in place there, in an actual, real sense, I did not belong; my home was not there. I had no home there where I was at home. There, where I belonged, I had become a foreigner, an outsider.

This was illustrated for me with even greater and more painful sharpness a few weeks later, walking in the early evening in Vienna's Volksgarten along the Ring on my way to the theatre, a Burgtheater production but not given at the Burgtheater. Like the Staatsoper, the venerable house for classic drama had been badly damaged and performances were held at temporary auditoriums, the Theater An Der Wien for the Opera and a theatre off the Ring, I can't recall its name, for the Burgtheater. The Volksgarten, always crowded in my childhood days, was quite deserted. Two young men were sitting on a bench I was approaching and as I passed them I heard one say to the other: "*Schau Dir diesen ausländischen Snob an*" ("Just look at that foreign snob"). They had assessed me entirely from the way I was dressed. I said nothing, but all through the performance of Shaw's *Major Barbara* (in German, of course) it haunted me: a sentence in its dual meaning—to be a foreigner wherever I was.

▶6

We had relatives in Paris. Though only distantly related—Sonya was my father's second cousin, her mother having been my grandmother's first cousin—there was a clannishness among some European families and the fact of the distant tie didn't really matter; a third cousin belonged as much to the family as a first. It was part of the tightness of Jewish family life. For example, Sonya's mother, a wealthy widow, used to travel a good deal visiting her daughter, who had lived in Hamburg before 1933, and her stepsons in London and Cairo. On these trips from her home in Poland, she made it a point to stop off in Vienna to visit her cousin, my grandmother, and we called her Tante Gelcia. Perhaps because she had a sister living in Vienna then, her daughter's wedding was held in Vienna, at the Hotel Metropole (the Gestapo headquarters during the Nazi period and bombed during the war), and my five-year-old brother with long, golden locks served as a white-satin-clad page. During the war, she, her daughter, and her family hid in the south of France, as many French Jews had done, and soon after liberation they returned to their Paris apartment, a large, dark, densely bourgeois affair, on rue de Grenelle near the Champs de Mars, where I had dinner with them once or twice during my sojourn in Paris.

They had survived but their lives too had been shaken and marked for good. The enormity of what had happened to European Jewry, not only at the hands of Germany but other countries guilty in complicity, rattled the survivors like unrelenting shockwaves. Not only Jews released from camps were gripped by anguish but those who had survived in hiding and had now returned to pick up the pieces, as it were. It was difficult enough for many non-Jews who had lived under occupation to find again their balance and reestablish the accustomed order of their lives; it was that much harder, and often impossible, for Jews. Many of those completely uprooted and stripped of everything, including their trust and faith in their former countrymen, left Europe for America, Australia, Israel, Canada, etc. Others, like my Paris relatives, attempted to be connected again within the pattern to which they had once belonged. But, in those early years after the great catastrophe, a dismay, a breach in trust, an insecurity underlay their lives, their moods and actions. Sonya was visibly nervous. Spoilt and sheltered, she might well have been a neurotic all her life but her disturbed present condition soon turned into an illness. Her husband too, formerly a successful business man, had little of the control and composure he must have had before. The ordeal had simply unleashed everyone's anxiety. And it was not over; the emotional strain was for many beyond rehabilitation. A few years later Sonya died in England where they had joined her husband's brothers and had tried to resettle. Their children, a son a few years younger than I and a daughter my age, stayed on in Paris, the son eventually becoming a physician and the daughter marrying one.

In retrospect, the encounter with my relatives, the evidence of deep estrangement that had continued to haunt European Jews, must have affected any desire I might have had to return to Europe for good. And as I went on to Vienna it became clearer and clearer that Europe, just rising from its ashes, could not provide the framework I had envisioned for my needing spirit as I lay musing on the deck of the *Nieuw Amsterdam*.

I took the train to Vienna after a month in Paris. I knew I would not find the city as I had left it, but what I did not know and could not have expected because I had not yet experienced such a confrontation was that a cold, almost brutal detachment would pervade me and that, oddly, I would not only welcome it but would even enjoy it. A stupor of indifference in the face of shifts of perspective brought on not only by the finality of change and time but by a city's misfortune for which I found I lacked any sympathy. True, there had been heavy bombings, the damage worse than had been known, gaps in the streets, debris not cleared away, the former "temples"—the Staatsoper, Burg-theater, Dianabad and others—gutted; still, on the whole, the streets were the same. The city's terrain, its flowing expansion from undramatic hills to vineyards, river basin, and flatlands, unchanged, the horizons from the Leopoldsberg or Kahlenberg, the same. But war and defeat had scrubbed the city grey, had wiped off its former life-fabric like cobwebs; what lay behind was grim like naked corpses. The city I had loved was dead. Dead. Killed, and guilty. And as one turns away quickly from the evidence of life's coarseness, I didn't stay very long; I think about ten days.

➤7

My parents had met me at the Westbahnhof, the same station from where we all had fled ten years before. Wherever I went, whatever I looked at, the reminders persisted. Walking down Kärntnerstrasse toward the Stephansdom—part of its steep roof blown off—I saw in my mind the joyous Viennese, swastikas on their sleeves, swastikas on their lapels and in their hands, cheer-ing, cheering, cheering Nazi slogans, anti-Jewish slogans, and I, in utter dismay, watching from across the street, early on, after the Anschluss, only a decade or so before. I saw betrayal in everyone's face I passed, now beaten, shabby and unashamedly unfriendly. Where was the former forced politeness, the faked *Gemütlichkeit*? Not there then, in July 1949. The Viennese were sour, and I did not regret it. I frankly delighted in seeing the Russians, who then controlled most of the *Innere Stadt* and whose headquarters was the Hotel Imperial, force the Viennese off the sidewalks near it, who with what glee had dragged Jews from their homes or off the streets and made them wash the sidewalks on their knees. I was not ashamed of my pleasure when, nearing Vienna, Russian control guards, whose zone we had entered, came into the compartment and demanded to see everyone's papers. How they scowled beneath their brush and feather-trimmed Tyrolean hats and mumbled inaudible words of displeasure, and how I gloated handing the guard my American passport for all to see and turning to address the Austrians in their own language—by which they knew at once my story, and their own. Taxi drivers and streetcar conductors growled at us, only those who had to be polite, the maître d'hotel and waiters in the restaurant where my parents dined daily, the salespeople in the few good shops still left, maintained the burden of their obligations; but the politeness was entirely perfunctory. My mother found it very difficult to be there. She was naturally well dressed and when she talked to people in the streets or shops they knew at once that she was someone who had returned. They could not abide to see Jews back whom they had driven out ten years ago, whose wealth they had appropriated to themselves and who were now, in their eyes, well off again while they had had to endure the rage of defeat, of the Russians, and had now to struggle to survive. My father was untroubled by their conflict. He was working with a lawyer to obtain reparations and didn't mind at least the displeasure with which his competitors had responded to his return. He was doing well and wasn't bothered by their feelings. His former pal from Graz, Herr Strutz, who had foreseen that the Nazis would follow us to America, came groveling back. My mother, who had cursed him vehemently for his unashamed gall and open betrayal as soon as he had left our apartment the last time he had visited us in 1939, now took no pleasure in his pathetic behavior.

My parents were living in an apartment on Kohlmarkt, in the same building as the renowned Demel—a tea shop unlike any other, famous as much for its pastries and unusual delicacies as its interior; the original Demel had been Imperial Courtbaker (the entrance to the Winter Palace at the Michaelerplatz was just up the street). Their life was comfortable; they dined well in a still elegant restaurant, the only one of first-rate quality in Vienna at that time, and went almost nightly to either the Opera, a theatre, or a concert. But my mother hated being in Vienna and early in 1950 she went to Israel, where most of her surviving relatives lived, and stayed there for a year. From then on, whenever she accompanied my father, she was in Vienna as little as possible— she did go with him to Yugoslavia but was not granted a visa to follow him to Prague—and she spent most of her European sojourns visiting relatives in Antwerp or Paris, or at the Austrian resort Bad Gastein.

➤8

My childhood memories while there? They were, curiously, dormant. The reality of the grim present dominated. Scenes from my childhood that had run through my dreams and had contrasted so drastically with my surroundings in America I could not impose upon the city of my birth. Not one of my old friends was there. They had all escaped; only one of my former classmates had come back from London. The son of a family of furriers—whose shop off Kärntnerstrasse was so well known for so long a time the Nazis had kept its name, as they also had of the large, Jewish-owned department stores—he had become an ardent communist during the war and had come back to Vienna for political reasons. When we met at a café he talked of nothing else; our interests were, obviously, too divergent for any sustained communication and our meetings stopped.

Of our many relatives who had once lived in Vienna only one

distant cousin of my mother was there. She was a sister of the jolly Tante Anna who had said in 1938 that she would rather die than leave and who, alas, had not survived. Helene, an older sister, did and was living with her husband (she had met and married him in a concentration camp) in an apartment facing the Danube Canal where, before the war, another sister, the young and beautiful Erna whom I remember well, now also dead, had lived. Helene's first husband had been the first Nazi casualty in our family. Soon after the Anschluss he had been sent to Dachau, long before the mass murders. A few months later, Helene was summoned to Gestapo headquarters and handed an urn containing his ashes. Of all the people I saw in Vienna who had formerly been part of our circle of friends and relatives and who had survived in England, America, or Palestine—another of my mother's distant cousins who had owned several apartment houses in Vienna, a friend from Queens who had once been the owner of one of Vienna's largest shirt-manufacturing establishments, each of them there to reclaim their properties, or, in the case of my schoolfriend, to work for revolution—none appeared as cheerful as Helene and her husband. They could not as yet have been in good health, Helene even walked with some effort, but without saying it, they made one feel that these two people had returned not to former properties, but to life. They had entered again into a realm of existence that transcended materialistic interests or political activism. They lived simply, but gladly. Never once did I hear them talk of their camp experiences but only of their current life and of their children, one in South Africa, one in Australia. They had acquired a small cottage in the country near Vienna and they spent weekends there growing flowers and vegetables; eventually they moved there altogether.

The nostalgia I had had for the city of my birth was not abolished; on the contrary, having been there enhanced it. But a shift occurred. It was, from then on, not nostalgia for place that became intensified, but nostalgia for *home,* for a past not connected with the grimness of the present I had met there. That the

Vienna I had known in childhood had already been saturated with a heavy nostalgic mood, a longing for a past then only dimly evident, for it was no longer a vital force, I learned only in subsequent years when a seminal experience I shall refer to later on—a cleansing and clearing confrontation—revived in me home's true origin and I traced back my cultural background.

But in that summer of 1949, the tenuousness, the dimness of the past in the present had been lost and extinguished. Only the sounds from the streets, of churchbells, cars, of children calling, brought forth in me something of the deeply familiar life that I had missed. But the sense of that, when I woke, usually late in the morning, and looked out across the roofs of the Kohlmarkt, dissipated all too soon. After I left Vienna, I spent a week in the Tyrol, at Igls near Innsbruck where I looked up Hanna's friend, the graphic artist, Paul Flora, and his wife, with both of whom Hanna and I traveled together from Rome, via Siena and Florence to Venice, when I returned from India in April 1955. Even Innsbruck had been far less oppressive in 1949 than Vienna—to where I have gone back only twice and each time briefly, in 1958 on an assignment for *Industrial Design* magazine where I was then an editor, and in 1974 with a friend who had never been to Vienna and with whom I drove to northern Italy from there.

But during the past twenty years, I have been in Europe nearly every summer, always in the south—Portugal, Spain, Italy, Yugoslavia—and, ever since Hanna settled there, for the past ten years, in France, the Loire Valley where she lives, or Paris, and Vence: the basin of the civilization I came to know and value long after I fled history's worst epoch.

In 1949, I sailed back to New York on the *Nieuw Amsterdam* in late July, determined to make America my home and to start in earnest to become part of its life, to be as American as though I had been born there. That was my uppermost thought on the trip back. I did not return to Europe until November 1954, and then only for a few days, to England to embark from there for Bombay.

THE CULT OF THE PERSONAL LIFE

►1

As shoots move up through cracked soil in early spring, as the child crawls, then walks, I had found myself long ago quite unconsciously on the path of individual development and growth. I knew that an independent life had to be shaped independently. When I was about twenty, I remember a sudden, significant realization, however obvious it may seem once it is told. I was lying on the couch below a window in my room, looking out at the building, or more precisely, the sidewalk across the street. A book I had just finished lay beside me. It was a biography of Sibelius, an inferior book, really; but it dealt with the forceful, courageous shaping of a great artist's life and work. I knew, suddenly, that I would never get across the street, would never take the step up the curb and onto the sidewalk, would never cross from one side to the other, would never get there and experience what that meant unless I actually did it, unless I took whatever steps had to be taken to accomplish the passage across. I knew then that in the realm of action everything was up to me. Very simple. And when, in 1949, I was back in the United States, I was resolved to be active in this next, a dual, struggle: to become part of my current world, and to secure the stand, the stance, that would permit me to accomplish my obligation to a principle—without which my participation, as I envisioned it, could not be achieved.

I had not yet come upon a statement by Wallace Stevens I now never fail to tell my students when I lecture on his work, that in "an age of disbelief . . . men turn to a fundamental glory of their own and from that create a style of bearing themselves in reality." But even if I had, even if I had read it, what could that have meant to me at twenty-five? How! How was I to assume such a stand? How was I to discover my own fundamental glory? The most I could do then was to desire it—the experience, the affirmation that would result in this radical, inner turn.

At first, quite naturally at that age, I was very eager for my experience of what the world around me had to offer, so that this process of desiring, so essential in moving onward toward that "fundamental glory," was gradual and increased only as my disillusionment in my immediate surroundings and my despair at discovering this *feeding* source within it, increased. How could I have known then that my personal dilemma was in fact a collective one, the spiritual struggle some of America's writers, and especially its poets, had engaged in and recorded? That I discovered only gradually, and mostly once, many years later, I began to teach.

►2

Headlong, I threw myself into the current art life, the only one of interest to me for the intellectual and spiritual nourishment I craved; in addition, the only facet of contemporary American life into which I could hope to shift successfully, where my own background would be at least not a hindrance, nor an embarrassment. My professional life—an engineer until 1954 when I left it for good and became, first a magazine, then a trade-book, editor and, finally, a university professor—helped in giving me a decent living but it did not extend into my personal life and in no way determined it. Without exception my friends and acquaintances were in the art world in some capacity or other: poets, novelists, playwrights, painters, gallery owners, editors, publishers, etc.

The first thing I did, in the fall of 1949, was to move into an apartment of my own; a studio on West 25th Street near the engineering office where I worked. I moved from there to West 11th Street near Sixth Avenue, to the Rhinelander Buildings, a row of New Orleans-style houses—porches, iron grillwork, gardens off the sidewalk—and eventually took an apartment on Second Avenue and 58th Street where I lived until I returned from India in 1955.

About a dozen years after I had responded to my first observation of an American suburban street with an intense shudder and had been seized by a despair like a shock, an intimation of a condition that exists here beneath the surface, I was walking one evening in the narrow park that runs along the East River at Sutton Place. Only a block away from the noise of the city, the lit windows in the tall buildings, from the rush of people, the many restaurants in the side streets, the bars on Third and Second avenues. It was before the Third Avenue elevated had been dismantled and there were none of the present towering office buildings but mostly low, narrow red-brick tenements, a dingy bar, badly lit, in many of them. Around six in the evening, on my way home or to an appointment, the neighborhood swarmed with young professionals, many stopping off at one of the bars, others heading for cocktail parties, as I often did—they were much in vogue.

I didn't care for the bars. They were dark, sawdust on the floor of some, windows unwashed, a faint smell of disinfectant coming from the toilets, and always a few drunks standing against or sitting at the bar who seemed to have been there all day long; inevitably there would be some sort of a row, usually harmless but sometimes one of the drunks would be taken by the collar and thrown out the door—an atmosphere of simmering depression, lingering frustration and hopelessness, the few times I had gone into one of them with friends. I could never understand the attraction these places below the rumbling elevated trains had to Ivy-league graduate students or young college instructors who insisted on going there, and often on getting drunk there, when they were in town. At the other extreme for an emotional outlet in a public social context were the cocktail parties, where noise, smoke, booze, and shrill, often clever chatter replaced the dreary depression of the bars with frenzy and, usually, groundless expectations. Not only had I gone to many such parties, I had given many. And they were fun in a way; an often glittering balloon that always burst as soon as the last guest had left and the place was filled with empty, or half-empty, glasses with floating cigarette butts and packed ash trays. A sour emptiness. A drifting loneliness the relative quiet along the East River embankment could not relieve, the glitter and noise of the interior streets could not conceal. I stopped along Sutton Place, looked below the railing at the cars streaming past in both directions, at the dark river, almost black, at a barge coming by, at the bridge, its stationary lights and those of the cars and trucks moving across. In the dark, the sky was not discernible in the water, only the lights from the bridge and the embankment bobbed up and down; there were few people about, some with dogs, others walking briskly past, one or two lingering by the railing, as I was.

Here, in the open, at the river's edge of the city, here was none of the intimacy I knew as a child or had felt more recently in Paris, of a city-life woven with human realities, changing though unchanged in their cycles, extensions, peaks and losses, pomp, joys, frailties and failures. Here were only disconnected splashes, distant sirens, steam from giant funnels; here was the fragmentation that follows intense activity on the surface when there are no interlocking connections beneath. An outer reality constantly shifting according to one's ego-needs and potential, an inner one uncultivated, unattended: how create a foothold, how grab on to either? So empty, so lonely the reality beneath the surface, so desolate the inner terrain, where but within another individual lay any hope for rescue, who but another person equally afflicted had the power to redeem one's loneliness? Years later, a Portuguese friend told me in Lisbon one summer about his first trip to New York. He had loved the city. Why, I asked? It's the most ego-centered city in the world, was his reply. He was talking of the cult of the personal life.

➤3

Had I, at fifteen on my first encounter, received a hint of the soul's desolation here? Was I, in my mid- and late twenties experiencing surface activities and expressions of a fundamental, inner emptiness? The pieces could not have fit the puzzle then, but I was certainly aware of a frantic despair. I had not the appetite for its destructive manifestations—heavy drinking, obsessive sexual promiscuity, disastrous personal relationships based more on neurotic than romantic needs, fights, wrist-slashings, overdoses of sleeping pills—and in no way could it feed my need for constructive self-assertion.

In this mood, an irony had entered my work which brought it attention but which I felt to be an obstacle and a dead end. I was not content to satirize society, to be clever about its obscene, Philistine interests and empty surfaces; nor was I competent, experienced, mature enough to deal with the human anguish brought on by this malaise. But the poems won me early recognition, awards, praise from critics and, what is even rarer, from other poets emerging then. And it was a generation of very considerable talents. In a survey of the postwar generation of poets in *The Saturday Review* in early 1952, Horace Gregory wrote of me as "the only younger poet that I know of who in spirit has the promise of a new and unpredictable avant-garde in America. No poet under forty in this country has a better command of dramatic form in poetry; and in his poems, several of which are vividly placed within a European setting, no young poet has shown greater inventiveness in creating new verse forms." And such attention came not only from a former teacher. Several roundups of the then young poets included me, such as *Poesia Americana del dopoguerra* edited by Alfredo Rizzardi and published in Milan, or "Ten Young Poets" by Hayden Carruth in *Perspectives USA #12* (also represented were Anthony Hecht, Daniel Hoffman, William Burford, James Merrill, W. S. Merwin, Hy Sobiloff, May Swenson, and Laurence Josephs). A few years later, I was one of twelve young poets in the first of a series of Introductions at the 92nd Street "Y" Poetry Center which included such upcoming poets as James Wright, Galway Kinnell, Denise Levertov, and Carolyn Kizer and Ned O'Gorman, with whom I read, introduced by R. P. Blackmur. When, during intermission, I came into the lobby, I was astonished to see Marianne Moore and Allen Tate, to whom Betty Kray, the Poetry Center's director, presented me. Clearly, they hadn't been there to hear three young poets read their work, but must have come out of respect for R. P. Blackmur, perhaps the best poetry critic this country has produced so far.

Most of the dramatic poems Horace Gregory alluded to were published by Hayden Carruth and, later, Karl Shapiro in *Poetry* magazine, still the premier poetry publication, but I was discontent with the ironic stance which did, however, contain a tragic undertone. I eschewed social criticism, I desired compassion, the impersonal regions of the heart; I sought to praise; tradition, the obligations of my culture had urged me on in this way. I was aided, as already mentioned, by taking as models masters whose works expressed and confirmed, and fed, this direction. My first poem published by *Accent* in 1949, shows a combination of those influences. Entitled, "Of Caligula, Bach and the Seascape" it aimed for a fugal pattern, the tones of a chorale, used terse, opulent imagery in the manner of Stevens, and touched on human cruelty against the impersonal background of time and the seasons. "A heritage quite complicated/ quite without question." It was a poem in which I wished to present ideas rooted in incontestable observation by means of vivid, direct imagery and unexpected juxtapositions. I suppose the strongest influence came from Stevens' early masterpiece, "Peter Quince at the Clavier," which I knew by heart, and still love. A few of my poems in that musical, reflective mode were published by Ted and Renée Weiss in the fine journal, *The Quarterly Review of Literature*. When, shortly after the issue containing them came out, I met a young woman named Holly at a Village cocktail party, she said, "I have something to tell you that should please you." "Oh?" I responded. "My father came to me the other day with a magazine that had some of your poems in it; 'Watch that man' he said." "Who is your father?" I inquired; "Wallace Stevens" was her striking answer. Not long ago, I had dinner with Holly Stevens at the Algonquin and I was tempted to have her verify this incident for me. But I didn't bring it up. I just wanted to make sure it hadn't occurred in one of my dreams of the miraculous. I feel quite certain that it did happen, for I remember the man who gave the party and the house on Morton Street where it was given, the large downstairs rooms, the candles in the opulent crystal chandelier, and that it was my good friend Ted (Edgar) Bogardus—the young poet and protégé of John Crowe Ransom who died tragically not long after—who had taken me there.

But my attempts at praise and the reflective, reverential mode were feeble. While they were not imitations they sprang more from influences rather than my own uncontestable knowledge obtained from experience. I had no doubt of the direction I had to take—I was as arrogant and cocky about what mattered as ever—but I did not know how to set about to gain it, where to turn to confirm my needs. Only dreams brought me visions of desired happiness, landscapes, seascapes drenched in the colors of harmonious blending progression, scenes of wingless flights above streets, incidents of union—a mélange of nostalgia that kept the music going, if my actual experiences did not.

➤4

I didn't fare well within my new milieu. Outwardly, it wouldn't have appeared so—superficially, I did belong, but in a real sense, from the root up, so to speak, I felt I was not part of it. I knew many people, was out a great deal—it's a wonder I got anything done, but I did—saw the plays that mattered, went to the ballet, concerts, to gallery openings. I knew the art world especially well, from Thursday evenings at Sari Dienes' studio on 57th Street and Sixth Avenue—the Sherman Studios, now torn down—where everyone gathered on one Thursday or other, Mark Rothko, Robert Rauschenberg, Julio de Diego (the former husband of Gypsy Rose Lee), Jasper Johns, Franz Kline, and many others gaining prominence within a small circle long before the commercialization of modern art had set in and these painters' personal fortunes were made. The hostess was also among these prominent artists showing her finely tuned abstract watercolors and large oils of street and wall surface rubbings at the Betty Parsons Gallery, the foremost showplace then. I saw Sari the other day, very vigorous and essentially unchanged at eighty-three. Of course she is stooped now and her hair—which she always wore like an erect, crownlike circle of fibers—once yellow-white is now totally white. But she is as inveterately rooted in the avant-garde as ever—as, no doubt she was when, a staunch anti-bourgeois rebel, bred by the Hungarian upper bourgeoisie, she was part of the Parisian art scene in the twenties, as she was of the art scene here in the forties and fifties. In 1949, when I first met her, she introduced me to the inexpensive Bocce restaurant on Thompson Street where the specialty was spaghetti with green sauce, a highly garlicky pesto. And just recently, when Sari invited me to dinner, it was the same sort of place more than thirty years later, on the extreme western edge of Soho, frequented by young bohemians, struggling television writers, painters and others to whom the life of art is synonymous with bohemianism as it has always been with Sari.

It never was for me. Well dressed and well paid in my job as an engineer, I always felt out of place in the cold-water flats in the Village or along Third Avenue where many of the people I knew then lived, by choice or not. To many the anti-middle-class exterior was the only artistic one that qualified for the good, true life. I knew the daughter of the one-time pearl-king of Europe, who had been raised in the glitter of Parisian wealth and celebrities in a mansion off the Champs Élysées but whose idea of the *good life,* as she called it, was a platform bed in a vast, almost empty, not centrally heated loft in lower Manhattan; which was where and how she lived as soon as she could get away from her parents' duplex on Central Park South. In her, and her world's view, she was then living as an artist, though she really didn't perform as one. Her work as a painter and dancer never came to much.

While the cold-water flat bohemia was not my style, I was hardly more comfortable in another extreme, in what *Flair*—a chic magazine that didn't last long—called the "upper bohemia," the well-furnished apartments of art entrepreneurs, collectors, and others who, mostly born into wealth, dabbled in the arts, some successfully, most not. True, the form of veneer that dominated there allowed me to blend with its life more easily but I soon despaired of the superficiality and lack of seriousness that were part of this, mostly Upper East Side style. At a garden party at Ruth Stephan's Greenwich, Connecticut, home—Ruth, poet and biographer, years ago had edited a splendid magazine, *The Tiger's Eye,* and I had met her at one of its publications parties at the Gotham Book Mart—Betty Parsons, one of the guests, sat doing a watercolor while some men near her talked. At one point, she turned to them, and said: "I hate you, lawyers. Always facts, and they are always black or white for you, either this or that; whereas the truth is in between." I cheered what she said. It certainly applies to the life of the artist—it need not, and very often does not, lie in either sphere.

The pursuit of the personal life and a clear breach with a snobbism toward conventionality and the ordinary world, characterized both bohemias. I had no use for American middle-class taste, manners, and values but an arrogant stance rooted in snobbism, mud-flinging, nose-thumbing, attention-getting exhibitionism didn't suit me either. I thought it adolescent, if not infantile. Certainly it did not suggest, as it should, an intellectual and moral superiority—which was my sense of the artist's obligation. Instead, a form of enfant terribleism prevailed, especially among some of the New York poets. This does not mean that they were not intelligent and well educated; in fact most had gone to Ivy-league schools and some taught there. But, except for the members of their own clique, they were frankly insolent toward everyone including the "common" man (later, some claimed to espouse Whitmanism), were seen in sneakers at dinner parties or the ballet, and formed a coterie, an "in" society, of giggly silliness. In poetry, this was sometimes expressed under the guise of surrealism or a New York–styled Parisian urban experimentalism. It was for that reason that my work then received their attention. For to them it merely sneered at society; but had they in fact read those poems carefully they would have felt the pain beneath the irony. And part of that pain was precisely that I did not want to sneer. I sought to praise, to stand for collective ideals. The world of most of my contemporaries with whom I came in contact in the early fifties was too insular for that. To have as one's foremost obligation making the impersonal personal, to put the struggle toward absolute verities ahead of irritations, grievances, ego-interests as the masters of former generations of poets had done—*griefs, yes; grievances, no,* Frost had said—was not a position they espoused; in the main, they shut their ears to it. I must suppose, as they were indigenous and many of old American stock, that the recognition of a fundamental emptiness, of a soil that needed nothing less than their soul—"The land was ours before we were the land's," Robert Frost had read at the inauguration of John F. Kennedy—had not hit them as a sudden despair as it had me the very day of my arrival in America. Emptiness was part of their condition at birth; they were born into it and would react differently to it than I for whom there had been no such absence at birth and for the first fifteen years of my life. And therein lay my dilemma, my refugee dilemma once again.

The responses of native Americans to the way life was lived and being shaped around them was of necessity different from mine. The angles from the past were different, hence the perspectives ahead. It also meant that they understood one another in a way that I could not; something fundamental that is taken for granted and need not be said. It is how I feel in Europe. Sitting at a café in Paris, Vence, Estoril, or any of the places where I have spent most of my summer vacations, I understand the people around me in just that fundamental sense of which one need not, and probably cannot speak. It is like being within one's family: one knows where one comes from and what all of that implies. It is this basic ease of understanding that has always been lacking for me here, as it must be, for it is a rift endemic to the condition of cultural uprootedness. Suffered by all of us, not only the Nazi and war refugees but by other waves of immigration. It simply has to be so; and cannot be reconciled. And, of course, this incurable rift had to have had its effects on subsequent American-born generations. But that is a social science inquiry beyond my range.

►5

The personal life that I saw as a cult in the fifties was a refuge from prevalent social and cultural modes. It tended to cut one off from current public issues but gave one the satisfaction of leading one's own life in ways that may or may not have been sanctioned by the rest of society. Its exclusivity and self-centeredness never suited me and became an obstacle in my attempted—and much desired— integration. Certainly such a "cult" life was not understood by my parents and their world. And that too was troublesome and painful for me. I could only describe to them some of the activities of my life, people I knew, parties I attended and gave, but they could not participate in them, would have felt entirely out of place at one of those large gatherings. My apartment had a terrace bigger than its living room and this enabled me to throw crowded cocktail or evening parties. Once during the winter, we strung colored Christmas lights across the terrace, made outdoor fires in tall metal cans as construction workers do to keep warm; we served mulled wine among regular drinks and most of the guests were out on the terrace in the winter air. There was a good French restaurant downstairs and this allowed me to give small dinner parties, food being sent up and served by the restaurant. I would describe these occasions to my parents who didn't know and wouldn't have understood that entertaining was one way whereby

I could imitate belonging. But it also pleased me to have this close contact with my contemporaries in the arts. It satisfied my notion of the proper place in my world to have such accomplished artists as Rosalyn Tureck, Mark Rothko, Robert Rauschenberg, Jasper Johns, Theodore Stamos, John Cage, Muriel Rukeyser, James T. Farrell, Merce Cunningham, Ram Gopal, Tambimuttu, and many others prominent around 1950 mingle at my parties. Once, Howard Griffin, poet and one-time secretary of W. H. Auden, who lived around the corner on 59th Street and himself gave many literary parties, brought Christopher Isherwood and his sixteen-year-old friend to one of my large cocktail shindigs. At one point I overheard Ylla, the renowned animal photographer, introduce Isherwood to the people she had been talking to, and turning to his friend, said: "And this is Mr. Isherwood's son." I was out of earshot to hear his reply.

In short, I was participating in my world as fully as I could manage to do, but those joys of freedom I had envisioned as a boy coming upon the American family at the Hotel Excelsior in Vienna, or when I had observed in the subway not many years after our arrival here the easy demeanor of two young men my age—that condition of elatedness, of harmonious oneness with my world, had not happened. On the contrary, I felt distressed, burdened by rifts, an unhealed split—and also, in a more immediate, practical sense by the continued pursuit of a profession where, I knew, I did not belong. I had enjoyed the theoretical aspects of engineering in college, but in practice it did not express my general interests, caused a further split in my life, and I was determined to leave it as soon as I could. All of these circumstances, and above all, my sense of alienation that increased the more I got to know and tried to be part of the society in which I lived, deepened, despite my aims at adjustment, my feeling of displacement, and intensified my loneliness. This in turn affected my personal relationships and my love affairs, such as they were, were troubled and short-lived. I thought, as does everyone, especially when still in one's twenties, that love for and of another would heal me. It didn't. It couldn't. I needed and longed for an integration of self that no personal relationship can provide.

I thought of psychoanalysis, for I had reached the point when what was happening around me seemed to have no connection with me, did not reach into me, seemed unreal and I knew that this was a grievous state, for one is in fact connected to the things and events around one and not to feel it is a severe dysfunction. But I also knew that what I was troubled by, though very personal, was not a psychological disturbance. In the realm of the psyche, yes, but of the soul rather than the mental, psychological being. I realize now how closely linked the two are, but I felt at that time that my healing lay elsewhere than on the psychiatrist's couch. For I knew, even then and certainly remembered, moments of feeling totally hale, in childhood, in dreams, and most significant for me then, in the instant of the creative act giving rise to the work, but also when absorbed in music and literature, or in a sudden recognition in someone's eyes, and the deep belonging and longing for it that reached up out of dreams. But such instants were only instants; they did not last, I did not live in them, could not return by my own efforts; they were given and I floundered in between. If I were centered, I argued, rooted at the source I am now only close to in its unpredictable reflections, I would then not depend upon them for the nearness they gave off. Regardless of its manifestations, I would be there as, I was certain, others, certainly the masters in art who fed me, had been. And that is what I desired: the confrontation that would secure me there. Such were my thoughts on my way home through the lonely, deserted East Side streets, having seen Albert Finney in *Luther*—was there anywhere on earth a figure, as those inspiring the major religions must have been, in whom throbs, is alive the total reality, the totality of existence and through whom the force of existence itself is experienced: I would journey, would go wherever needed, for such confrontation.

➤6

Among my friends was a young painter, Sam Spanier, whom I had known from my "radical" days—we met at a leftist camp in Connecticut in 1944—and who had been living in France for some time. He had been in Paris when I was there in 1949 and he knew many of the new breed of young expatriates; one day, on our way to lunch, on rue Monsieur le Prince, he introduced me to a young poet, slim, intense, handsome, Edward Field, who was then "bumming around" Europe and was about to leave for a year's stay in Greece, and who has now long been among my close friends. While in Paris, Sam had also met ardent followers of the Gurdjieff adherents and he spoke to me about this when he returned to New York in the early fifties.

Talk of spiritual matters as such was alien to me. I rejected notions about mind expansion and control, sharpened sense perception, or any pose whereby one supposedly improved one's performance in worldly matters and penetrated life's mysteries. My aim was to be in harmony with existence and not to have a mental grasp of its complexities—this seemed to me futile, ego-oriented, and vain. Furthermore, I did not seek to improve my knowledge but my quality of being. Intuitively I resented the imposition of matters of the spirit upon, essentially, worldly interests. This is not, by any means, a judgment of Gurdjieff's teachings, of which I know nothing; it is simply how I reacted to Sam's talk of it and to his infatuation then with spiritual cliques (his mother had been a Christian Scientist). Sam, who today is a devoted follower of the teachings of Sri Aurobindo and runs a retreat for its adherents he founded on a large wooded property near Woodstock, N.Y., was by no means alone in this pursuit. There was, in fact, a sizeable group of Gurdjieff-Ouspensky devotees here who used to meet in a townhouse in the East Sixties or worked on a farm near New York—in Connecticut, I believe.

In a way, theirs was a secret society for one could not participate in their meetings unless initiated, and the members, many of whom were successful professionals and were among New York's trend setters in the arts and fashions, did not discuss principles of the teachings with outsiders. Their "infiltration" in the current *haut monde* reminded me of the indoctrinations into a secret society revolving around Sir Henry Harcourt-Reilley by the proselytizing Julia in T. S. Eliot's fashionable play, *The Cocktail Party,* which was then running on Broadway. There was a significant difference, however. In the play, the psychiatrist, Sir Henry, leads his patients back toward the healing source within an existing Christian tradition from which contemporary life had departed, or which it ignored, while, as far as I could ascertain, the New York infiltrators belonged to no such discipline whereby the spiritual current that underlay their own cultural world would be revived. The *In Search of the Miraculous* (the title of Ouspensky's book) had no interest for me. The world held sufficient wonders which, I felt, would be available were I to be part of it more deeply. I was convinced that the miraculous would reveal itself in the ordinary, daily things of life were I to find in myself the right attitude whereby the veil covering the one and only miracle would be lifted. It was the world I wanted and not the secrets of a secret society.

For that reason, I was more attracted to Zen Buddhism, which lies at the root of a culture's tradition, stresses the *here* and *now,* and which was then taken up by a number of people in the art world. I hoped it would perhaps permit me to assume the existential position I trusted but needed to be grounded in by means of direct experience. John Cage and Sari Dienes had introduced me to the *I Ching* the Chinese *Book of Changes* and I used to consult it often, throwing three pennies to obtain the hexagram in response to a problem, a request for direction. The advice, or "The Judgement" as it is called there, stated like that of an oracle in cryptic terms, terse, vivid imagery, and often exquisite lines of Chinese poetry, sought always to put the inquirer in harmony with the cosmic dynamic reality of nature and the elements, and this appealed to me greatly no matter what the specific content or immediate relevance. Nature and time set the example for human conduct and humility, and this constant reference to *things as they are,* to a diminishing of ego and strengthening of cosmic self—the one life-principle everpresent—attracted me and suited me. But, while consulting the book was uplifting and often soothing, it didn't really stir the waters; it couldn't have done that for me. The pleasure was more in the realm of art than a stirring in the depth of the soul.

The major spokesman among artists for Zen was John Cage. I admired him greatly, his sharp intelligence, terseness, personal charm, and above all, his application of his conviction to the way he lived and the way he was. The aesthetic of Zen suited his tastes and own manners and was, moreover, in harmony with his own background; he is from the West Coast which seems to have absorbed more cultural influences from the Orient than the Occident. His aim in his work was, or such is my interpretation of it, to prod his listeners into an emptying of the mind, so central in the practices of Zen, the demolishing of limiting perceptions, by stressing the underlying emptiness, the sacred nothingness (no-thingness), and the resulting freedom of appearances and sounds not restricted by conventional structures but happening in a natural fashion, haphazard, chaotic, or not. No imposition, no artifice, that was the aim. The water drops from the wet bough, a splash in the quiet pond. The principle of cosmic naturalness espoused by Zen applied to the practice of art. For example, Cage and the pianist David Tudor would appear on stage, dressed in tails, holding a score; Tudor would sit down and Cage would be ready to turn the pages. The piece, entitled "Ten Minutes, Sixteen Seconds" or some such time designation, would start, not a key was touched, not a sound made and after the time designated as the title of the piece had passed, the two men would get up and bow to the audience. Or, enormous speakers would be set up around the auditorium, near-deafening sounds would bring the listener at the center of the whirling noise, to near demolition of his sound-sense. Or, Merce Cunningham would assume the conductor's pose, would lift his arms in graceful motion while twelve musicians, a radio in front of each, turned the dials in arbitrary directions, I believe. The result was a mélange of sounds presumably freed of "old-fashioned" structure—for me certainly not music but a lesson of sorts.

Cage's brand of seriousness and demonstration of his concepts had a marked effect on some of the painters then emerging—and now world famous; I am thinking in particular of Rauschenberg and Johns—who felt from his concepts a widening of perspective and a clarification of artistic attitudes appropriate and indigenous to their own backgrounds and environment. Clearly, they were not so for me. Assuming them would have been precisely what they were against, artificial and an imposition. Our backgrounds and natural expressions were simply too different. Though intrigued by it, and on friendly and close terms with some of its members, I could not identify with the Cage circle either.

The interest in Zen had been stirred in Cage and others by the presence in New York of D. T. Suzuki, the eminent Zen scholar and its most effective and respected spokesman in the West. His books and commentaries on Zen were widely read, and a practical application of it, *Zen in the Art of Archery,* by Eugen Herrigel, for which Suzuki had written an introduction, was a favorite topic at Sari Dienes' Thursday evenings and at similar social gatherings. Suzuki was lecturing at Columbia on, if I recall correctly, Thursday afternoons, and I attended a number of his talks in the early fifties.

Talks ill describes the sessions. Suzuki, in his eighties by then, was hard to hear, he didn't enunciate with precision, and had a habit of letting his words trail off—as if they didn't matter but what they faded into, the silence without and within, did. It took considerable practice on the part of the listener to catch the words that emerged from the mumble. But that didn't matter, for this rising and falling of words was part of the experience of listening. And the mood that soon settled over the classroom was extraordinary. In the same manner in which his words faded,

Suzuki invariably drifted into slumber, for half a minute, perhaps longer. He was not a Zen master, he emphasized that again and again; he talked of the masters, of their commentaries, of their lives. And always in terms of some incident, some story that illustrated a Zen principle, the Zen way. He talked of the monasteries, the arduous disciplines, the koans, the deeds of the masters, the trials of the monks; and underlying all the anecdotes or commentaries was always the beauty of compassion, the incomparable condition of the ultimate existence, the fired, joyous heart, the tears of the masters at a disciple's *satori*—the piercing of the veil, the annihilation of the limited mind, the union with the mists, with the drop falling from the bough. And then, Suzuki would drift into slumber, or would ascend from slumber, his head slowly falling or rising; the late afternoon sky, the early winter sunset penetrating the classroom sunk into itself, for a moment everyone present reaching the silence where resounds assent, the secret of home.

These sudden transformations, so simple, so subtle, gave the occasion the reverential clang of ritual. They meant the most to me, in those days of my restless dissatisfaction. But, again, they slipped by; when they were over, I could not hold on to them inwardly; the turmoil I was in took over.

There were other spokesmen of Oriental thought and religious-philosophic attitudes in New York then and some, like Krishnamurti, had considerable followings. When he lectured here, the session I attended at the large Washington Irving High School auditorium was jammed. The Vedanta Center on the West Side and the Ramakrishna Society on the East Side also had loyal supporters. The mass turnings toward Eastern thought that occurred about twenty years later with Transcendental Meditation, the Hare Krishna sects, and various others was, perhaps, anticipated by these far less numerous and certainly not flamboyant or exhibitionistic but, from their appearance and behavior, serious inquirers. In addition to the Krishnamurti talk, I attended a few others on Vedanta, the religious-philosophic system at the root of Eastern religious tradition, but these had no particular effect on me. The mood from the Suzuki afternoons wore off; I remained needy and skeptical.

► 7

One afternoon, in the spring of 1952, I went to a cocktail party given by an attractive former actress, Ann Harrison, a close friend of Sam Spanier's, whom he had brought to my apartment on 25th Street and whom I had seen infrequently since. She had been married to a prominent New York newspaper executive, so that when she divorced him, the papers covered the trial in flashy detail. Evidently, she had felt herself drawn, irresistably, to a spiritual force and she had set about pursuing it and heeding its mysterious call. She gave up her opulent way of life and set out for India. When she returned to New York she took an apartment at an East Side hotel where the cocktail party took place. She was charming, had the quality of innocence and openness encountered in young film actresses projecting a wholesome American image; but what she was doing, moving about from ashram to ashram, seeking out obscure wandering *sanyasins* (monks) in the Himalayas to whom she was directed mysteriously, and how she talked about it, with unflinching openness and insistent joy, made no serious impression on me. Her talk, too sweet, lacked objective clarity and intellectual substance. I didn't take it all that seriously then; however, in subsequent years I came to realize that she had been perfectly sincere. Unfortunately, her insistence on obeying her own mysterious guidance rather than that of someone by long and tested tradition qualified to guide appears to have resulted in serious mental troubles.

At the party on that spring afternoon, I remember in particular the painter Rudolf Ray and his wife, Joyce, who became good friends of mine, and the widow, an old lady by then, of Hector Guimard, who had designed the decorative portions and entrances of the Paris Metro (he had evidently been a great deal older than she was). At one point, the door opened and in came two young Indian women of striking appearance followed by their husbands; one was Rajeshwar Dayal, India's Ambassador to the United Nations, and the other, his brother-in-law, Sonny Srivastava, son of Sir J. P. Srivastava, one of India's industrial tycoons. Susheela Dayal was Sonny's sister and the other woman, looking precisely as one would imagine an Indian princess—slender, reticent, sparkling, mysterious—was Sonny's wife. Ann had met Sonny and Sir J. P. at the airport at Khanpur, the city where the Srivastavas had their main residence. Ambassador Dayal had then only recently been appointed to New York from Moscow; his became a distinguished career, which included being Hammarskjold's deputy in the Congo during its main crisis, Ambassador to Pakistan, to Paris, and finally India's Foreign Secretary, a post he held until his retirement.

I had been sitting on a couch facing the door when they came in. After the introductions, Mme. Dayal (Susheela, as I soon came to call her) sat down beside me and I said to her—spontaneously, the idea unmeditated, the thought as though come about of itself: "You are fortunate to belong to a country whose traditions are not only old and tested, but still alive, so that you can turn to them, can avail yourself of them, should you need to and desire to do so!" (I knew next to nothing of India; the country in the East that had always held fascination for me was China and, since Suzuki, though much less so, Japan. But what I had done to Susheela was obviously to blurt out my own dilemma.) Susheela replied, "Yes, you are quite right. But that tradition is available not only to us; it is available to all." And she at once began to tell me of her teacher, a great Vedantic sage in whose presence she had been only a few days ago, having just returned from India by air. And she slid down, sat on the floor against the couch, her arms enfolding her knees, her head slightly lowered, and she spoke, in a voice bright and sonorous as bells, her words precise as a performer's sounds.

One does not in India talk of the sacred but standing or seated cross-legged on the floor. Her posture, her words, had a clarity that springs from reverence and humility, the diminishing of personality, the rising tones of authenticity.

What had not opened up for me that afternoon as Susheela had stood in the doorway, had come, from the reaches of home, to my despair? O world, O homeless, O fortress . . . out of my depth, to me then in my depth of alienation . . .

The choice had been Moscow again, or America. *You must go to America,* she was told, she told me, in a different connection, years years later.

Faces, women's faces above me, over my bed, when I was three, burning with fever. I had an aunt, Aunt Laura, round face, waves in her hair, a standing up fur collar; she pinched me and I laughed in her arms . . . I cried to see her face above me . . . and she came and held the infant . . .

I climbed up on a rock out of a storm;
I saw my mother nearby;
I cried for her help, to secure my return;
I was an adult and this was a dream;
she could not help me . . .

I had walked by the water at night;
I had stopped to look; I could not see my face in it,
only the river splashing against the stones,
the lights from the bridge and the refuse bobbing up and down;
I had looked to see myself and couldn't find myself
. . . O father, father . . .

► 8

Later that year I had, what I considered—too aware of the irritating, frustrating circumstances within which I had lived—a physical breakdown, hepatitis, not as common then as it has since become. I was in the hospital for three weeks, recovered for two at an inn near Woodstock, N.Y., and stayed a month with my parents, then in New York. My father had had some alarming symptoms, warnings of a stroke, which fortunately did not happen. But my mother was distraught, the more so since I too had to check in at a hospital. I entered it on a Sunday, it was Misericordia Hospital on East 86th Street, which is no longer there. It was run by nuns and, for some reason, though I dreaded being in a hospital, I was euphoric. As if, with the collapse of the body, things that had plagued me were also removed, at least for a while. I hardly slept the first night; unaccountably, a joy had welled up, an excitement of sheer being revived, for I had known it, remembered it only too well from childhood and those intense moments when at work on poems that had succeeded.

I had brought with me to the hospital two books, Frazer's *The Golden Bough* and Gurunathan's slim volume *Atma Darshan,* which Susheela had given me; *Gurunathan* was how her Master's followers addressed him and referred to him. His family name was Sri Krishna Menon and his spiritual name is Sri Atmananda. The title of the book, *Atma Darshan,* means "Self Realization" or "The Means Toward Self-Realization" and, added to it, underneath the title is "At The Ultimate." But I was too weak, at times too nauseated to read and I gave myself up, gladly and fully, to revery.

The condition of my body, its nausea, seemed to me to be an apt expression of, and reaction to, the world from which I was then withdrawn. I knew that there were other areas in us than worldly cares and I turned to those, let myself be drawn into them with joy. I felt pulled again into a landscape of dreams. They had already been portentous, magnificent in the last months ever since I had met Susheela and they continued even more so during the hospital period. If home was no longer a possible condition for me in my world, it was affirmed and recovered in these dreams. I had read in Gurunathan's book of the predominance of the "I"—a sharp distinction is drawn there between the "Real I" (Atma or Self) and the "apparent I" (personal self or ego)—over body attributes and characteristics which when seen from its supreme angle, at the Ultimate, are illusory and nonexistent; and I had felt confirmed in this, confirmed that I had glimpsed a glimmer of its monumental and unassailable triumph, in some dreams—and even in very early childhood experiences of which I was reminded as I lay retracing my past and path in the hospital bed.

In one of these dreams that I had not long before entering the hospital, I had fallen into a deep sleep. There was absolutely nothing in the dream, yet I was conscious of its nothingness so that it was a dream of nothingness. In the process of waking, just before reaching wakeful consciousness, I rose upward, shapeless, out of and into nothing, no forms, no colors, nothing sensory, only presence, being-ness, triumphant and joyous. I awoke in bliss. The background (my home?) had shone in its own invisible light. It was there, I could not doubt it, I experienced it. Now I must stay there, I must, I must . . . I repeated this to myself in the days that followed. I returned to it in my hospital relaxation and excitement.

In another dream, I was on my way to somewhere; just where that was was not important; that I was going there was, that I was on my way there, to the direction ahead like of a compass needle. It was equally clear in my mind that I was leaving whatever it was that was behind me, behind. I was determined to leave it behind and to be on my way onward, to whatever it was that lay ahead. I was walking on a country path, grass on both sides and in its middle. I was walking ahead on the pebbly parts when the thought entered: Why? Why leave your world behind you? You don't know, can't be sure of what you'll find. Go back. Turn back. Wait a while. You aren't ready yet. Don't give up what you've got. Go back for now. I turned around. The path backward was gone. Only overgrown wilderness. Now I had no choice. I must go forward. I turned around to go forward again; I could not. The path forward was gone; only overgrown wilderness ahead. I could not go backward, I could not go forward. The earth began to open around me, a deep chasm on each side; in an instant I would fall, would slip; and I slipped and fell. But suddenly, all anguish was over, a joy shot through me; I felt myself being held as though enveloped; there was nothing there, but I was not crashing down into a void . . . and I woke. Gradually I knew that if there was no true home for me outside, I must find it, locate it within; I must reside in my own sphere; in my own birthplace within.

Susheela came with Raj, her beautiful sister-in-law, who was also Gurunathan's devoted follower. The nurse put the long, dark red roses in vases all around the room. I told Susheela and Raj of a dream I had had while in the hospital. Through a break in a wall, I was looking into a courtyard. Women dressed in long garments like the Indian sari were moving slowly and rhythmically in a circle as in a ritual dance, each carrying a lit candle on her head. They kept circling around in this ritual solemnity in front of a blue figure painted on the stone wall across from where I stood. I knew the figure was Gurunathan, his upper body bare, the blue pants tied at the ankles. As the women were turning, Gurunathan moved forward toward me without ever leaving his place within the frame on the wall. I woke.

I had never read any books on Indian mythology or art and, to the best of my knowledge, had never seen a photograph of a representation of Krishna, the much-beloved Indian deity so often shown in blue, and with whom the color blue is hence associated. Nor did I know then that Gurunathan had, in fact, at one time, when he was a young man, been a Krishna devotee. Many years after this dream, while browsing through some paintings in an Oriental antique shop, I was astonished to come upon a detail from a North Indian fresco showing Krishna as he stepped outside the frame of a painting. On inquiry, the dealer told me that this was one of the traditional ways in which Krishna is represented in some parts of India.

O symbolism of the intimate, of the unapprehensible nearness, of return to where one has never left . . .

Though I had never seen a picture of Gurunathan's house, Parvathi Vilasom in Trivandrum, I dreamed of that also. Of the courtyard where his followers and sometimes his family—he was a householder, had children and grandchildren—gathered around him, of the stairway to his room, of his room. I saw him standing with his disciples, each in a long white cloth—the dhoti of Southern India—and I saw him enter his house. I told Susheela that what had impressed me so strongly in that dream was that as he left, the love he bestowed on each of his disciples was one and the same. I was happy. I knew, then in the hospital, that I would have to make the journey.

But, of course, when I was back in the habits of my daily life, I wavered, as I had done in the dream. After all, I was practical, responsible, level-headed; I had no interest in spiritual hocus-pocus. But I knew in my depth that this did not apply here; this was no hocus-pocus; Susheela was no hocus-pocus, and what is more, I could not deny what had happened to me already; how could I have taken my experiences, my dreams, as anything but indications, pointers? The only really happy moments during those few years after I had returned from Europe, determined to make America my home, had been in connection with Susheela and the direction toward which she, without ever suggesting it, had pointed me. She was no proselytizer, no propagandist. If I was meant to go, I would go. The choice was mine. There had been clear, powerful indications; the rest was up to me.

In the fall of 1953, Susheela returned to New York from a short visit to Trivandrum, then the capital of Cochin-Travencore which is now the state of Kerala, on the beautiful, lush Malabar coast. She had told Gurunathan about the indications I had had and asked him if these were adequate. His reply was: "Instruction must still be given." There must be the actual, physical confrontation. A year later, Rajeshwar was appointed India's Ambassador to Yugoslavia and Roumania and he and Susheela left New York in the autumn of 1954. On November 3, I sailed aboard the *Queen Mary* for England.

THE CULT OF THE PERSONAL LIFE → 213

My parents were in Vienna but there was not enough time to see them. I had booked passage on the P&O liner *Corfu,* scheduled to depart from Tilbury for Bombay in a few days. They wished me bon voyage on the telephone. "If this is good for you," my mother had said—she sensed but could not have known how tortuous, during these past five years, my struggles had been—"it must be good for us." John Cage, David Tudor, and, I believe, Merce Cunningham were in London and I attended one of Cage's "Sound Happenings"—huge speakers all around the hall emitting disjointed, ear-splitting sounds. I knew that I was off, once again, to more coordinated harmonies.

I spent my thirty-first birthday on the ship passing through the Suez Canal.

The mountainous desert on the left side, the fertile, bright green patches and dark-veiled women riding on donkeys on the right; the warmth in winter; the jasmine scents in the ports; the wail-like songs repeated on and on; the boys in their long garments with caps like yarmulkes on their heads driving the goats; the enormity of the sun rising from the water early in the densely peaceful dawn in the harbor of Bombay; the turbaned stevedores waiting to come aboard, squatting, looking indrawn, reminding me somehow of fawns drinking at a pond—all of these were already suggesting patterns of a reflected unity I had been without, and had missed, for far too long.

A few days after my arrival in Bombay on November 30, I saw at a large reception given by Susheela's sister, Shakuntala Masani, for the Council of Cultural Freedom that had met that year in India, Joseph Campbell, the well-known writer on, among other subjects, Indian art and mythology, whom I had known slightly in New York. He asked me why I had come to India and when I told him, replied, "How courageous of you." I did not see it that way; it had not been at all a matter of courage—I had come out of nothing but necessity.

V

INDIA, PARVATHI VILASOM

I am staying at Vidyuth, in Karamana, on the outskirts of Trivandrum at a boarding house, a modern, European-style villa, run by Wolter Keers, a young Dutchman, son of a pastor. A few, six or seven, of the Westerners there to be with Gurunathan are staying at Vidyuth as well. Wolter has a staff of the customary servants, a cook, a sweeper, a watchman, and two boys, about twelve years old, who are all-around helpers.

There is no ashram at Gurunathan's. There is at Parvathi Vilasom, his white, large, Indian style villa, or bungalow as it is called here, a spacious covered yard called *pandal* where those who come to be with him gather to hear him in the early evening. There is, as one enters the gate in front of the house, a dense, tall mango tree, to its right a shed where a calf is kept, led about in the garden by an attendant, a young ebony-colored man, slim but muscular, bare but for a short dhoti, and looking more like a satyr or a faun than the youthful Brahmin that he is. There is a wide balcony supported by pillars that form a small arcade at the entrance where sandals—shoes are rarely among them—are lined up against the wall; no southern Indian household is entered with feet covered. From the balcony, where the Malayali, the local inhabitants, visitors from other parts of India, and the Westerners (Europeans, Americans, and South Americans) sit in something like a lotus posture on mats on the tile floor—to the pandal, before the talks, chairs are brought for the Westerners—one sees as though into a valley (the house is situated on a downhill slope) the tops of a variety of palm trees, the long leaves, either serrated or of oval shape, swaying like the waves of the sea further below, both driven by a fine wind.

Evenings are long, white during the silence, when the temple horns mark the sanctity of the hours of change, the crows caw as they do all day, and the huge bats, flying foxes that have hung until this hour in the trees, rise screeching into the sky; then the evening colors ascend, at first pale, then gradually darkening.

We sit on the balcony after the talks. Poonama sings the *Kirtanams,* devotional songs, for the mind, stirred, brought to its ultimate, now rests, and the heart absorbing it as the sea its waves, responds with praise, with gratitude tonal but inadequate.

In his room beyond the open door, Poonama sits as she sings and chants on a mat on the floor to the side of the bed where Gurunathan lies on silken sheets. One or two others of the household are standing around the bed. After Poonama finishes we take our leave, in the Indian manner, hands folded at the slightly lowered brow; Gurunathan, now sitting on the side of the bed, his feet dangling, responds in like fashion. We find our sandals, we walk out into the dark, our words, our humming perhaps, in tune still with the silence.

There is no ashram.

When the Rockefeller Foundation people came and offered to set up a Vedanta Institute, Gurunathan said: "No. I am here. No institute."

When some of the devoted brothers wandering through Italy with Francis of Assisi proposed establishing an organization, he objected: "Only by example, only by example shall we teach."

No ashram. Only his presence.

When reporters came asking about his biography, important details of his past, he said: "I have no biography. I have no past."

When visitors came with recording machines, with stenography pads to write commentaries on his illuminations, he forbade it.

Words are pointers; without the directive force their power is lost, the aim obscure, the horizon diffuse. The magnitude is too extensive, too inclusive, the discourses, ever-unfolding, reaching too deeply into silence, into the silence beyond silence, into that which is more than, other than an absence of sounds, to be described, to be recorded as words on paper, as sounds on tape. He would not have it. Only his utterance, the presence of his utterance. No ritualization: the ritual unadorned; the light in its own glory.

No institute. No superimposed organization. No ashram.

"For how long have you come?"

"Two, three months."

"That is all right. Susheela wrote about you. Where will you stay?"

The observation, the care, the penetration as total, as detailed as light—or its absence—that settles everywhere.

When I asked, after having been with him about two months: "Supposing one has grasped at least some of the teaching, should one then know how to expound it?"

"No! It expounds Itself!"

Orthodox non-dual Vedanta: He called it, the science of perception; the "Real I," the changeless, unifying principle at the core of being, transcending even the object-subject tie, the *oneness* of the two. No form without seeing, no sound without hearing, "the light of consciousness in all thoughts and perceptions; the light of love in all feelings."

I stayed at first at the Mascot Hotel, a comfortable leftover from the British raj (rule); beds surrounded by mosquito nets; large fans suspended from lofty ceilings; swinging doors out on a wide, covered balcony; European bathrooms (not common in southern India); high-turbaned, elderly "bearers" bringing early English breakfast, tea and bananas, at daybreak. In the tropical

South life starts at daybreak, the birds, an immense variety, chirping, trilling, gaggling high up in the dense, still dark, trees. Then, after two weeks at the hotel, I moved to Wolter Keers' boarding house on the hilly outskirts of Trivandrum.

A walk, with Wolter, in the evening along the wide avenue leading to the Vidyuth compound reached by a driveway in whose circle stands an immense pepper tree, its trunk consisting of myriad stems twisted like upward-reaching snakes; the tree shades the lawn and the upper balconies, even the flat roof that is surrounded by a railing from where I have often looked down on the exotic gardens—exuberance, peace, joy seem to flow like an invisible mist from the very soil and ample growths.

It is dark along the road, an occasional tonga comes by—the horse-drawn carriage that looks like a wagon from the days of the old American West, but covered with wood and not tarpaulin—or sometimes it is a bullock cart that passes us. We carry flashlights for there are snakes about, but they will attack only if stepped on or otherwise threatened.

(One day, professional snake charmers came to Vidyuth. Wouldn't we want to have the grounds cleared of snakes? Wolter agreed. They went around the lawn and gardens with their flutes and about four vipers and rattlesnakes came out from the bushes. Gladly, we paid the men what they had asked. When we told Gurunathan about it in the evening, he roared with laughter. They were "professional deceivers" he said. They had brought the snakes in their baskets and planted them first.)

As we walk on, there is a dense darkness all around spotted only here and there with lights from flashlights, lanterns on the carts; also some of the windows in the low mud houses we pass are dimly lit with oil lamps or candles; there is electricity only in the villas like Vidyuth and they are all hidden from the road by deep gardens. But on the crude verandas of most of the huts there are still the flickers from oil lamps that had been set out earlier just before the advent of the white time between day and dusk—the holy hour observed.

Further south of Trivandrum, at Cape Comorin, India's southernmost tip where three oceans meet, a holy place, the populace, there on pilgrimage, waits to rush into the water from the rocks or beaches, to cleanse the body—it is auspicious to do so at the holy hour, the timeless moment where godhood dwells in between time.

Earlier, here in Karamana, the women swept the courtyards, the grounds in front of their houses, and the steps with crude brooms of twigs; they also swept around their shrines inside the compounds or the public ones and temples, lit the oil lamps, many of the local people going to the temple pools, men and women nearly naked performing the daily ritual of bathing to be cleansed—cleansed of the world; and then smeared ashes across their foreheads.

Now the young women with flowers braided in their full, long hair, seated on the porch steps or behind the windows, are chanting in the night, of yearning, of devotion. One doesn't have to know the meaning of the words, and we don't, to sense the emotion, to respond to the feeling. The sky sparkles; Krishna steps from his frame; the earth is resting.

"Satva," translated, is "Thought turned toward Atma (the Self)." When the Indians speak of something being "satvic," they mean that an object, an environment so referred to, speaks to the inner being, induces one to turn inward, allows one to converse with one's soul. Presumably, an object or environment created from that angle, shaped out of the spiritual posture to praise Atma, the One Self, incorporates, contains, and gives off Atma's own characteristics as something felt rather than seen—though the harmony this induces becomes almost perceptual.

So Francis of Assisi rebuilt the broken church, stone by stone; . . . the Jews each time their temple; . . . so the Greeks built cities for their gods; . . . anonymous architects and masons, a populace, the French and others, the great cathedrals; . . . and so, creation absorbed into spirit, the animals sit in contentment, and the soil gives off invisible beneficence.

I spent three months near Parvathi Vilasom. What occurred there cannot be recreated. What cannot be said, cannot be said. "It expounds Itself!" That has been my challenge.

When I left, my past had been restored, seven generations before, and seven after.

VI

EPILOGUE: ESSENTIAL TRANSFORMATIONS

► 1

Following my arrival back in New York in June 1955, I didn't go to work for eight months. I had at last left engineering and needed to make the transition, not only professionally but to the New York environment, to which I returned with great trepidation. I gave up my apartment and moved in for a few months with my parents; my mother was back from Vienna, my father staying on in Europe until the winter.

Would what I had gained sustain me? I feared it might wear off. I could not have known then when I returned, and had to face the demands of my ordinary life as one does when waking from dream imagery of brightest harmony, that what I had been given, what had been revived, released within me like a conflagration, would sustain me, would not leave, as I had been foretold. "You will never be alone!" A few years later, in May 1959, when I received a cable from Susheela with the news that Gurunathan had left "his mortal coil" (those were not her words but that is how Indians refer to the death of a sage), and I sent a note to Joseph Campbell to inform him—he had had an interview with Gurunathan while I was there in February 1955—he replied that he was indeed sorry to hear it but that, even though the conversation had lasted only a half hour, it was continuing still. I had been there three months. Instruction had been given, as Gurunathan had told Susheela it had to be. The birthplace, or birthright rediscovered—home—was now centered within. The discipline was clear, the direction firm; the rest was up to me.

One evening at dinner, my parents, who had not voiced any real objection to my journey but who were, understandably, curious, asked me if I could tell them what it had meant to me and just what I had gained. They had already sensed, and had mentioned it, that whatever it was that had happened, its beneficial effects were apparent. I thought a bit, and said, "When I was a child you know that I was, on the whole, very joyous."

They agreed.

"Well, that meant that I was in a condition of naturalness. New things, new impressions, new names came to me each hour, each day. Experiencing the world emerging was a joy, even if there were moments of fear, as of course there were. But it was all part of a full, single flow; no separateness, only a continuous connection. As I grew older, this sense of the oneness of things grew weaker, and when we came here it was altogether broken. But now this break has been repaired. I feel again connected, and not cut off."

Conversations of this sort, of religious-philosophic import, were not uncommon at my parents' dinner table. And they reacted well to what I said. These may not have been the exact words, but it was the exact meaning. My mother replied, "Yes. I do understand that."

My father, too, nodded.

They never questioned me again. Quietly they shared my gladness.

►2

During this transition period, I wrote all the time; it lasted until January 1956 when I went to work for Plenum Books (then Consultans Bureau), the firm of my friends, Fran and Earl Coleman, which specialized in highly technical books, and took an apartment on West 14th Street. It again says something about my mother's superior values that when I had to choose between two job offers, one back in engineering, the other in publishing at exactly half the salary, she urged me to take the latter. But before joining the publishing firm, I wrote a book for children. I had learned the very day I returned to New York that Ylla, the animal photographer, had been killed in an accident while photographing a bullock race in northern India. There is a large game reserve near Trivandrum and when Ylla came there to take pictures, she had stayed with us at Vidyuth. I was the more startled to hear of her death because of an incident that had occurred then. One day, a young man who had befriended a number of us at the boarding house, a local Brahmin from one of the leading Trivandrum families, came to drive us out to a nearby village to consult the astrologer who served his family and others of similar social status. When I asked Ylla to come along, she laughed and said: "No. If he's going to tell me I will die soon, I don't want to know about it!" I was startled. She was only forty and at the peak of her very successful career. She had spent a few months in India and had left behind a great many photographs. Her agent, Charles Rado, had asked me, not long after my return, to write the text for a book of elephant pictures selected from the great quantity she had taken. It became *The Little Elephant* and was published by Harper & Row (then Harper Bros.) the following year. (The book is still in print.)

I enjoyed doing it, but most of my time, especially during the first two months, was given to reflecting on the welled-up feelings, the fresh calm, the vastness and reality of the experience, the shielding it from disturbance. I feared—needlessly, as it turned out—its vulnerability, the new child in alien arms. Poetry was the proper, nourishing enclosure, the nacreous shield, and I wrote and wrote; and tried and tried for the singing rhythms, the syllables that would vibrate and shine on the surface containing the unsayable wonder of gratitude and praise. No irony, no sad mockery, for it was not a tone of departure the new poems conveyed but of return. "These are poems of an interior perspective, curiously weightless, poems that levitate, so to speak, in their own language, pulling all upward," Hayden Carruth wrote of them in *Poetry London-New York* when they appeared as a book in 1957. And James Dickey, in the *Sewanee Review:* "It is impossible not to be impressed by Gregor's unearthly quietism, and by the sincerity and intensity of his self-searching."

The irony was over. When I sent the twenty poems done during these first two months to Tambimuttu, the flamboyant, princely, irrepressible editor of the wartime magazine *Poetry London,* who had started it again, this time from New York, he not only took the long title-poem and others for the magazine, but also offered to do them as a book, and *Declensions of a Refrain* inaugurated what was to be the Poetry London-New York Books series. Though this happened in the winter of 1955, the book did not appear until early 1957.

The readjustment after my return was not accomplished in a few months, nor even in a few years, for that would have meant to be immovable, fixed in the new identity: *To be in the world but not of it.* But experience now lay at the center of my existence. The statue that the culture—once, long ago, rooted in that very commitment—had grown in me, and that had kept me from the freedom I had glimpsed as a boy and youth, now lay in pieces, cracked of its own accord. The source freed, its confinement lay demolished. The forming of the new, the right containment had from now on to be aided—the *new* posture, the radical posture I had for so long sought to encourage and to make my own.

►3

In the continuing process of adaptation and assertion that followed—a subject all its own—it has become increasingly apparent to me over these many years that the shock of personal alienation I felt like a shudder the very day I arrived here in 1939 originated not only from my own condition. *Something was missing;* why else my despair? In one form or another, this shock—trauma, split—must have been experienced by everyone transplanted here from an old culture in which the unity of being, harmony with cosmic law, had been once upheld as man's ultimate achievement. But the acute discomfort—and, more than that, the psychic disturbance that the absence of this potential within an existing cultural framework has caused those sensitive to its need—has been felt not only by refugees and immigrants but by native Americans as well.

In the first chapter of *After Strange Gods,* T. S. Eliot—St. Louis-born of an old New England family and a resident of England from 1914 until his death in 1965—says of his return to America in 1931 by way of Vermont coming from Canada:

> It is not necessarily those lands which are the most fertile or the most favored in climate that seem to me to be the happiest, but those in which a long struggle of adaptation between man and his environment has brought out the best qualities of both; in which the landscape has been molded by the numerous generations of one race, and in which the landscape in turn has modified the race to its own character. And those New England mountains seemed to me to give evidence of a human success so meagre and transitory as to be more desperate than the desert.

The adaptation between man and his environment is the crucial point here, the *satvic* principle, the transformation of material into essence, into an *expressed* oneness, the spiritual act of *connectedness* only man can accomplish.

Other American poets of the past have roused us to this awareness—Emerson, Whitman, Dickinson, Robert Frost, Wallace Stevens, William Carlos Williams, Marianne Moore, Hart Crane, Jean Garrigue.

The terrible loss the refugees felt—especially during their first years in exile when they clustered together on the sidewalks of the Upper West Side in New York or around tables in the few cafés that existed here then—was that they had come from an environment in which this transformation had occurred and been established into one in which it had not.

► 4

In February 1958, on my way back to New York from my second journey to India (by air this time, and only for two weeks in Trivandrum), I stopped in Rome before going on to Vienna, where I was to do an article on a leading industrial designer for the magazine *Industrial Design*—a glossy, handsome journal of design principles and application, the *Bauhaus* legacy in the fifties—whose technical editor I was. My friend Jean Garrigue, in the forefront of contemporary American poets, celebrated for her intensity of spirit, wit, metaphysical perceptions, and power of ornamentation, was in Naples during one of her frequent and always lengthy sojourns in Europe. I took the train to Naples and the next day Jean and I spent on Capri.

The time of year, sea and sky alternating between wintry moodiness and the brightness, clarity of the seasons ahead, stormy one moment, sunny the next; the crowds of local inhabitants going out from or returning from the mainland, the scarcity of tourists as we drove up the steep slopes in a horse-drawn carriage: All of this gave the occasion an invigorating sense of reality—a richness of scenery and the full human response with which daily, ordinary life can be lived. Necessary transitoriness against a background of permanence; the human expression enhanced and eased by the spiritual penetration achieved at the sight and absorption of the physical surroundings—structures of time-withstanding embodiment, light-reflecting stones and darkened spaces, almost audible harmonies that console and meet human necessity. Conflicts, needs of which Jean was acutely aware, which the European environment brought into focus each time she was there and which her poems contained.

But the reality around her both inspired and tormented her. It contrasted too drastically with her own background and environment, to which she feared to return but toward which she felt a total obligation. For a century, Americans of such finely tuned sensibility have lived with this torment. Jean was (*was,* alas, for she died in December 1972) a descendant of a Huguenot family that had fled to America in the seventeen-hundreds, and she lived in two worlds, the one of ideals for which her ancestors had come here and, of necessity, the one of her own period dominated by altogether different societal values. The American ideals, the Bill of Rights, the true democratic spirit, she stood for, but the misuse of them, their exploitation she resented bitterly. She knew that her country's turning more and more—openly and unashamedly—to an exclusive materialism, that extracting its physical resources while not only ignoring its spiritual ones but viewing such development with disdain, was ruinous, a nation's suicide in history. She expressed her dismay in her work, though it was not anger at her severely departed society that gave it its truly outstanding character, but her steadfast maintaining of ideals. In her long poems, and a number of shorter ones, she achieved an instructive, metaphysical insight hardly matched by her contemporaries. She rejected the notion, the limited vision of the visible as the absolute and only acceptable proof and projected in her poems the unity of life at the root and ecstatic height of direct experience. Though in her more mundane ones she rails against the stupidity and narrowness of self-centeredness and promotion (small *s* in self), the distortions of the American ideals she cherished—and which even I had sensed, as though their aura had come across to me when I was a boy still in Vienna—by a current code placing personal interests ahead of theirs, her work itself showed no such taint. For it was foremost a remarkable achievement in her art and not a vehicle for anger. As Jean's editor at the Macmillan Company (which I had joined in 1962 and whose poetry list, among many other books in a broad cultural category, I was responsible for) I sent galleys of her *Selected Poems,* published in 1967, to Marianne Moore, who replied: "Music should be directed by the ear; poetry by the imagination . . . Jean Garrigue must have heard of the Philistines, might have spoken to one. If so, no imprint of any such meeting has been left on her."

I will never forget seeing Jean in Naples. A friend of hers was with us in the evening when we went out to dinner. This was Harold Norse, a poet I had also known in New York and had seen in Paris later, in 1961. After we had left the restaurant, Jean walked ahead. She was wearing what I knew was a favorite dress of black velvet which I, too, thought was especially becoming to her. As Harold and I were talking, she stopped in front of a house, those old stones of the Neapolitan streets, turned toward us and seemed, for a split second, to be listening to something and, in doing so, to be lifted out of herself. It was as though something invisible had flowed through and across her. She looked transported, her presence luminous, the blackness shimmering.

But that day in Capri, even while reading me some of the poems she had been working on—that magnificent "For the Fountaineers and Fountains of Villa d'Este" which appeared in her next volume, *A Water Walk at Villa d'Este,* the following year—her anguish was in her face and in much of what she said. Her European experiences had once again affirmed her own being, the European background given her the setting permitting her to achieve in her work a depth of resonance her own native environment could hardly provide. Though I knew that her personal dilemma was the collective, cultural one of her own world, was indigenous to present-day America and had to be expressed, had to make itself known through the poet's spiritual intensity and acute insight, I flew off from Rome the next day saddened to have found her in this mood and plight.

For I had just come again from the source of reconciliation. The turmoil that is the world seemed needless and far away.

➤5

If the European background, the accumulations in the soil and stones resulting from religious-spiritual attitudes and practices—and what but the exhortation toward the transcendent, time-free realm lies at its core—could yield for Jean and other native Americans what it did, and still does; could provide a stirring and an affirmation at the center of one's own being—would it not be natural for me to gain the same from it, who had been shaped by its tradition? And, the war damage long repaired, my center relocated, my perceptions renewed, I have returned almost yearly to its origin, its southern regions.

If, by the eighties in America, billions of dollars are poured yearly into the new industry of so-called self-encounters (soul-repairing EST, Lifespring, and other groups) because, presumably, the separation between man and nature, man and his environment has become so acute, the environment not reflecting any of his inner needs but running counter to them, that he has become isolated, has lost any sense of the intimate connection he needs so badly; if the framework of the culture he lives in has become so "dehumanized," "depersonalized," so "fragmented" he must resort to technology-emulating systems to break out of his loneliness however temporarily: then how much more grievous is the situation for many a European wartime refugee, for my Aunt Greta and Uncle Martin, reaching eighty, who had once lived within a structure that had bred connectedness between man and the creation, and who have never become accustomed to living without it, as those born into a world that never cultivated it can also not live without it. The alienation they experience—those native to it and those not—is the same; only the way of relating to it, dealing with it, functioning within it, differs.

►6

At first I was disappointed when I was shown to my cottage in Vence, for it was situated in a forestlike wilderness in a valley deep below Le Vieux Mas, the main building on the large grounds of the Karolyi Foundation where Mme. Karolyi lives— Countess Catherine Karolyi, the widow of Count Michael, the socialist premier of Hungary directly after the collapse of the Austro-Hungarian Empire, in whose memory the foundation for writers and painters had been established. I had been in the vicinity before, in the summer of 1977 when, while at Hanna's at St. Firmin sur Loire, I traveled down to Provence to stay for a week at St. Paul de Vence, at a delightful *auberge* consisting of white, green-shuttered cottages and a large garden just below the old town's ramparts. This time, three years later, I had come to spend the month of July at the foundation in Vence, a few kilometers further north in the Alpes-Maritimes.

St. Paul de Vence had been vivid in my mind ever since Ada Louise Huxtable, then the architecture critic of the *New York Times,* had talked to me about it, and I later read about it in the concluding essay of her book, *Will They Ever Finish Bruckner Boulevard,* published by Macmillan in 1970, shortly after I had left the company, and of which I had been the editor. Witty, brilliant, charming, and to my surprise when I first met her, petite—I had foolishly associated the enormous scope of her mind with a frame of equivalent proportions—Ada Louise talked eloquently of the beauty, the harmony with its undulating surroundings, of a town, its buildings at least three hundred years old, its earlier ramparts dating from the reign of Francis I, which the French, keeping intact what was of value from the past, had declared a national monument. Like Jean, she spoke out sharply, and in that essay with irony, against a discontinuity of time-tested harmonizing principles perpetrated in favor of artificial expediency and trends of the moment. The center-spread illustration of St. Paul in her book speaks forcefully for her argument: round, clipped trees and hedges in the foreground, an awning-covered terrace of a newer building whose style nonetheless resembles that of the old houses beyond the ancient ramparts rising straight up above the shrubbery; the sloping roofs in the old town, relating to one another as do the surfaces in a many-faceted jewel or crystal, ascending toward the square tower of the old cathedral rising in the center to a considerable height above them into a cloudless sky. Everything connected, an entity like a beehive—shrubbery to building, building to rampart walls, walls to houses, roofs to steeple as though grown out of, bred by the town, steeple to sky. A marvel of unity, a habitation of extensions into fading distances. And when, in the summer of 1977, I actually approached St. Paul de Vence from the auberge Le Hameau slightly below it, I saw not only the picture ahead of me, but what was equally important to this aggregate of unity—which the picture could not show: namely, that the town itself grew out of the landscape. The angles of the fields and vineyards, of sloping roofs between cypresses, the large gardens of lavender, each sloping toward the sea, created a natural structure, an interconnectedness which the town up on the hill also expressed. And from there, from its ramparts, there were, from all sides, visual extensions limited only by the sky and the horizon. And every inch of the land below had been worked, had been lived with and cherished for centuries. Something grew from this, something invisible but present, from these extensions, from the unified, cultivated earth, from the old stones and the newer ones, something like a human expression, the *human persona,* the spiritual *Gestalt* that the earth too embodies and, if extracted, provides. This is the character of the South, of the Mediterranean basin: sea, the earth in its natural exuberance, the warmth, the spires, the human habitation. This was so of Dubrovnik on the Adriatic, of Assisi, of so many a town in Tuscany, Provence, and other regions, other small towns not designated for historic significance or celebrated personages: the oneness of man with creation, his unique position within it, the unifying towers he has built, his obligation.

When I arrived at the Karolyi Foundation three years later, I had anticipated a month in the midst of this exuberant cultivation. At first, however, I felt disheartened when I was taken to my cottage, situated on a slope that led to a river and which was, in consequence, cut off from the elaborate views relating to one another as the roofs of St. Paul. Also, the part of the Foundation where the cottage stood was uncultivated, a wilderness of pine trees, olive trees, of untrimmed yellow bushes, the broom, of boulders, of prickly and overgrown paths. Only from the kitchen window did I have a view of the mountain in the distance, its lower parts dotted with gardens and red-roofed, pale-colored houses.

But it did not take long, and my misgivings gave way to an ever-deepening contentment: I was, during that month, to experience nature in a way that I never had before. For this was not after all nature cut off from man and his cultivation; it was merely a part of the varied grounds where wilderness flourished that was, nonetheless, surrounded by land forms the earth provided and ample evidence of the earth's poetic talents extracted and nurtured by man into fields of roses, paths of red and white oleander, honeysuckle clinging to some walls, blue, red, white blossomed frail shrubs falling across others. And in the midst of this were the animals and insects: a family of domesticated hares on the grounds near the Countess' house, a stray dog that befriended me, others that barked in unison across the valley at any intrusion, the birds high up in the branches, the cicadas chirping.

And when they all slept, there was a silence of such denseness—the equal of my favorite cathedral's interior, the basilica at St. Benoit not far from Hanna's village, whose central part dates back to the ninth century. Never since my nights at Vidyuth had I slept surrounded by such a depth of silence, of calm. When I woke, as I occasionally did, during the night, it was almost frightening, almost too awesome to hear this silence. I felt then in tune with the essence that is one and the same in all and reigns, undisturbed, when creatures sleep. This was the core of connection, the unity from which extend the related surfaces of hills and homes.

As I looked in the day at the changing views from the grounds above, at the haze of the sea below, at the intricate design of colors on wildflower petals, as I watched the hare permitting me to approach only this far, as I looked into the eyes of the stray dog who, when told that I would have to leave, turned sadly to go; as I listened, listened, listened to everything and everything lived, the soil, the air, the mountain, the sky clouded or clear—I knew that the essence was one and only the natures of fauna and flora many. And I knew also that in man that essence has risen to conscious awareness: *in* him, the radiating center.

In the midst of this naturalness and blissfulness, I was reading John Cheever, nearly all of his corpus, for I had read only some of his short stories before. In recent years I had given my summer reading—on a Mediterranean beach or in Hanna's garden—to the entire work of one author, to E. M. Forster, to Proust for two summers, and others, thereby entering not into a segment but the whole of their world. Cheever's made me shudder, and the despair and hopelessness his work suggests reminded me of my first response to my experience of alienation, the terror I felt looking out on a suburban street the first day I was in America. For Cheever chronicles brilliantly—and in his novels in most inventive ways—the anguish of the indigenous but nonetheless alienated man, alienated from himself, from what could bring meaning and value to his life—the condition imposed upon him by a society departed seriously and damagingly from human, soul-enhancing values by its exclusively materialistic pursuit. A world hopelessly split between the virtues upheld by the farming, or whaling, seafaring forefathers and the societal ambitions promoted today, coast to coast.

Sitting outside near my cabin, the denseness of trees and foliage all around me, no sounds but of birds out of sight and of insects chirping, to my right, as I looked up from the book, a sudden glow, a view of the distant mountains of the Alpes-Maritimes bright in the cloudless sky, I read Cheever's outrage and frustration with his society's madness, a fragmentation gone awry. "I said again and again that if American capitalism continued to exalt mercenary and dishonest men, the economy would degenerate into the manufacture of drugs and ways of life that would make reflection"—such as I was having then—"any sort of thoughtfulness or emotional depth—impossible. . . . I see American magazines in the café and the bulk of their text is advertising for tobacco, alcohol and absurd motor cars that promise—quite literally promise—to enable you to forget the squalor, spiritual poverty and monotony of selfishness. Never," (and here comes the clincher) "never, in the history of civilization, has one seen a great nation singlemindedly bent on drugging itself." So speaks one of the characters in Cheever's novel *Bullet Park*.

And I think of the many times I've had lunch with just the type of trapped man Cheever so often writes about, public relations or advertising executives who used to invite me out to one of the expensive midtown restaurants when I was an editor on *Industrial Design* magazine, or, briefly, on *Business Week,* in the hope that I would write about a client's new product my host was paid to promote. How often, after the second martini, his human plight would begin to show, would leak through: the expensive house in the suburbs, the kids in college, the pressures in the office from others out for his job, the upgraded product he didn't care a whit about—and where, where in all this was *he?* Where his gain? Where and how could he gratify a craving he could probably not name? Only the emptiness was his; a constant, gnawing ache.

How easily, almost unconsciously, the inner being picks out and takes, absorbs what it needs—if provided. Every human being needs to be replenished in his human aspects. Who can manage on his own? Even the brave can only succeed so far; it is the culture within society that must provide this feeding. In man are his surroundings mirrored. The clearer the source, the clearer the reflection.

➤ 7

Summer after summer, in the midst of what was once of consequence—practices that strengthened connectedness—I hear and absorb echos not of something being said but of a condition, a presence that, once established, cannot be annulled. And hearing them, sensing them, I become once again aware of contrasts, of what it is to live where they are, and where they are not: where, in place of their source, their origin, there is only emptiness, a void.

Something is missing: I sensed this more than forty years ago.

The force within the environment that ignites the imagination and rests the soul.

Expressions of power and energy, however attractive and stimulating—as I at first found them in America and still do—the hectic activities on life's surface, do not lead one inward. This the poet knows, not only the poet by practice but the poet alive within human consciousness.

"Music," wrote Marianne Moore, "is directed by the ear; poetry by the imagination."

The poetic reality in every human being is stirred by those expressions within the environment—like the broad, tree-lined avenues that revolve around an obelisk or an arch in the middle of a wide circle—that lead one on to self-recognition and compassion. The power of communion, generosity of spirit generated, the sense of feeling deeply at home that is created when the heart, tending outward to immense expansions, feels itself received.

Toward the end of his life, William Carlos Williams, pediatrician in industrial northern New Jersey, innovator in metrics, master of the glimpse, which included the American industrial scenery, perhaps the major figure in the movement of modernist American poetry, seeing space travel as an ego and power extension and not, as it should be, an amorous adventure with the creation, said of the moon landing:

> What
> do they think they will attain
> by their ships
> that death has not
> already given them? Their ships
> should be directed
> inward upon . . .

➤ 8

In 1966 it was my great pleasure and privilege to get to know Marianne Moore. Macmillan had been her publisher through her *Collected Poems* in 1951, when Miss Moore changed to Viking. The company kept the book in print and each time the stock ran low a new printing had to be authorized. As I was handling the poetry list, the form approving a new printing came to me. There wasn't any question about the decision, I signed the form, but it occurred to me that an edition also including all of her work published with Viking since ꞏ1951 would be apropriate by then, and of immense value. I also discovered that Miss Moore was to celebrate her eightieth birthday in Novermber 1967. I went immediately to Gerald Gross, head of the trade division, and he agreed that we should aim for a volume on her birthday consisting of her complete poems. In those early days after the merger of Macmillan with a corporate giant—Crowell, Collier & Macmillan—the company still continued its long-standing obligation to publish the best in contemporary poetry. Judicious selection had brought the company over the decades not only luster but hefty profits. For it had on its list of poets the works of William Butler Yeats, Edwin Arlington Robinson, Thomas Hardy, Vachel Lindsay, John Masefield, Rabindranath Tagore, and Sara Teasdale. All of these went into many printings—even the Teasdale *Collected Poems* sold about a thousand copies a year, years after its original publication. The sums taken in over the decades from book sales and permissions, especially for poets like Hardy and Yeats, were staggering. Yet, when Yeats' centenary was to be celebrated in 1965 and I urged the company to take a full-page advertisement in the *New York Times Book Review* to celebrate the occasion, my request was continually rebuffed by the corporate hierarchy until, with the intercession of Gerald Gross, they relented and the celebratory ad appeared.

My first step toward a combined volume of Miss Moore's work was to query her. Yes, she would welcome it, she replied on a postcard, the message typed, a number of words crossed out and corrections written in, or typed in, above. This, as I discovered in the communications that followed, was characteristic of her replies, each terse and exact and, evidently, a struggle to have it so, for some words were always corrected. As her response was affirmative, Viking agreed also to the joint venture, by no means a common occurrence in publishing, one that took a great deal of consultation with company lawyers before the complicated contractual agreement was concluded.

I don't recall my first meeting with Miss Moore but I do, and clearly so, subsequent ones. Yet what has remained vivid in my mind is the impression she had made on me when I first called on her at her apartment on West 9th Street. She was a luminous presence, no other way of putting it, physically the lightness of air, intellectually, spiritually the strength of steel. The subtitle of one of her late books, *Tell Me, Tell Me,* is *Granite, Steel and Other Topics.* She had come into considerable public prominence by then, mostly because of her interest in baseball and her television appearances in that connection, but she had nothing, absolutely nothing of the celebrated personage about her. Certainly, knowing her work, one would not have expected that of her, however well deserved it might have been considering the eminent position she had held by then in literary circles and the secure place she had achieved in a cultural tradition she not only continued but had moved forward. Her behavior was all kindness, courtesy, generosity of attention in the way she faced one, greeted one, spoke to one. She had a clarity, a nobility about her that not only excluded any trace of egocentricity but would make it unthinkable. She was, what even the masters in art are not always, the living example of her work. She was at once intimate and aloof, not by design but by her nature. As she does, of course, in her poems, she talked in observations so that one had the impression of being at first addressed in an impersonal way, but her comments were so directly projected to the person she was talking to that one soon felt involved in a most personal, intimate exchange. She made the observed fact, the abstract thought, direct and real. She spoke at length about humility, quoting Winston Churchill and others; and she acted it out from the moment she opened the door for me, told me to take whatever I wished to drink from a kitchen cupboard where an enormous variety of bottles friends had brought her stood, mostly unopened, led me into the living room, talked to me, facing me always—who can ever forget those sparkling, smiling, clear eyes—and finally, when I got up to leave to get back to the office, insisted on taking me downstairs and seeing me into a taxi.

I never asked her, but I can well imagine what she must have thought of writers openly out to "make it," promoting themselves with "self-advertisements" and exhibitionistic readings. Her likely response is in her poems. She understood only too well what was corroding the basic values—"Values in Use," the title of one of her poems—she had upheld unconditionally in her work and in her life. She mocked egocentricity; she praised creatures in creation that perform their duty in an unquestioned act of harmony, do what they have to do not for selfish motives but in response to nature's dynamic mechanism. "Blessed is the man," she says in a poem of that title, "who does not sit in the seat of the scoffer . . . Blessed the geniuses who know/ that egomania is not a duty." She starts her poem, "The Paper Nautilus" with:

> For authorities whose hopes
> are shaped by mercenaries?
> Writers entrapped by
> teatime fame and by
> commuters' comforts? Not for these
> the paper nautilus
> constructs her thin glass shell.

Squarely she puts the blame on those who have succumbed to the society-endorsed pursuits of fame and fortune and have thereby betrayed their talents and fallen seriously short of their duty. For if the spokesmen of true values, those who have it in them to keep alive distinctions, who have it in them to be in the world but not of it, will not speak up, will not take their stand in the obverse of worldliness, the obverse of the materialist's interests their society promotes, who will? She fought the alienating trends not only by speaking out against them but by proceeding in her life and in her work from that which unifies. And strengthening that, it became a force in her, and those around her felt it. She was, indeed, regal.

An amusing incident took place around Christmas 1967 when I took her and Jean Garrigue, her great admirer, to dinner at the Coach House in the Village which, Marianne had once mentioned, was one of her favorite restaurants. It is a charming place that resembles an old-fashioned New England inn—not too large a room, fireplace, polite waiters, understated home-style decor, excellent food. Before setting out for the restaurant we had a drink at Marianne's apartment. She had a fire going, was dressed in a marvelously becoming pale blue wool suit, and was, as usual, attentive and witty. On a low table in front of the fireplace were piled up some books, among them a novel I had just read—

Ken McCormick who was then my editor at Doubleday, which had published the book, had sent it to me. The book deals with an older man experiencing, vicariously, the love affair of a young couple staying with him; the imagined love scenes, depicted in precise detail, were not always orthodox. I asked Marianne if she had read the book. "Yes," she said. When I told her that I too had read it, she replied, "Oh," and added, emphatically, "I wouldn't have let you!"

Soon after she got ill, about a year or so later, I had a dream about her. I was sitting with a woman in an auditorium, very much like an old-fashioned school auditorium—or, now that I think of it, like the church in Brooklyn Marianne had belonged to for many years and where shortly after her death in February 1972 a memorial service was held for her. In the dream, Marianne sat a few rows behind us. I turned around once or twice to see her; she looked radiant. I said to the woman next to me: "Isn't it marvelous how well Marianne looks." "Yes," the woman replied, "that's because she is loved so." Afterward, when I repeated this to Marianne, she broke into tears.

She had prepared for her death, every detail including the programs for her services, the psalms that were to be sung. A sense of timelessness, of utter simplicity, of a high purpose achieved, settled over the church, a summing up of her life, as everything she wrote had been a summing up, a totality of observation.

With her ended the generation of poets who understood still that unless we transform material into essence, absorb the world around us into us as a sea absorbs its waves, object and subject into oneness, the presence in the environment without which the soul cannot be at rest will not be established.

➤ 9

In mythology, as in cultural history, the hero representing the sacrificial act central to the health of his society overcomes the obstacles in his path to meet his challenge of self-enlargement, or the threat to the collective health of his people. Whatever the mission, the achievement lies in clarifying and restoring distinctions.

What is a domestic animal without a domestic situation; what the earth, the soil, the planet without husbandry? *"Was wirst Du tun Gott, wenn ich sterbe?"* ("What will you do, God, if I die?") asks Rilke in his poem, uttering a thought central to his tradition—wherein man assumes the role of God's coworker.

Something is missing where this has not been collective practice; where a nation's true heroes—and we have had them—have gone largely unnoticed. But, across the land, there is increasing evidence of a widespread yearning. To let distinctions shine. To cultivate the invisible so that it is felt within the visible. "The image," says Wallace Stevens, "must be of the nature of its creator," thereby returning *him* to us "anew, in a freshened youth . . . in the substance of his region, wood of his forests and stone out of his fields . . ."

This past winter I took the bus up to Mt. Tremper, near Woodstock, New York, where, for some years now, Sam has been running Matagiri, a retreat for followers of Sri Aurobindo. Just before reaching my stop, a young woman told the driver she wanted to be let off at the monastery. This turned out to be a Zen monastery which Sam showed me the next day as we were driving past the former mansion which is now the Zen retreat. There are other such centers, he told me, in the area, including a Tibetan Buddhist monastery. No doubt, Woodstock is not the only rural community in America where such organized retreats for inner concentration for the recovery of the Self have been established. It is a vital task. The waters must flow or the land parches.

On my short walk, on the wintry mornings, from the guest house to the retreat's main building, I would see a snow-covered mountain of the Catskills ahead, the fields and slopes on both sides of the road also covered with snow, dry shrubs sticking out from the blanketed ground, now food for fire but, like fossils which they resemble, reminders of what has been—dim associations in innermost recesses, of chestnut trees in bloom, of a row of statuary in silent, sunlit, leafy paths. A chalky whiteness, loose bark. How it invites the soul to revery, nature's long sleep . . .

To my left, before turning into Sam's property, I would see a horse grazing in the winter pasture. Only patches in the brook are frozen; a clear stream, like notes of a bright melody, runs around the icy chunks. The dogs are coming to greet me, barking, tails wagging. Wisps of smoke from the stoves in the meeting and dining hall up ahead.

Ongoingness surrounds me, ongoingness that brings to me the intimacy it contains. Clear, clear echos, the canal winding, the bridges into the old city, childhood's undisrupted closeness. The background echoing, reclined shapes, godlike, lulling—home that is never lost.

> The emptiness of a world
> . . . .
> does not wipe the secrets out
> the link that I cannot trace back
> the murmuring as of a distant sea
> the gold-leafed symmetry
> the looks of supplicants
> the smiles of those whose inner glow
> on stones and peeling canvases
> shines on in spite of centuries.

←←←←

> The skipper's port of call
> is not diminished in the storm.
>
> What was will be again.
>
> Streets of repose that lie ahead
> are undisturbed and wrapped
> as always in pale light.
>
> Return is never lost to man.*

*From *The Past Now* by Arthur Gregor (New York: Doubleday & Co., 1975).